FAIR AND BALANCED,
MY ASS!

FAIR AND BALANCED,
MY ASS!

An Unbridled Look at the Bizarre
Reality of Fox News

JOSEPH MINTON AMANN
& TOM BREUER

NATION BOOKS
NEW YORK

FAIR AND BALANCED, MY ASS!
An Unbridled Look at the Bizarre Reality of Fox News

Copyright © 2007 Joseph Minton Amann and Tom Breuer

Published by
Nation Books
An Imprint of Avalon Publishing Group, Inc.
245 West 17th Street, 11th Floor
New York, NY 10011

AVALON
publishing group incorporated

Nation Books is a copublishing venture of the Nation Institute and Avalon Publishing Group, Incorporated.

Library of Congress Cataloging-in-Publication Data is available.

ISBN-10: 1-56858-347-8
ISBN-13: 978-1-56858-347-1

9 8 7 6 5 4 3 2 1

Book design by Bettina Wilhelm

Printed in the United States of America
Distributed by Publishers Group West

For Brett Somers and Charles Nelson Reilly

Contents

▼

PART 3: The B-Squad

PART 4: The Case Studies

PART 5: A Final Thought

INTRODUCTION:
The Fox News Viewer

▼

I think you people are absolutely disgusting. I love Bill O'Reilly. You're nothing but a bunch of commies. You asshole Canadians, you let all these people in. You don't give a sh. . . . You're anti-Christ up there. You're a bunch of atheists. You're nothing but a bunch of assholes. I can't stand people like you. Freedom of speech, okay, thank you for my freedom of speech, but I can't stand you damn Canadians. You assholes, I love Bill O'Reilly. What the hell are you doing? . . . You . . . Fuck off!

—Brenda Watson, Ashland, Oregon

FOX NEWS VIEWERS are an interesting lot. From our work on *Sweet Jesus, I Hate Bill O'Reilly* and sweetjesusihatebill oreilly.com, we've come to know many of them over the past couple years, usually through their rabid e-mails or enraged voicemail messages, such as the one above. We submit that Ms. Watson is not unique. In fact, we believe that she is the quintessential Fox News viewer.

Note the trademarks of the fervent Fox News Channel devotee:

1. They invoke the name of Christ . . . usually right before they tell you where you can shove his cross. They tell you

you're an atheist, yet give no support for this. Apparently, criticizing anyone at Fox News is tantamount to blasphemy and will get you booted right out of Canaan.

Typically, they know little about their own religion, and so their faith is based on an amalgam of televangelist sound bites and faith-based bumper-sticker slogans. They defend the secular images of our society as if they were religious icons. Suddenly, Santa represents the Christian faith no less than the Baby Jesus himself does.

2. They claim to love freedom of speech and other tenets of democracy, but it's a fickle love. Dissenting views are met with a full-frontal assault that invariably ascribes unpatriotic beliefs and traitorous motives. Words like "commies" are bandied about. Senator Barbara Boxer and Howard Dean are synonymous with Karl Marx and Fidel Castro. Political dissent, civil liberties, and the separation of church and state are the bastard stepchildren of the Fox News family and they will never nurse at the teat of Sean Hannity.

3. They hate Canadians. We're really not certain why. They just do. Maybe it's that trademark Canadian devil-may-care attitude. Maybe Canada's relatively moderate views on taxes, homosexuality, and religion are just too infuriating for God-fearing, gun-totin' Americans to handle. Yet our neighbors to the north are not alone. Fox News seems to foster hatred of nearly all foreigners. Sure, they offer the occasional reach-around for those who aid us in military action, but they still wanna be the top, baby.

Now, this isn't a book about the insanity of Fox News viewers. We could write that book, but stores tend not to stock volumes that require forklifts to get them out to your car. Anyway, to attack Fox News viewers is to address the symptom, not the illness. And Fox itself is deeply, deeply ill. Indeed, there is much to explore in the nearly unfathomable depths that Fox News has sunk to. It's an adventure of sorts. Twenty thousand leagues beneath the seas of journalist integrity.

It's a scary journey, to be sure, but it also promises to be a visceral thrill, a catharsis—and, if you just happen to be Brenda Watson of Ashland, Oregon—a glorious, long-prayed-for awakening.

Yes, Fox viewers are most definitely the victims, not the perpetrators. Their words are merely the froth and delirium of rabid, sickened souls. And as the cliché goes, if we can save just one soul, this will all have been worth it.

You ready, Brenda? Okay, let's begin.

THE TECHNIQUES

THE DEVIL WEARS
A FOX NEWS PRESS BADGE

ROUGHLY **SIX THOUSAND** years ago, according to the best minds of creation science, a man named Adam and a woman named Eve were led astray by a right bastard from the wrong side of the Euphrates, and mankind was forever routed from Paradise.

Ironically, the man and woman ate from the Tree of Knowledge, but all they really learned was: if you do for some reason run into a talking animal in the forest, for God's sake don't follow its advice.

It's been an uphill climb ever since, and the closest anyone's come to perfect happiness since then is when we all got to read the transcript from that Bill O'Reilly sexual harassment lawsuit.

But whatever grace we as a species have achieved on our own during that span has been hard-won. Our intellect has lifted us above the law of the jungle and helped salve the wounds from our toils. And our collective knowledge is now not an albatross but a savior.

Indeed, one of our greatest assets has been the free flow of information, brought for the benefit of man by honest brokers.

Or so it was in the beginning, until . . .

Our story begins, fittingly enough, before the fall of modern broadcast journalism. We start with a quote from a more sincere time—the height of television's golden age.

It's a speech contemporary audiences will recognize from George Clooney's provocative Oscar-nominated film *Good Night, and Good Luck:*

> We must not confuse dissent with disloyalty. We must remember always that accusation is not proof and that conviction depends upon evidence and due process of law. We will not walk in fear, one of another. We will not be driven by fear into an age of unreason, if we dig deep in our history and our doctrine, and remember that we are not descended from fearful men—not from men who feared to write, to speak, to associate and to defend causes that were, for the moment, unpopular. This is no time for men who oppose Senator McCarthy's methods to keep silent, or for those who approve. We can deny our heritage and our history, but we cannot escape responsibility for the result. There is no way for a citizen of a republic to abdicate his responsibilities. As a nation we have come into our full inheritance at a tender age. We proclaim ourselves, as indeed we are, the defenders of freedom, wherever it continues to exist in the world, but we cannot defend freedom abroad by deserting it at home. (Edward R. Murrow, *See it Now,* March 9, 1954)

Take a moment to reflect on the eloquence of Mr. Murrow's oration—its profound understanding of our nation's founding principles and unique place in history; its soaring prose and stirring call to invest hope in our better angels; its moral clarity and vigorous defense of our Constitution, of our venerable and indispensable tradition of intellectual freedom, and of each citizen's right—and duty—to dissent and to nurture a healthy distrust of our leaders.

Then read this:

MANCOW: Guys, I do want to do one serious thing today. Howard Dean ought to be kicked out of America.

BRIAN KILMEADE: Absolutely.

MANCOW: He ought to be tried for treason. He is the enemy. These people, these Dummy-crats—I'm not a Republican. I'm a Libertarian . . .

STEVE DOOCY: What did he say, Mancow, this time?

MANCOW: He said yesterday—it was late-breaking news—I, I've never done this before in my life. I was calling radio shows. I've never done that. I called Sean Hannity and Alan Colmes last night [and said]: "You guys gotta get on this. Howard Dean said we're going to lose the war."

KILMEADE: Yeah.

MANCOW: This is the head of the Democrats!

E. D. HILL: Hey, Mancow . . .

MANCOW: These people want every boy to die. They're blood-thirsty animals. Howard Dean is a vile human being. I can't believe it.

KILMEADE: Many people can't. His quote was, "The idea that the U.S. will win the war in Iraq is plain wrong."

DOOCY: Mancow, we have invited Howard Dean on this program many times and he has declined.

MANCOW: Because you'll ask him questions. You'll ask him real questions. And if I sound like I'm ranting and raving and furious, well, it's because I am. But this guy, this guy is blood-thirsty. He is evil. I'm telling you, I really think every time you report another dead body in Iraq, they go, "Hoo hoo, it's perfect!"

HILL: Well, that's it. You get the sense that people are rooting for the U.S. to lose the war.

DOOCY: For political purposes.

MANCOW: We know the enemy is watching the news.

DOOCY: Mancow, thanks very much.

(Fox News's *Fox & Friends* interview with shock jock Erich "Mancow" Muller, December 6, 2005)

Now, whatever your political stripe, it's hard not to note stark differences between the above excerpts. However, most disturbing is not the contrast between the above speakers' politics, their stances on each citizen's right and responsibility to hold unpopular opinions, and their general worldview, it's that in fifty years of assiduously refining its craft, broadcast journalism has apparently progressed from "We cannot defend freedom abroad by deserting it at home" to "What did he say, Mancow, this time?"

That's like discovering penicillin and then, half a century later, perfecting a state-of-the-art procedure for drilling holes in people's skulls to let the demons out.

Of course, some of you might already be crying foul. It's easy, after all, to spotlight snippets of dialogue to buttress a point. For instance, if you were to conclude from a politician's remark about our shaky prospects in Iraq that he was "vile," "bloodthirsty," and "evil" and was actually rooting for American casualties, without noting that he was really making an impassioned appeal on behalf of our soldiers' safety and welfare,[1] well, in a more enlightened time, your on-air hosts might just call you a big fat ignorant prick.

But Fox News has become the safest of safe havens for Mancow's brand of reactionary twaddle. (Indeed, Fox would later give Mancow his own hour-long special on the network.)

Still, if your appraisal of the hugely successful Fox is limited to its politics, or even its howlingly funny disavowal of those politics, you're seeing at best half the picture.

In *Sweet Jesus, I Hate Bill O'Reilly*, we showed how it was

O'Reilly's insanity and stupidity, far more than his dishonesty and obvious rightward tilt, that made him overripe for satire.

We laughed a lot while writing that book. Indeed, every time we thought Bill could become no more ridiculous—that he had at last ascended to the throne of eternal dumbass in Plato's World of Forms—he managed to top himself. For instance, at one point in our O'Reilly book we wrote a cheeky reference to the Nixonian enemies list we imagined Bill was nurturing late at night deep within the seamy viscera of his computer's hard drive. Not long after we wrote about it, O'Reilly actually did publish a media enemies list on his Web site.

We left the reference in. If Bill was going to go to that much effort to outsprint satire, who were we to question him?

Be assured that O'Reilly is the spittin' image of the network that fathered him, as are Hannity, Gibson, and all the rest. And as Isaiah 14:21 says, we must "Prepare a place to slaughter his sons for the sins of their forefathers; they are not to rise to inherit the land and cover the earth with their cities." (Okay, so maybe that's a bit harsh.)

Still, many will no doubt try to preempt our critique by dismissing us as liberals with an axe to grind, or by accusing us of distilling the worst of the network into the pages that follow.

We have three responses to this:

1. Fox's conservatism is at least to some measure beside the point. It's the network's insanity that most concerns—and, indeed, delights—us. While many will dismiss Murrow v. Mancow as an unfair fight, we could just as easily have contrasted a random 1968 William F. Buckley *Firing Line* excerpt with Fox's decision to endlessly loop film of a dirty-dancing, bra-and-panty-clad accused pedophile to the tune of "Hot for Teacher"[2]—as resident liberal Alan Colmes calmly introduced his show in the background.

2. While we're certainly dedicated to bringing you the best and worst of Fox's nut-job reporting, we're not exactly Woodward and Bernstein—or even Kitty Kelley, for that matter. Indeed, digging for dirt on Fox and its personalities would be like

panning for gold in El Dorado. This stuff springs up daily, like early-morning dew or the veins on O'Reilly's temple.

3. Fox is not just provably stupid and definitively crazy. By objective measures, it's also a failure as a news organization. Sure, as infotainment, it's a balls-out, rip-roaring success. Indeed, Fox can sell a dishonest meme like Ron Popeil can sell a Set-It-and-Forget-It Rotisserie. Both make you feel great about buying it but neither is really doing you any favors.

Take the widely cited October 2003 study from the University of Maryland's Program on International Policy Attitudes. The study concluded that people's knowledge of the issues surrounding the Iraq War depended in large part on their primary news source. And while the study trotted out numerous data and comparisons between consumers of the various major media, trust us when we tell you: its main conclusion was essentially that Fox viewers are morons. And they weren't necessarily born morons; that's the sad part. It was Fox that made them that way. As the study's authors pointed out, "Variations in misperceptions according to news source cannot simply be explained as a result of differences in the demographics of each audience, because these variations can also be found when comparing the rate of misperceptions within demographic subgroups of each audience."

This is just a dry, academic way of saying if you rely on Fox to inform you about world events, you might as well be watching *Maury*.

A couple of numbers did stand out, though. According to the study, 80 percent of people who watch primarily Fox News held at least one key misperception about issues surrounding the Iraq War, far exceeding those who got their news primarily from NPR or PBS, of whom only 23 percent held a major misperception.

Normally the market would punish people who sell a product that works four times worse than its competitors'. Clearly, this study was saying that Fox viewers would be better off information-wise if they watched no news at all—a fact that should have gotten a bunch of people unceremoniously canned. After all, if you're in the business of conveying information and you're actually conveying disinformation, you really, really, *really* suck at your job. If you taught school and you left your students with the impression that Dale Earnhardt was a celebrated twentieth-century Russian neoclassical composer and that Sergei Prokofiev was just some guy who drove his car into a wall and died, you probably wouldn't get tenured.

But in the wake of the U of Maryland study there were no high-level beheadings at Fox. The network's anchors were not suspended or replaced outright with people willing to do their jobs capably and diligently. There was no public mea culpa from Rupert Murdoch, accompanied by a solemn promise to restructure the organization from top to bottom.

No, the beat went on, as they say. That's kind of odd, unless you consider the possibility that Fox is really not all that interested in reporting but is very interested in, to paraphrase the alarmingly prescient film *Broadcast News,* being *salesmen.*

WELL, THAT'S YOUR OPINION!

THOSE OF US who watch Fox News professionally, or simply to unwind at the end of the day with a few well-earned belly laughs, dismiss the network at our own peril.

While there may be a considerable measure of Schadenfreude involved in tuning in to, say, *The O'Reilly Factor,* it's hard to overlook the fact that he influences millions of people nearly every day.

Indeed, watching Fox can be a little like watching *Jeopardy!* during kids' week. Even if you know more than they do—and you probably will—it's hard to feel good about yourself for the experience.

But it's not like the leading lights at Fox actually *enjoy* turning America into a nation of fatuous morons. If they could accomplish the same goals by not making their viewers morons, they'd probably do so, just as the tobacco companies would probably prefer their products didn't cause cancer, and Ann Coulter probably wishes the sound of her voice didn't make young men's and small animals' testicles shrivel. But none of that is going to stop any of them from making their money and spreading their propaganda.

To be sure, Fox News's sensationalistic brand of personality-and opinion-based journalism is a well-crafted sales strategy. And whatever else you want to say about them, they're excellent salesmen. Indeed, with just about any story on Fox, you can ask yourself three questions: are they pandering to their viewers, peddling right-wing propaganda, or both? [4]

Now, preaching to the choir can be quite lucrative, particularly if the choir has an almost unlimited budget for Rascal Scooters and Civil War chess pieces. And there's not necessarily anything wrong with it. Lots of media outlets preach to the choir. For some, it's their bread and butter. *The Nation's* not going to solicit a commentary on Social Security privatization from Grover Norquist, after all, and *Us Weekly* is certainly not going to report that Brad and Angelina *aren't* hot.

But most people who are engaged in some form of advocacy journalism—be they Rush Limbaugh or Al Franken—have the decency to admit it. Fox not only doesn't admit it, they famously cloak themselves in a tawdry veil of objectivity, endlessly shouting their "Fair and Balanced" and "We Report, You Decide" slogans until their viewers are finally programmed, *Clockwork Orange*–like, to believe them.

But again, by objective measures, Fox does a demonstrably poor job of presenting the cold, hard facts in a spin-free fashion. For instance, according to the Project for Excellence in Journalism's 2005 State of the News Media report, 24 percent of the stories on MSNBC's *Hardball with Chris Matthews* contained the host's opinion, compared with 97 percent on *The O'Reilly Factor.* The report also analyzed coverage of the war in Iraq, finding that 73 percent of Fox's Iraq War stories contained opinion, compared with 2 percent for CNN and 29 percent for MSNBC. Fox was also around twice as likely as its competitors to run positive stories about the war and far more likely to run positive stories than negative ones.

So what we're seeing more and more in today's news business, and particularly at Fox, is that personality and opinion sell. Not reasoned and informed opinion but blustering, loud, obnoxious, in-your-face opinion. Archie Bunker opinion. We're right and you're wrong. We're going to heaven and you're going to hell. We're patriots and you are traitors. We're men who love women, while you, my good sir, are a homo.

Of course, Fox News's one saving grace is that it's hilarious. Watching Hannity pummel Colmes won't make us better people, but it's kind of like seeing the school bully beat up the really irritating kid. It's not right, but you don't really want anyone to stop it. Seeing O'Reilly get his panties in a bundle when someone questions his ratings is always a good laugh. And having those three loons on *Fox & Friends* spout hateful lies with racist overtones is like music—sweet Clay Aiken music.

But Fox can be frustrating, too, because its employees are so unswervingly dedicated to denying their true nature. If your local weatherman dressed up as a Viking every day, called himself Hjørt Bjornsen, and told you there was a 60 percent chance of snow flurries and a 30 percent chance that Thor would rain fire and canned hummus from the sky during mid-morning rush hour—all the while claiming he absolutely *was not* dressed as a Viking—eventually it would stop being cute. That's essentially what it feels like to be sane and reasonably intelligent and tuned in to Fox News. It's hard to look away, because there's a guy on TV making a complete ass of himself while saying obviously untrue things. But it would be nice to get the forecast every once in a while.

So we understand your pain.

And we're here to turn that frown upside down.

I SEE YOUR STUPID ARGUMENT AND
I RAISE YOU MICHELLE MALKIN

LET'S START OFF with just one concrete example of Fox's special brand of lunacy.

While the commentators and anchors at Fox do the bulk of the heavy lifting, they're not afraid to farm out some of their dirtier work to subcontractors. And this is where Fox loves to be an equal-opportunity employer. A person of color on Fox is certainly something to behold, yet these are not your traditional minorities. This is the rainbow coalition of far-right conservatism and apologetic liberalism—and they're given free rein to be even loonier than their WASPy counterparts.

Take, for instance, Michelle Malkin. Malkin is a rising right-wing star who has, ironically enough, authored books on how liberals are unhinged and out of control as well as how the forced eviction and imprisonment of innocent Japanese-Americans during World War II was a pretty solid idea. If she still doesn't ring a bell, picture a pilot fish following a shark around cleaning scraps of shredded cabana boy from its host's teeth, and that will give you a good sense of why she shows up on Fox so often.

Watch Michelle Malkin for any length of time, and it's hard not to want to actually put her in one of those internment camps she's so fond of. Of course, we wouldn't actually support putting Malkin in an internment camp, even though she does pose a clear and present danger to Western liberal democracy. To paraphrase Voltaire, "We disapprove of what Michelle Malkin says, but we will defend to the death her right to say it." Then again, we'd also defend to the death your grandmother's right to say Kelly Ripa is sending her coded satanic messages through her television. That doesn't mean O'Reilly should book her on his show.

But the fact that O'Reilly does book Malkin on his show—over and over and over again—is as good an example as any of how Fox conducts its business.

Attractive in a superficially intellectual way? Check. Toes the party line? Check. Mirrors the viewers' fears and core beliefs? Check. Blustering right-wing demagogue? Check. Nutty as a holiday cheese log? Check.

And while an appearance by Michelle Malkin offers just the right blend of pandering and propaganda for the perfect Fox stew, on May 8, 2006, it took a vigorous stir from that big homophobic spoon she carries around to really get things cookin'.

On that bright, sunshiny, gay-bashing spring evening, Malkin and O'Reilly did their level best to misrepresent a California bill that dealt with public school history curricula and sexual orientation. Essentially, the bill amended a law that was already on the books prohibiting curricula that discriminated based on such things as race, sex, creed, or handicap. The proposed bill simply added gays and lesbians to the list of protected groups. The bill also said social sciences curricula should include "an age-appropriate study of the role and contributions of both men and women, Black Americans, American Indians, Mexicans, Asians, Pacific Islanders, and other ethnic groups, and people who are lesbian, gay, bisexual, or transgender, to the economic, political, and social development of California and the United States of America."

So it was merely a recognition that gay people shouldn't be smeared for their sexual orientation and that prominent gays should be duly recognized for their contributions to society. Pretty simple, really.

And likewise, it should have been pretty easy to grasp, unless you're congenitally dishonest, a rank homophobe, or stupid.

Here's how Loofah Man and Internment Girl framed the debate:

MALKIN: Well, this is much more radical than ensuring that homosexuals and other people of minority sexual orientation status are respected in the schools. It's already against the law in California to discriminate against anyone based on their sexual orientation.

I looked this bill over very closely, and it is a very radical, very extreme, dangerous bill. It says that no teacher can even say anything that would, quote unquote, "reflect adversely" on anyone, a historical figure, whatever, based on their sexual orientation.

And so, now, there are real concerns that this could be interpreted broadly in the liberal Ninth Circuit Court of Appeals and other liberal courts as saying that you can't even have sports teams, for example, that discriminate based on gender. And this is pure political propaganda.

O'REILLY: Well—and also, if you are a teacher, what are you—you're not going to be able to say bad things about Jeffrey Dahmer? He's a cannibal, a gay cannibal, and you can't say, "Well, that's wrong." I mean, if what you're saying is true, teachers would not be able to cast aspersions on even villains if they were homosexual.

MALKIN: Yeah, that's right . . .

Okay, there's so much bullshit stuffed into those five paragraphs, you practically need a ZIP file.

Now, if you actually want to research the bill instead of taking Malkin's and O'Reilly's word for it, that's fine—though unnecessary. We promise you, there was nothing in there about special rights for gay cannibals.

All the bill said is that you can't trash historical figures *because of* their race, gender, religion, or sexual orientation. So basically, a teacher can't stand in front of his class and exclaim, "You know what they're saying about Alexander the Great, don't you? *FLAM*-er!" Similarly, you can't say JFK was a dirty papist, or use the n-word when referring to Martin Luther King Jr. That just makes sense.

And if you're taking art history and learning about the ceiling of the Sistine Chapel, it probably also makes sense to discuss Michelangelo's homosexuality. Is it absolutely necessary? Probably not. But if you're discussing his life, and his impact as an artist on sixteenth-century Europe, then you should probably mention that he was a gay guy. This fact had a significant impact on his work. Is it necessary to read his love poems to Tommaso dei Cavalieri? No. Let's face it, gay love letters from the 1530s are kind of a snoozefest anyway.

Furthermore, *what the fuck?* Really, what's with the gay cannibal crack? Is O'Reilly really imagining a bleak futuristic dystopia where gay cannibal history is brutally suppressed by sinister government jackboots and where kids can't be told that storing your homosexual lover in your Sub-Zero is frowned upon? Oh, how will our children ever be able to compete in the world marketplace?

Anyway, what history class are your kids taking where they're learning about Jeffrey Dahmer? Seriously, if you happen upon a copy of your son's American history syllabus and it says, "Sept. 7: Ideological Foundations of American Revolution in New England Agrarian Communities in the Early Colonial Period. Sept. 14: The Fabulously Gay Cannibalism of Jeff Dahmer," you should probably move to a new school district.

We grant you, it was a long time ago, but when we were in school we're pretty sure we never had classes where we learned all about John Wayne Gacy . . . our Trapper Keepers filled with gruesome crime scene photos and sketches of creepy birthday clowns.

But this argument is actually quite typical of Fox News—the ugly twin heads of pandering and propaganda are out there in the open for all the world to see.

Malkin went on to say, "And in any case, I think school teachers in California and everywhere else ought to be paying more attention to whether or not third graders can find, oh, Sacramento or Washington, D.C., on a map than what the sexual orientation is of historical figures in America."

Be assured, Malkin and O'Reilly are a lot more concerned about whether kids know Henry David Thoreau was gay than whether Jeffrey Dahmer was. Or whether they can find the Castro District on a map, for that matter.

IT'S LIKE NEWS FOR FOURTEEN-YEAR-OLDS

OF COURSE, THE above is just a small sampling of the cornucopia of insanity you get every day from Fox.

But O'Reilly's thoughts on gay cannibalism are actually the deep end of the pool compared to the stream of inane chatter and bright, shiny things the network likes to toss at TV screens minute by minute.

"News with a pulse . . . News not boring" was the old mantra of Shepard Smith's *Fox Report*. Somewhere along the line he's dropped it—probably because it's an awful slogan. Yet it really sums up the Fox approach to journalism.

While the "elite" media bore you with straightforward news couched in civility, Fox is like the dentist who tries to lure people to his practice by handing out fudge and Snickers bars.

Flashy graphics and bombastic music, women who look like they may have started out in the soft-core porn industry, and stouthearted men who talk loud enough to cover up the fact that they don't know what the hell they're talking about—*that's* Fox News.

As Fox News anchors go, we like Shepard Smith. Of all the network's personalities, he's one of the few who dares take little digs at O'Reilly and he still appears to be walking around with two intact legs. But let's face it, he's running the McDonald's of the news world.

His show has taken the already dummied-down approach of Fox News and hammered it into a thin film that can be eaten like a Fruit Roll-Up. The graphics are bolder, the music more intense, and the copy even "hipper." You'll hear stuff like, "Now with your G-Block Quick Hits." What does that even mean? It's the sort of thing you'd hear if they made Ashlee Simpson managing editor of the *CBS Evening News*.

Rest assured it's much the same throughout the broadcast day. For instance, on nearly all Fox News Channel shows, random local car chases have become programming staples. And we're not talking about the ones featuring wife-murdering football stars. Those are kickin'. We're talking about the guy who steals a Camaro from the parking lot of the Travelodge in Van Nuys and spends the next fifteen minutes driving down Sepulveda. Will the guy get shot? Will an innocent pedestrian get creamed? Will the police drag one of those spiky things across the street to blow out his tires? How far can he drive on the rims?

Most important, why is this a national story? And why is a

report on nuclear disarmament talks being interrupted to cover it? Is this news for people who find *Deal or No Deal* too intellectually taxing? And why, when we do return to regular programming, is there a little box in the corner of the screen to show you exactly how things are going back in Van Nuys?

But that's Fox for you. When it's trying to be serious, it's laughable. When it's trying to be light and breezy, it's like a railroad spike in your frontal lobe.

The sad part is, this lowest-common-denominator approach to journalism is working. Whatever else you want to say about him, O'Reilly's right when he says his show is crushing his competition. The easy response to that is it doesn't matter. After all, what do ratings really have to do with running a respectable newsroom? But it does matter. We should all be concerned when so unworthy an enterprise triumphs—whether in the marketplace or, even more crucially, in the marketplace of ideas.

In this introductory chapter, we've given just a few examples of Fox's unbound hubris, stupidity, tawdriness, fearmongering, and not-so-subtle bigotry. Ah, it is but an aperitif. We hope you'll follow us to the feast, where we'll serve up the full smorgasbord of crazy, insipid, inane, oafish, dishonest, didactic, quasi-entertaining delights that together make up Murdoch's nightmare.

As they say in the publishing world, if you like Bill O'Reilly, you'll *love* Fox News.

Now, if you were able to hop in a time machine and go back twelve years to warn the people of 1995 about Fox, and they asked you to describe this dreadful new phenomenon, you'd probably say, "It's as if you approached G. Gordon Liddy and the *Entertainment Tonight* crew and asked them to go cover the war in Bosnia."

Indeed, this is where the sacred of old-school journalism meets the profane of pop-culture disinfotainment.

Truly, Edward R. Murrow would not be amused. But that doesn't mean you shouldn't be.

Enjoy . . .

NOTES

1. After saying that the "idea that we're going to win this war is an idea that unfortunately is just plain wrong," Dean went on to say, "I've seen this before in my life and it cost us 25,000 brave American soldiers in Vietnam and I don't want to go down that road again."
2. This really happened.[3]
3. No, seriously.
4. When watching *The O'Reilly Factor,* it's actually four questions, the fourth being, "At precisely what point will he try to sell you a sleeve of No Spin Golf Balls or beg you to buy his latest book?"

2

WHY BENJAMIN FRANKLIN WOULD NEVER WATCH FOX
(Even If He Had Digital Cable)

Well, there are these two kinds of patriotism. There's blind patriotism, unflagging patriotism. And then there's the patriotism that says I live in a democracy and it's very important for the health and the life of this democracy that it get better all the time, not get worse. Because when a democracy gets worse, it can get worse and worse and worse. And the nightmare in every democracy, the very nightmare, is if it gets worse and worse, we could end up totalitarian.

—*Norman Mailer on* Hannity & Colmes, *March 1, 2006*

When is it okay to whack them around?

—*Brian Kilmeade* of Fox & Friends, *interviewing New York police commissioner Raymond Kelly about the handling of protests during the 2004 Republican National Convention*

BEING A PATRIOT means different things to different people, but if there's one pillar of our democracy that's truly indispensable to our way of life, it's the Constitution.

This daring and inspired document helped enshrine the revolutionary spirit and core values of our Founding Fathers, guaranteeing broad individual freedoms through its Bill of Rights. Among these, of course, are freedom of speech, freedom of religion, freedom of assembly, the right of due process, and the right to be secure against unreasonable searches and seizures.

Unfortunately, Fox views certain of these rights and freedoms in much the same way the Bush family regards Neil. Yeah, he exists, but it's best not to draw too much attention to him just now.

Indeed, while Fox explicitly and implicitly promotes itself as the pro-America alternative, the truth is that it's the opposite of patriotic. O'Reilly, Hannity, Gibson, and the rest are at best Potemkin patriots. They love the colors, the victory cheers, and the bombs bursting in air but they don't much care for the country itself. They adore the flag but they hate the Constitution.

Essentially, they're like children who prefer to play with the box their toy came with because they're not yet mature enough to appreciate the gift itself.

This shouldn't really be all that surprising when you think about it. Fox is in the lowest-common-denominator business. A shady used-car salesman doesn't try to sell sketchy El Caminos by donning a tweed jacket, clenching a rustic ivory-stemmed pipe between his teeth, and regaling his customers with tales of John Locke, Thomas Jefferson, and the philosophical underpinnings of the Bill of Rights. No, he throws on a glittery red, white, and blue hat, waves a miniature department store flag, and screams that people better buy what he's selling or they'll regret it forever.

Such is Fox. The network's loud, terrifying graphics, the ubiquitous flag in the upper-left-hand corner, and the bizarre spectacle of E. D. Hill dispensing homespun foreign-policy advice is proof enough that it's more interested in PR than true patriotism.

Indeed, Fox relies on at least three tactics to demonstrate how patriotic it is, only one of which is even superficially pro-America:

1. larding broadcasts with patriotic imagery, jingoism, and catchphrases until viewers basically have America leaking out of their orifices;
2. promoting blatantly anti-American philosophies and tactics and presenting them as pro-American; and
3. disparaging their countrymen's patriotism at every possible turn, up to and including accusing them of treason.

WIRETAP THAT ASS

IN DECEMBER 2005, the *New York Times* disclosed that President Bush had approved a warrantless domestic wiretapping program in apparent violation of the Foreign Intelligence Surveillance Act (FISA).

The revelation sent chills up the spines of civil libertarians, and even some Republicans—most notably Arlen Specter, the then-chairman of the Senate Judiciary Committee—considered the president's program suspect and possibly illegal.

Well, in the next couple of months, Fox went to work on the story like Lynndie England with a gimp mask and a box of hot nipple clamps until it pretty much said what they wanted it to say.

Indeed, in defense of what was pretty clearly a violation of both the spirit and letter of American law and the Constitution, Fox let loose a barrage of misinformation that would have made Joseph Goebbels soak his Übermensch Underoos.

Just days after the FISA story broke, Fox correspondent Jim Angle regurgitated the administration's chief justification for the program—that secretly bypassing FISA courts was necessary to move quickly on threats—without noting provisions in the FISA law that already allowed for emergency surveillance (under existing law, FISA warrants can be obtained after surveillance has already begun):[1]

ANGLE: So the president authorized the National Security Agency to intercept international calls and e-mails—but only those linked to Al Qaeda—even if one end of the conversation was in the United States. Some argue that requires a warrant from what is known as the FISA court, which operates in secret. The president suggested that would have been too slow.

BUSH: (video clip) The people responsible for helping us protect and defend came forth with the current program, because it enables us to move faster and quicker.

ANGLE: But congressional critics argue the president has taken the law into his own hands, that he doesn't have the authority to order electronic intercepts of anyone in the U.S. without getting a search warrant. (*Special Report with Brit Hume,* December 19, 2005)

A little tip to reporters: It's okay to provide context if the president says something misleading. Not every story has to slavishly adhere to a he said/she said structure. Indeed, one wonders how far a Republican administration would have to stray before Fox reporters actually showed an interest in reporting:

ANGLE: So the president authorized the Department of Health and Human Services to send Americans to federal cyborg-run Soylent Green factories—but only those citizens of advanced age. Some argue that Soylent Green is people.

SUPREME CHANCELLOR JEB BUSH: (video clip) Soylent Green is not people.

ANGLE: Back to you, Shepard.

When Fox reporters weren't suggesting that bypassing FISA was necessary (even if blatantly illegal), they were saying the surveillance program was terribly popular (even if blatantly illegal).

On January 2, 2006, Stuart Varney, substitute host for *Your World with Neil Cavuto,* informed his viewers that the president's wiretapping program was supported by 96 percent of the population. That's right. Ninety-six percent.

His source? An unscientific online poll from a Web site affiliated with a think tank headed by a former Reagan administration official.

You might as well run a poll on Teletubbies.com asking, "Is Mommy nice?"

VARNEY: Here's the news of the moment: America wants those controversial wiretaps. Just take a look at a new online poll by

FamilySecurityMatters.com. Ninety-six percent of the nation says, "Go ahead, tap away." Terror analyst Harvey Kushner is one of the group's contributing editors. Harvey, welcome to the program.

KUSHNER: Thanks, Stuart.

VARNEY: That's unusually strong support—96 percent.

KUSHNER: Well, it's strong, and we're not saying it's totally scientific. As CNN tries to imply, it's those who visited the Web site and put in their answer.

Oh, those slick hucksters over at CNN. Shame on them!

Now, as any first-year journalism student should know, you can get polls to say just about anything if you don't worry about selection bias. But if Varney had any sense at all, he'd know you can't *legitimately* get 96 percent of the country to agree on *who* the president is, much less what he does.

Still, it wouldn't matter if 99 percent of the visitors to the ACLU's Web site approved of the program. The law and the Constitution are interpreted by the courts, not by online polls.

But that's just the public. What do legal experts and members of Congress think? Well, if you watched Fox, you might get the impression that even über-left-wing Senator Ted Kennedy thinks the program is legal. And he's the second most liberal senator in Massachusetts!

On January 25, 2006, Angle was back reporting on the warrantless wiretapping story for *Special Report with Brit Hume:*

ANGLE: After three days of an administration offensive and weeks of debate and accusations, there seems to be some agreement on what is illegal and what is not.

KENNEDY: (video clip) When the president goes around and speaks and says we are monitoring calls from overseas from Al Qaeda to the United States, the NSA can go ahead and do that now under the law.

ANGLE: Though Kennedy suspects the eavesdropping is far more than that, what he says is legal is what the president says he's doing.

BUSH: (video clip) The intercept of certain communications emanating between somebody inside the United States and outside the United States, and one of the numbers would be a—reasonably suspected to be an Al Qaeda link.

Of course, you might think from the way Angle spun his report that Kennedy was basically supporting the program as it was structured. Unfortunately, when Angle reported, "Though Kennedy suspects the eavesdropping is far more than that," here, apparently is what he meant:

KENNEDY: . . . It isn't the Democrats that say that the president's exceeded the law, it's the Congressional Research Service. They're not Democrats, they're not Republicans, they're independent students of the Constitution and legislation. No one can read their declaration about the president's conduct and not question the president's activity.

Hmmm, that's a lot of missing information there. One might even say it flatly contradicts the entire slant of Angle's report. Indeed, Angle's reporting is practically a seminar on how to take quotes out of context to alter their meaning. Whiny politicians and celebrities everywhere should take note. *This* is out of context—not that thing you said about atheists and queers causing hurricanes.

But then, why should Fox viewers even care about the considered opinion of the Congressional Research Service when Bill O'Reilly has a magical law library in his shorts?

O'REILLY: . . . Here's my argument. And this is a winner all day long. The wiretap laws are set up to prevent criminal—criminal abuses, investigating criminal cases. This is a military matter. It's a military matter.

NEWT GINGRICH: Right.

O'REILLY: You can intercept anything you want, any kind of communication you want without a warrant in a war. And that's it. And that's what they should do. (*The O'Reilly Factor,* February 6, 2006)

Sometimes you wonder if Bill has a staff member specifically assigned to making up facts or if his employees just hate him that much. Needless to say, you can't intercept anything you want without a warrant in a war.[2] This would be true even if we *were* officially at war with the American public, which, officially at least, we're not.

So in the weeks after the *Times* story ran, Fox pushed the impression that the warrantless wiretaps ordered by President Bush were (a) necessary, (b) overwhelmingly popular, (c) supported even by Ted Kennedy, and (d) legal.

And they managed to do it with straight faces and with that electronic Old Glory flapping in the upper-left-hand corner over and over.

So when a Democratic congressman actually proposed holding the president of the United States accountable to the law and the Constitution, the groundwork was already laid to paint him as some kind of anti-American nut.

Indeed, March 16, 2006, was a red-letter day for America, as two familiar Fox personalities lined up to ridicule Senator Russ Feingold's call for censuring George W. Bush:

JOHN GIBSON: The far-left has once again grabbed the attention away from more realistic Democrats, and presented the country with the image of a Democrat leader, Senator Russ Feingold, demanding the censure, perhaps even impeachment, over something which most Americans actually approve. Is the NSA surveillance program illegal? New records from a secret spying appellate court say no, but it has become such a Democrat mantra that they are sure it was illegal. (*The Big Story with John Gibson*)

DICK MORRIS: Feingold's pushing the wrong issue. If he was censuring Bush over something like the—saying there were no—there were weapons of mass destruction in Iraq, there he might have a little bit of support. But the public overwhelmingly supports Bush on the wiretapping issue. They want that wiretapping because they think it makes them safe. And they don't believe the president should be censured, particularly not in the middle of war. (*Hannity & Colmes*)

Translation: Obeying the law and upholding the Bill of Rights are not polling well this election cycle, so try again, you dirty Constitution-lover.

START YOUR MORNING WITH
A NICE HOT CUP OF SHUT THE FUCK UP

NOW, MOST JOURNALISTS would see it as their duty to inform us of assaults to our civil liberties. But Fox seems to have a different take on government transparency—it's fine just as long as the government's occasionally encouraged to throw sand in our eyes.

On the June 29, 2006, edition of *Fox & Friends,* former *F&F* co-host and current *Fox News Live* anchor E. D. Hill had had enough of the *New York Times*'s informing its readers that their government was spying on them. She made this neat little suggestion in response to a *Times* report about a government program that tracked international financial transactions: "What about—in the past, we have had, at times, an Office of Censorship, where people review what is about—is something that was—it's going to be big, you've got to run it through and say, 'Okay, does this hurt our country or is it of, you know, news value?'"

First of all, E. D., you make Crispin Glover sound like Cato the Elder. Seriously, did you translate that from Klingon? You're a professional broadcaster, for God's sake. You sound like half a dozen lobotomy patients playing telephone.

Second, a news organization calling for the creation of official government censors is just bizarre. It's like McDonald's asking for a federal ban on beef and cheese.

Hill is right about one thing. There was an Office of Censorship during World War II. It immediately ceased operation when Japan surrendered and was abolished shortly thereafter.

We could argue all day whether it was appropriate to administer such a program under the dire threat of two ascendant powers bent on world conquest.

What the program definitely didn't do, however, was prevent media from telling Americans that their privacy rights were being shredded in the name of an open-ended campaign to stamp out an abstract noun[3] that could never be stamped out in a thousand years if we tapped every phone in the country and herded everyone but Dick Cheney into internment camps.

The same day that Hill made her mind-numbingly incoherent yet startlingly ill-informed proposal, her *Fox & Friends* co-host Brian Kilmeade was licking the same hallucinogenic toad on his Fox News radio show: "See, I'm more into the ends justifying the means."

Great. This is the kind of thing you want to hear from journalists. Kilmeade later continued:

> You put up the Office of Censorship. You get a consensus to journalists to analyze and then you realize what FDR realized early. Winning is everything. Freedom is—you don't have any freedom if the Nazis are the victors. You have no one to trade with if Western Europe fails. That's the reality. You're in love with the law, but I'm in love with survival.

Kilmeade's argument is certainly persuasive. How else will we survive without an Office of Censorship? But couldn't we use that argument to justify any violation of civil liberties? Full-body cavity strip searches at bus stops? Only if you want America to survive.

Hey, why don't they imbed computer chips into our brains when we're children? That way the government can always tell when we're contemplating thought crimes.

Well, if you love your country you'll support it.

Then again, maybe Fox is right. Maybe we need to give up personal freedoms to ensure the safety of our country. They're obviously leading the way. They're even willing to censor themselves!

What's a little sacrifice when so much is on the line? After all, what kind of anti-American lunatic would put his own needs ahead of the security of his countrymen?

But look, the bottom line is airline travel has just gotten worse. It's terrible when you get on the plane. It's terrible to get through security. Now you can't check anything.

I FedEx my stuff ahead. Can you imagine that? You've got to FedEx your stuff because you can't take it on the airline? I mean, it's out of control. (Bill O'Reilly, *The O'Reilly Factor*, May 18, 2005)

EGGS BENEDICT ARNOLD AND OTHER AMERICA-HATING BREAKFASTS

AH, TREASON. So easy to cook up and yet such a memorable meal. And the kids over at Fox News just love serving it.

Now, back in the day, treason was a rare and serious charge, but Fox throws it around like baby batter at a key party.

And who's guilty of treason? The horde of Republicans who harshly and openly criticized President Clinton while our troops were in harm's way during the Kosovo campaign?[4] Bwa ha ha ha ha. Nice try, commie. Treason is a distinctly Democratic affliction. Everybody knows that.

Sometimes it's an entire political faction that's got the fever:

And it shows how the left, in providing this aid and comfort to the enemy, is helping bin Laden plot the destruction of the United States, if he can. (Dick Morris, *The Big Story with John Gibson*, October 29, 2004)

Sometimes it's just their presidential candidate:

John Kerry knows he gives aid and comfort to the enemy. Every time they step up to the microphone and tear down our military they build up the insurgency. (Michael Reagan, *The Big Story with John Gibson*, December 5, 2005)

Sometimes it's a war protestor:

Coming up next, meet an Iraq War widow who says Cindy Sheehan is committing treason. (Alan Colmes, *Hannity & Colmes*, April 19, 2006)

Sometimes it's a lowly senator:

Meanwhile, it is a time of war. And the Democratic leader of the U.S. Senate is calling the commander in chief, in his words, dangerously incompetent. Does this border on treason? (Neil Cavuto, *Your World with Neil Cavuto*, March 23, 2006)

Now, it's hard to conceive of anything so unpatriotic as rebranding legitimate political dissent as treason. As we noted, prominent Republicans were quite a bunch of sassy pants during Bill Clinton's Kosovo campaign, and Fox and its favorite guests didn't accuse them of hating the country.

But in the 2000s, war has suddenly become political Kevlar. Apparently, some pundits believe you can't criticize the president during a war, no matter how ill-conceived it is or how much of a clusterfuck it turns into. After all, that would give aid and comfort to the enemy!

So what if Bush attacks Iran next? Doesn't matter. He's your president. Venezuela? Oh, they've been asking for it anyway. What if he wants to send your kid to Nepal to nip the Sherpa threat in the bud? There are some things you just don't do, and one is criticizing your country's commander in chief while our troops are high in the Himalayas bravely dying on yaks for your freedom. What if he wants to unilaterally invade England to reinstall King Ralph as sovereign? Come on! Do you support the war effort, or are you a traitor? Choose! Now!

Of course, it's possible that ascribing treasonous motives to roughly half of Congress is just pure right-wing agitprop and was never really meant to be taken seriously. Whole political parties can't really hate their own country. Only individuals and entire Ivy League colleges have that kind of moral agency.

> Does Yale hate America? I mean, should we be mad at Yale? Eighty-five percent liberal. That doesn't seem fair and balanced to me. (Bill O'Reilly, *The O'Reilly Factor*, April 4, 2006)

Let's break that down.

"Does Yale hate America?"

Of course it does. But Yale also likes pudding and hopes for a *When Harry Met Sally* sequel. Also, Yale sometimes drunk-dials its ex-boyfriend late at night after watching *Mystic Pizza*.

"I mean, should we be mad at Yale?"

Yes, we should. It hates America, right? And all those late-night phone calls. Ugh. In fact, we should just give Yale the silent treatment.

"Eighty-five percent liberal. That doesn't seem fair and balanced to me."

Nor to us. In fact, if Yale is using "fair and balanced" in its promotional materials, Fox News should sue. How can they lose?

DON'T PEE ON MY TROOPS AND TELL ME IT'S RAINING

ON THE FEBRUARY 20, 2006, edition of *Hannity & Colmes*, Sean Hannity gave us this "we report, you decide" take on the Democratic Party:

> Your party has undermined the war on terror every step in the way. They are consistently, repeatedly, almost on a daily basis, not only wrong, but they're hurting the war effort. They're hurting our troops. They're hurting our commander in chief.

And you know something? I think you're hurting yourself politically as a result of it.

Yeah, Sean has never been much for subtlety. Girls Gone Wild
commercials are known to show more nuance than this. You
might as well get your news from Hilary Duff's MySpace page.

Of course, this is not just the opinion of Sean Hannity. It's the
semiofficial stance of Fox News. It's not meant to spark a debate
on how we should approach terrorism. It's a firm declaration that
those who support the Bush administration are right and everyone
else is screwing over the country.

Unfortunately, there is no adequate sound-bite response. "Nuh
uh, no we aren't" just doesn't cut it. But it's not designed to
engender discussion. Like much of what's said on Fox, it's meant
to marginalize and degrade the opposition.

Now, this is a slippery slope to be sure. Saying an opponent is
wrongheaded on an issue is one thing. Saying he's a pox on the
nation and an affront to our fearless leader is quite another. But to
Sean, criticisms of our president are no less blasphemous than
Galileo's proclamations were to Pope Urban VIII. Unfortunately,
Sean and Pope Urb were about equally astute.

Really, what would Hannity see as an ideal alternative to healthy
debate? A one-party system? Or would he prefer a two-party system
where the Democrats are so thoroughly marginalized they become
the obliging Tom Willis to the Republicans' domineering George
Jefferson? Say it ain't so, Weezie. Say it ain't so.

WEDNESDAY IS KARAOKE NIGHT FOR TERRORISTS

IF YOU MADE a list of what Fox News pundits love most about
America, it might go a little something like this: (1) the flag, (2) the
troops (abstract), (3) patriotic songs, (4) the Fourth of July, (5)
parades with old VFW guys wielding ceremonial rifles and young
babes handing out Domino's coupons, (6) any Founding Father
who ever publicly mentioned God or Jesus, (7) Ronald Reagan
silver dollars from the National Collector's Mint, (8) the Pledge of

Allegiance (pre-commie), (9) advanced military technology that the Reagan administration never sold to our declared enemies, (10) the troops (actual).

On a good day, the First Amendment might just barely squeak its way into the top five hundred, somewhere between Tom Clancy novels and all-you-can-eat night at Long John Silver's.

So when free expression goes up against a beloved patriotic song on *Hannity & Colmes,* you just know that tune's gonna make the First Amendment its bitch.

On July 7, 2006, Sean Hannity reacted to an antiwar parody of "God Bless America" as if he'd just watched Osama bin Laden and Saddam Hussein perform the Kama Sutra on Betsy Ross.

The song played on in the background as Hannity metaphorically loaded his knickers: "Climbing mountains, crossing oceans, and invading foreign soil. God help America, no blood for oil. God forgive America, no blood for oil."

One of the show's guests that night was Diane Wilson of the antiwar group Code Pink. She offered an unapologetic defense of both the song and the sentiment behind it: "Well, first of all, I think that was the Raging Grannies who sang that, and that was the first time I had heard it. But I think the Raging Grannies are very tough, patriotic women, and I think there is freedom of speech in this country, and I've got no problem with them doing it."

Fox's other guest was Republican strategist Karen Hanretty. She responded, "You might not like the war, you might not like how the war is being conducted, but I don't think that most people out there look at these Raging Grannies or Code Pink or any of these protesters who go around making fun of, you know, American patriotic songs."

Notice how the argument has been reframed. Instead of a group protesting its government's actions in the Middle East, you now have a fringe element "making fun of" patriotic songs. Who could possibly support that?

Of course, the Raging Grannies were hardly making fun of "God Bless America." They were simply appropriating a familiar national totem to further what they interpret as a classically patriotic aim, like when Bill O'Reilly sticks a flag on a ceramic "No Spin Grandma" mug and sells it to morons.

But Hannity was having none of it. Of course, rather than discuss the issue like an adult, he employed a familiar diversionary tactic.

Indeed, when he has no real argument to make, he will often pair his guests up with other, more polarizing liberals. Then, once he's established some faint unholy alliance, he'll question the actions of the absent party and ask his guest to defend them. It's not so much a "have you stopped beating your wife?" strategy as a "has Michael Moore stopped beating his wife, and do you support him?" strategy.

HANNITY: So you're supporting Cindy Sheehan's movement right now. You're supporting her fast. Correct?

WILSON: Yes. As a matter of fact, it was Code Pink that called the fast.

HANNITY: Okay, Code Pink. So you support Cindy Sheehan calling our troops rapists and calling our soldiers war criminals. You support Cindy Sheehan calling our president a lying, filthy bastard. You support our president being called the Führer. You support that Cindy says that our president murdered her son. You support all that, right?

WILSON: Well, I don't see how you can say that people that are in the political movement together, in a peace movement together. There's a lot of people in there that . . .

HANNITY: I didn't ask you that. Is it appropriate to call our troops rapists and war criminals and the president a lying, filthy bastard? Do you support that, yes or no?

WILSON: Well, I'll tell you what. I've got a nephew over there, and I know he's not a rapist . . .

HANNITY: I didn't ask about your nephew. I asked if you support the rhetoric of your fellow antiwar protestors.

WILSON: Well, I think she's got a reason where she's coming from.

HANNITY: All right, so it's okay to call our soldiers who did nothing but help defend this country rapists? It's okay to say that? It's okay to say that we're war criminals? Do you support that, yes or no? Do you support it?

WILSON: Well, I'm trying to tell you, if you'll shut up a minute. I believe she's got freedom of speech . . .

HANNITY: I didn't ask if she's got freedom of speech. I asked if you agree with it. Do you support it, yes or no? It's a simple question.

WILSON: I—I think Cindy Sheehan has been . . .

HANNITY: Yes or no?

COLMES: We've actually got to run. But I doubt that every Republican supports what Saxby Chambliss said that we showed earlier tonight. Or Conrad Burns. Thank you very much.

Of course, Hannity's "yes or no" technique is classic. Quite frankly, it's approaching vaudevillian status. It's fast becoming the "Who's on First?" of cable news.

Hey, Sean. Do you support Bill O'Reilly sexually harassing a subordinate employee? Do you support the Republican Party covering up a congressman's creepy e-mails to underage pages?

Yes or no? YES OR NO?

Third base.

TAKE THIS PROTEST AND SHOVE IT

MARK TWAIN ONCE said, "Patriotism is supporting your country all the time, and your government when it deserves it." While in a more whimsical (or perhaps just less conciliatory) mood, he also defined the patriot as "the person who can holler the loudest without knowing what he is hollering about."

Yeah, it's safe to say Twain would have hated Brian Kilmeade.

During a July 13, 2004, interview with New York police commissioner Raymond Kelly, the *Fox & Friends* co-host asked his guest about plans for security during the 2004 Republican National Convention.

Read this and judge for yourself just how much of it is good-natured ribbing and how much is a reflection of Kilmeade's actual beliefs. Then again, you have to wonder if those two dudes on *Fox & Friends* occasionally said stuff just to make E. D. Hill look smart:

KILMEADE: When is it okay to whack them around?

KELLY: Never.

KILMEADE: If they are not moving, if they are threatening you, can you whack them around?

KELLY: No, no, no. Believe me, we do things according to the Constitution and the laws of New York state. So that's not something we engage in.

(Crosstalk)

KILMEADE: I hate seeing these protestors.

God bless America.

NOTES

1. A February 7, 2006, statement by Wisconsin senator Russ Feingold read, in part:

> The administration has said that it ignored FISA because it takes too long to get a warrant under that law. But we know that in an emergency, where the attorney general believes that surveillance must begin before a court order can be obtained, FISA permits the wiretap to be executed immediately as long as the government goes to the court within seventy-two hours. The attorney general has complained that the emergency provision does not give him enough flexibility, he has complained that getting a FISA application together or getting the necessary approvals takes too long. But

the problems he has cited are bureaucratic barriers that the executive branch put in place, and could easily remove if it wanted.

Moreover, if the administration thought the FISA process was too cumbersome, it could have sought changes in the law instead of simply deciding to unilaterally ignore it.

2. The FISA law specifically addresses this. It says, "Notwithstanding any other law, the President, through the Attorney General, may authorize electronic surveillance without a court order under this subchapter to acquire foreign intelligence information for a period not to exceed fifteen calendar days following a declaration of war by the Congress." So O'Reilly's argument is a winner all day long for fifteen days, after which he reverts to being a dumbass under both the FISA statute and the Constitution of the United States.

3. A tip of the pen to Terry Jones for this characterization of Bush's grammatically tenuous "war on terrorism."

4. Incredibly, on April 9, 1999, George W. Bush, then a presidential contender, said, "Victory means exit strategy, and it's important for the president to explain to us what the exit strategy is." In the same interview, he also called the Kosovars "Kosovoians." If a leading Democrat hypocritically demanded exit strategies only from wars started by Republicans and then proceeded to call the Iraqis "Iraqimuffins," it would be kinda hard to take him seriously on matters of foreign policy. But blissfully we sail along.

THE WHORE OF BABYLON
HAS A CABLE NETWORK

And I am a Christian, sir.

> —Sean Hannity, March 3, 2006

Look, I'm a Christian.

> —Fred Barnes, February 12, 2006

I have seen cartoons that have attacked my faith, Catholicism. I'm a Christian.

> —Sean Hannity, February 6, 2006

You know I'm a Christian.

> —Sean Hannity, February 2, 2006

I'm a Christian.

> —Rich Lowry, December 22, 2005

I'm a Christian, you're a Christian. Okay.

> —Sean Hannity, December 12, 2005

I'm a Catholic.

> —Sean Hannity, July 25, 2005

I'm a Christian. I'm a Catholic.

> —Bill O'Reilly, June 23, 2005

Just as I believe that it was a real event, because I'm a Catholic, and that's what I believe. I choose to believe it.

—*Bill O'Reilly, May 18, 2005*

Reverend, I'm a Catholic, and I disagreed with the pope on the issue of war.

—*Sean Hannity, April 5, 2005*

I mean, because I think—one of the things—when I say I'm Christian, I'm a Catholic. But there's no distinction in my mind.

—*Sean Hannity, February 25, 2005*

T HE UNITED STATES is, like all vital twenty-first-century democracies, a religiously pluralistic nation.

We count among our citizens Christians, Jews, Muslims, Buddhists, Hindus, Sikhs, Baha'is, Zoroastrians, Taoists, Shintoists, Jainists, Scientologists, Wiccans, Rastafarians, and Native American traditionalists who worship the Great Spirit. We have atheists, secularists, deists, and pantheists living happily alongside UFO worshippers, New Age devotees, spiritists, animists, mystics, neopagans, apocalyptic cults, and Voodoo practitioners.

Among these broad categories exist numerous offshoots as well. For instance, counted as at least nominally Christian are such diverse believers as Catholics, Lutherans, Methodists, Baptists, Evangelicals, Pentecostals, Anglicans, Eastern Orthodox, Jehovah's Witnesses, Mennonites, Quakers, Amish, Seventh-Day Adventists, Mormons, Jews for Jesus, the 700 Club, and Gary Busey.[1]

So as you can see, sectarian believers range from the traditional and common (Catholics, Lutherans, Jews, Muslims, Buddhists) to the trendy and rare (Branch Davidians, Heaven's Gate cultists, Busey).

Many of these religions to this day consider fellow believers with competing doctrines to be virulent imposters. All consider their belief system to be more or less the correct one—which is part of what makes them religions.

So it's no mystery why most mainstream news outlets tend to take an essentially don't-ask-don't-tell approach to religion. For instance, if you go on the air and announce that Catholicism is the one true faith, the animist lobby will put a boot so far up your ass you suddenly won't know the doctrine of transubstantiation from a hole in the ground.

But Fox News takes a decidedly nontraditional tack when it comes to journalism and America's pluralistic ideal. Far from distancing themselves from the sectarian conflict that still simmers among some in the body politic, the folks at Fox have thrust themselves right into the middle of it, casting themselves as frontline shock troops in the culture war. And while the network has generally positioned this cultural rift as one of religionists versus secularists, this is actually a pretty feeble dichotomy. After all, you're not likely to see Fox's anchors putting down prayer rugs in the studio and giving a quick shout-out to Mecca in the middle of Hoveround commercials. No, in Fox's eyes, the "culture war" is without question a clash between Judeo-Christian forces (taking care to keep it light on the Judeo) and those who either aren't religious or who work to preserve a religiously neutral public sphere.

Indeed, at Fox, there's really only one true faith, and the message is clear: Christians rule, Muslims and atheists drool.

Perhaps Fox News anchor John Gibson summed it up best during a November 2005 appearance on the *Janet Parshall's America* radio program: "I would think if somebody is going to . . . have to answer for following the wrong religion, they're not going to have to answer to me. We know who they're going to have to answer to."[2]

Folks, he ain't talkin' 'bout L. Ron Hubbard.

AND THEY'LL KNOW WE ARE CHRISTIANS 'CAUSE WE NEVER SHUT UP ABOUT IT

THERE'S NOTHING WRONG with being Christian. We want to make that perfectly clear. There's something terribly wrong, however, with being a bad Christian, just as there's something terribly wrong with being a bad hairstylist or a bad wedding DJ. It's tacky, and you bring suffering unto the world.

Of course, there have always been those Christians who prefer to focus on Christ's admonition to love one's neighbor and care for the least among us—volunteering at food pantries and homeless shelters, visiting prisons and hospitals, and sending money to underprivileged children overseas.

And there have always been Christians who are more interested in how their neighbors behave and believe—volunteering at antigay rallies, harassing school boards that happen to think J. K. Rowling's *not* a witch, and sending money to the guy who puts the guano in batshit crazy, Pat Robertson.

This latter category tends to find fresh assault in every media message that runs counter to their own worldview—such as the worldview that a group comprising nearly 85 percent of the population and controlling nearly every government body in the country is being systematically persecuted by a sinister minority elite, or the worldview that Adam and Eve's sons raised sheep and wheat under the watchful gaze of velociraptors.

Of course, before Fox News came along, reporters and anchors almost never blurted out their religious affiliation. It was like they hated God or something.

To this day, most major news personalities continue to spit in God's face by neglecting to mention on the air whether they hate Jesus or love him.

Honestly, isn't it kind of odd how one can sit through news program after news program on nearly every major network and not be filled in on the religion of the hosts?

Even off camera, such things are rarely discussed among the media cognoscenti. Sure, while partying with Lou Dobbs, he may, at that crucial tipping point between the seventh and eighth St. Pauli Girl, pull out that ridiculous diagram of Noah's Ark he's been working on for years and, for the fifth time in as many weeks, walk you through every friggin' animal pen, inevitably drawing your attention to the bizarre "tick and mite room." And who hasn't stayed too late at Chris Matthews's pad only to make the mistake of dropping blotter acid with Doris Kearns Goodwin and suddenly having to face the prospect of lying around on a futon with "White Rabbit" blaring in the background, enduring yet another maundering tribute to the Bhagwan Shree Rajneesh?

But otherwise we're left in the dark. And rightly so.

But it's a different story at the United Church of Fox News. There, we're constantly reminded that both the network's commentators and contributors are indeed Christian. Of course, their Jesus isn't the poor woodworker who went on to become an itinerant teacher preaching the virtues of peace, love, and economic justice to an oppressed and downtrodden people. If that Jesus ever showed up, Karl Rove and Fox would have him turned into a far-left, terrorist-coddling child pornographer before his publicist had a chance to book him on *The View*.

No, Fox's Jesus is more like Toby Keith—a prowar, pro–death penalty, pro–upper-class-tax-cut firebrand who wears his hair long and wild and speaks ungrammatical Aramaic in a reassuring Southern drawl.

Make no mistake about it, their Jesus kicks ass. The Democrats' Jesus is a wussy. Seriously, which one would you rather follow?

I USED TO HAVE A GOD LIKE YOURS . . . AND THEN MY DAD GOT A JOB

I mean, everybody knows that the Christian god is not a god of vengeance.

—O'Reilly

I will take vengeance in anger and wrath upon the nations that have not obeyed me.[3]

—God

NOT ONLY IS Fox's right-wing Jesus better than whatever girdle-wearing Jesus you happen to be worshipping, but Christianity is clearly superior to whatever time-honored, ancient doctrines the other four billion people are babbling at any given moment.

On June 23, 2005, Bill O'Reilly sat down with Billy Graham's son Franklin to cast scintillating star beams of enlightenment on a wanting world.

Oh, it went a little something like this:

O'REILLY: Now, the problem that many of us—I'm a Christian. I'm a Catholic. And the problem that we have is that our enemy, our primary enemy, is centered around Allah. And most media people sweep that under the carpet.

GRAHAM: Yes.

Is O'Reilly really saying there are Americans out there who don't know Al Qaeda and its confederates are Islamic extremists who draw inspiration from a skewed devotion to Allah?

Does he really think he's scooping his competition by pointing this out? Does he imagine Larry King and Keith Olbermann are going on the air every night reporting that Al Qaeda is really centered around Carol Channing?

Is he further suggesting Allah's the real problem, and not the wayward beliefs of a few of Allah's adherents?

Oh Lord, is he going to keep talking?

O'REILLY: But if Islam didn't exist, there wouldn't be a war on terror. That's the fact. Now, we know that Islam has been hijacked by extremists and that most Muslims aren't terrorists and don't wish us ill. We know that. But how do you deal with an enemy that is religious-centric?

O'Reilly makes a fascinating argument here. Insipid, but fascinatingly so. Of course, there would have been no Crusades or witch burnings without Christianity either. There would have been no KKK lynchings without Protestantism, and no priest pedophilia scandal without the Catholic Church. That doesn't mean you can pin—implicitly or explicitly—these crimes on Christianity. All it proves is that crazy assholes tend to be lazy and want their advance PR done for them. Jesus has a huge Q rating, higher even than SpongeBob SquarePants. Convince people you've got his endorsement, and your prospects will go through the roof, just as it's easier to sell indoor grills if people think George Foreman is involved somehow. But to justify something truly crazy, you can't rely on George Foreman. You need God. The criminally insane understand this. Bill's still a little unclear.

So what O'Reilly seems to be saying here without really saying it is that Muslims are nuts. Not all Muslims, mind you; just the nutty ones. They're also the ones who happen to be driving the hijacked bus that's carrying all the other Muslims.

GRAHAM: It's tough, Bill, very, very difficult. And I think a lot of our politicians and many in our military discount the religious fervor that these men have, who are willing to take their life. And they believe that, if they take their life, strap dynamite on, blow themselves up, and blow . . .

O'REILLY: Yes, they're going to heaven.

GRAHAM: . . . they're going to heaven. And so they believe not only are they going to heaven, but this is the only way that they can assure that they're going to heaven. The god that I worship is not the same god that they worship.

O'REILLY: But you can't convince them that your god doesn't want to kill themselves and others. We can't seem to do that.

First of all, it's hard for anyone to discount the religious fervor of Islamic extremists in Iraq, particularly if you *are* in the military and your left foot is currently flying through a falafel stand because your president decided to expand Al Qaeda's holy war to a place with better targets to bomb.[4] At the very least, you'll catch on to the "fervor" part of the equation right away. The religious part may take a few seconds to put together. Much like your foot.

Honestly, who in this country is downplaying the terrorists' religious extremism? How is this even possible? The religious fervor of Al Qaeda is so entrenched in Americans' minds at this point that the only way to downplay it would be to deliberately mis-characterize it. Maybe something like, "Four Iraqis and two Americans were killed today in yet another tragic conflict between East Coast and West Coast rappers." We all know these guys are religious nuts. Let's move on—and sincerely hope no more inno-cent Muslims or Sikhs in this country get their asses kicked because rednecks think their hats and beards look funny.

Secondly, are O'Reilly and Graham really setting down a dis-tinction between "our god" and "their god"? If you're going to start in with the "our god" and "their god" stuff, you're going to have to assume one of the following:

1. They are, in fact, one and the same god. Each side is simply interpreting a universal higher power in its own way, assigning it their own characteristics.
2. We're right and they're wrong. Yahweh exists. Allah, not so much.
3. They're right and we're wrong. Allah rules the universe and Yahweh is the world's biggest pyramid scheme.
4. There is no God and we're all screwed anyway.

Based on the conversation to this point, we're guessing O'Reilly and Graham are in camp one or two.

GRAHAM: But what I want the American audience to under-stand, the god that they worship is not the same god that we worship. The god that I worship gave his son for me.

O'REILLY: Everybody knows that.

Here O'Reilly and Graham almost seem to be talking as if both Yahweh and Allah exist and are up on a mountain like the Heat Miser and Snow Miser battling for control of the world.

Either that, or neither has grown a large enough pair to say what he really thinks: We're right and they're wrong. We're wor-shipping the one true God and they're worshipping nothingness.

Make no mistake; that is the message. They're as confident of this as they are of their knowledge of scripture:

O'REILLY: I mean, everybody knows that the Christian god is not a god of vengeance.

God of vengeance—Jehovah! God of vengeance, shine forth. (Psalm 94:1)

The righteous shall rejoice when he seeth the vengeance: he shall wash his feet in the blood of the wicked. (Psalm 58:10)

BEN FRANKLIN HATES "HAPPY HOLIDAYS"

Believing with you that religion is a matter which lies solely between Man & his God, that he owes account to none other for his faith or his worship, that the legitimate powers of government reach actions only, & not opinions, I contemplate with sovereign reverence that act of the whole American people which declared that their legislature should "make no law respecting an establishment of religion, or prohibiting the free exercise thereof," thus building a wall of separation between Church & State.

—*Thomas Jefferson's letter to the Danbury Baptists, January 1, 1802*

OKAY, REGARDLESS OF what the far-left bomb-throwing author of the Declaration of Independence might say, this country was still founded on Judeo-Christian principles, wasn't it? Haven't the secularists just gone too far? What of the aggressive assault to Christianity that's taking place in this country? What say you, Bill O'Reilly?

What do you think Benjamin Franklin and George Washington and Thomas Jefferson and James Madison would have thought about the ACLU, all right, Pledge of Allegiance, no God, Christmas icons out of the public arena? What do you think those guys would have thought about that? (*The O'Reilly Factor*, April 11, 2006)

Now, imagine that half a dozen or so of our Founding Fathers were teleported to the present day. O'Reilly would have you believe that the second they saw a Happy Holidays sign at City Hall, they'd suddenly bust out crying like the Indian in that anti-litter commercial from the seventies.

But the world's changed a lot since the eighteenth century, and as far as culture shocks go, we're guessing the dearth of nativity displays on public lands across America would be pretty far down the list for George Washington and his merry band of ye olden dudes.

First of all, they'd be appalled that black people are running around unshackled. Secondly, they'd wonder when all our women went crazy—giving orders to men at the Stock & Exchange Board; cavorting about in pantaloons and queer, midriff-baring blouses; making a cruel burlesque of our august republic by daring to cast votes in the hallowed halls of Congress. And if they saw two guys walking down the street holding hands? Forget about it. Jefferson would be thrown for such a loop, he probably wouldn't be able to have sex with his slaves for weeks.

And those are just a few of the social advances that would send them reeling. Imagine if you showed George Washington TiVo. In fifteen minutes he'd be too engrossed by the latest Real World/Road Rules challenge to give a flying fig about whether the associates at Sam's Club say "Happy Holidays" or "Merry Christmas." Honestly, if you could magically transport James Madison into the middle of modern-day Times Square, you wouldn't see a man disgusted by the ACLU. You'd see the father of our Constitution curled up in the middle of the street in the fetal position, pissing himself.

As for the Pledge of Allegiance, the Founding Fathers would probably have very little to say about recent court challenges to its constitutionality. Why? Because the Pledge of Allegiance wasn't written until 1892. And it didn't include any mention of God until 1954. So the Founding Fathers would have about the same reaction to removing "under God" from the pledge as they would to *Bewitched* switching Darrins.

The truth is, our Founding Fathers would have disagreed with a lot of the things we do. And many people today would disagree with a lot of the things they did—such as purchasing other human beings and growing weed.[5]

That's why we changed so many things. It was a different time and a different world. Was theirs better? No. Is ours perfect? Of course not. In fact, about the only thing that hasn't changed is that it was great to be a rich white guy in the 1700s and it's great to be a rich white guy today.

So O'Reilly and Hannity and Gibson and Hume and all the rest can tuck themselves into their Bella Notte sheets in their lavish homes every night, thank the Lord for their millions, and pray that He comes soon to save them from this secular hell.

THE FATHER, SON, AND HOLY RABBIT

This country stands for tolerance. We stand for tolerance for Muslims, Jews, Wiccans, Kwanzaans, and—and for Christians. Tolerance should continue in this country and it should continue even for the supermajority, which happens to be Christian. This isn't always the case. It's all too easy in this country to say, hey, no Christmas tree, fire Santa, ban red and green because they're just too Christian.

—John Gibson, The Big Story, October 25, 2005

AS WE DISCUSS further in Chapter 16, Fox is so appalled at this country's fake war on Christmas that they've thrown their full weight behind a very real counteroffensive.

But as this is a chapter devoted to Fox's peculiar brand of Christianity (which is in reality so heretical it makes the apocryphal Gnostic Gospel of Thomas look like the resolution of the Arian controversy following the First Council of Nicaea),[6] we thought we'd give you a taste of just how far off the beam these idiots fall in their defense of Christ.

Case in point: apparently no one has bothered to tell John Gibson that Santa Claus is a *secular* symbol. He may have originally had something to do with St. Nicholas, but today his religious roots are unrecognizable. He's a false god—the god of commercialism, consumption, and greed. Come on, if he were truly a religious figure, do you think he'd have ever ridden that electric razor down that hill?

In fact, the whole concept of Santa Claus should be an abomination to Christians. He's omnipotent, omniscient, and eternal. Sound familiar? Plus he has elves, man. That's just creepy.

Now, it's certainly magnanimous of Gibson to say that he's tolerant of Kwanzaans. If nothing else, it should reassure the Passoverans, Halloweenans and Labor Dayans as well. But what we don't tolerate in this country is stupidity and ignorance. And for good reason. They make people say stupid and ignorant things.

Still, on the stupidity score, Gibson has miles to go to overtake O'Reilly:

> Although some left-wingers in the media deny it, we have documented a number of cases where Christian holidays like Christmas and Easter have been attacked by secular interests. Lawsuits and corporate policies have proved this point over and over again. (Bill O'Reilly, *The O'Reilly Factor,* April 11, 2006)

Again, we'll delve further into O'Reilly's "War on Christmas" fever dream later. But the curious thing here is not that O'Reilly says things that demonstrate his paranoia about the modern secular jihad against Christian holidays. It's that he says them while sharing the screen with conspicuously secular symbols.

Indeed, as O'Reilly was flaying secular liberals for attacking Christendom's most sacred holy days, O'Reilly was doing his best to attack Christendom's most sacred holy days.

As he babbled on about this country's secular attacks on Christmas and Easter, the images of a department store Santa Claus and the disembodied head of a *Donnie Darko*–esque rabbit costume appeared onscreen. Beneath these two images was written the rather portentous "Under Attack."

Again, the Easter Bunny is not a representation of Christ's death and resurrection. That rabbit makes its annual appearance because Cadbury would have its pelt if it didn't. Let's face it, Jesus doesn't lose if the rabbit gets grilled—it's the people at PAAS who work year-round for the one week we all buy their egg-coloring tablets who are scared shitless that people might start catching on.

But this is apparently all nuance to O'Reilly and the rest of the Fox News family. Indeed, a couple of weeks earlier, on *Fox and Friends,* the network had already sounded its war trumpet.

While reporting that some stores were now calling the Easter Bunny the Spring Bunny, we were treated to onscreen headlines that said "Bunny Ban?" and "Bunny Backlash." Of course, this is another nonstory. If a tone-deaf retailer somewhere wants to call it a Spring Bunny, that's his business, but it won't rise to the level of a Bunny Ban until anti-Easter government brownshirts storm into private homes warning citizens that they better be thinking about the vernal equinox when they bite the ears off their chocolate rabbits.

The idea that stores across the country will start putting up Spring Bunny displays is absurd because there would be no context for it. When was the last time you walked into a store, saw a giant rabbit, baskets, eggs, and chocolates and thought, "What the hell is all this?"—then noticed the large sign that said "Happy Easter" and were suddenly bathed in understanding? The fact is, we're not gonna rename the stupid bunny.

Of course, the idiot brigade at *Fox & Friends* did have enough sense to point out that the Easter Bunny was not really a Christian symbol. But they also reported that the Catholic League was infuriated by this revolt against the rabbit. The message was clear: Christians should be upset by all this and should see it as yet another PC attack on the mainstream culture.

But Christians shouldn't be upset at all. They should rejoice at the prospect of eliminating the Easter Bunny as a popular holiday symbol. They should be reclaiming their holidays and doing their level best to scrub them of secular imagery and commercialism. For God's sake, Yahweh said we weren't even supposed to have graven images. What would He think of His followers sweating over guys dressed as giant burrowing mammals?

Can the highly paid journalists at America's most-watched cable news network possibly be this ignorant?

Seriously, is it too much to ask of the devout Christians at Fox that they should actually crack open a Bible before they presume to thump it?

NOTES

1. Much like Saul of Tarsus, Busey dedicated his life to Jesus Christ after being thrown from his ride (in this case, he became a Christian several years after a serious motorcycle accident). Unlike Saul of Tarsus, subsequent to his conversion, Busey did a movie called *The Hand Job* and contributed voice-over work to the notoriously Jesus-thin video game *Grand Theft Auto: Vice City*. Then again, Saul of Tarsus (a.k.a. St. Paul) is widely regarded as one of the most influential figures in Western history, whereas Busey is widely regarded as a nut.

2. Just in case you think this quote was taken out of context (as Gibson suggested Keith Olbermann had done in anointing Gibson the "Worst Person in the World" on his MSNBC program shortly after Gibson made it) or misquoted (as Gibson explicitly said a "former colleague" [Olbermann] had done), here's the full quote and some additional context:

   GIBSON: The whole point of this is that the tradition, the religious tradition of this country is tolerance, and that the same sense of tolerance that's been granted by the majority to the minority over the years ought to go the other way too. Minorities ought to have the same sense of tolerance about the majority religion—Christianity—that they've been granted about their religions over the years.

   PARSHALL: Exactly. John, I have to tell you, let me linger for a minute on that word "tolerance." Because first of all, the people who like to promulgate that concept are the worst violators. They cannot tolerate Christianity, as an example.

   GIBSON: Absolutely. I know—I know that.

   PARSHALL: And number two, I have to tell you, I don't know when they held this election and decided that tolerance was a transcendent value. I serve a God who, with a finger of fire, wrote he would have no other gods before him. And he doesn't tolerate sin, which is why he sent his son to the cross. But all of a sudden now we jump up and down and celebrate the idea of tolerance. I think tolerance means accommodation, but it doesn't necessarily mean acquiescence or wholehearted acceptance.

   GIBSON: No, no, no. If you figure that—listen, we get a little theological here, and it's probably a bit over my head, but I would think if somebody is going to be—have to answer for following the wrong religion, they're not going to have to answer to me. We know who they're going to have to answer to.

PARSHALL: Right.

So, out of context, Gibson appears to be saying people who don't worship the Judeo-Christian god may ultimately have to answer to Him for their failure to do so. In context, he appears to be saying that while he (Gibson) doesn't really understand what he's talking about, Yahweh will likely crush anyone who doesn't worship Him in accordance with Mosaic Law, or who doesn't accept Jesus as his personal savior.

3. Micah 5:15.
4. As many will recall, in a March 2004 *60 Minutes* interview, former presidential counterterrorism adviser Richard Clarke asserted that shortly after 9/11, the Bush administration was already agitating for an invasion of Iraq:

> Rumsfeld was saying that we needed to bomb Iraq. . . . And we all said . . . no, no. Al Qaeda is in Afghanistan. We need to bomb Afghanistan. And Rumsfeld said there aren't any good targets in Afghanistan. And there are lots of good targets in Iraq. I said, "Well, there are lots of good targets in lots of places, but Iraq had nothing to do with it."

5. Hey, you can look it up.
6. Seriously.

4

HOW LOW CAN THEY GO?

They make a living putting on video of old ladies slipping on ice and people laughing. That's their life. That's their life. They exist in a small little place where they count for nothing. The history will be made by those who have affirmative thoughts, who make, you know, innovative suggestions in life and are inclusive.

—Fox News's Geraldo Rivera about Comedy Central's Jon Stewart and Stephen Colbert

He practically slips through his harness there, and his pleas for somebody to stop the ride falling on his mother's deaf ears.

—Fox News's Trace Gallagher chuckling at video of an obese boy screaming for his life on a roller coaster as his mother sits next to him and laughs

ONE OF THIS book's main themes is that Fox is not merely a conduit for conservative talking points and propaganda—it's also a really bad news organization.

For example, as we noted in Chapter 1, at least one study proved that Fox News viewers knew far less about issues surrounding the Iraq War than people who relied on competing news outlets.

In other words, Fox is to broadcast news what Postum is to coffee. They both resemble the real thing, but they're really just wartime substitutes that for some reason continue to be popular with old people.

There are so many examples of Fox's bias, shoddy reasoning,

and meretricious warmongering that we could never possibly keep up with all of it. But sometimes the network strays so far from what might be considered legitimate reporting that you have to take special note.

One method we like to use for recalibrating our crania after too much exposure to Fox is something we call the "Can you imagine . . . ?" test.

It's a good way to readjust your expectations for what news should be.

Basically, as you watch Fox News and see supposedly impartial anchors twisting what should be straightforward stories into doughy neocon pretzels or witness pundits scrambling to find increasingly lower common denominators, you should ask yourself, "Can you imagine Jim Lehrer saying that?" or "Can you imagine Jim Miklaszewski filing that story?"

The answer, invariably, is "Christ, no," and so one is usually able to limp away with a surprising measure of one's cognition still intact.

Of course, Fox lowers the bar so far and so frequently that viewers tend to place them in a universe all their own. After all, once you see a giant white rabbit running past you, invisible grinning cats and talking playing cards tend to lose their power to alarm.

Indeed, there are times when Fox's reporting and commentary veer toward the eleventh-hour banter at a College Republicans keg party. It's the kind of stuff you might hear if you traveled back to 1972 and miked George W. Bush as he fumed in gridlock traffic behind an Amnesty International march.

FOX TAKES ON COMMUNISTS FOR KERRY

WE HAVEN'T WRITTEN much about Fox's Web site so far. It's a value-added feature—kind of like a complimentary aperitif or dessert wine, depending on how you use it. (A quick tip: if you're looking for real online entertainment, bookmark BillOReilly.com. It makes all other comedy Web sites seem about as funny as the Hindenburg explosion.)

In October 2004, correspondent Jane Roh filed an on-the-street reaction story for FOXNews.com to coincide with the first George W. Bush–John Kerry presidential debate.

That night, she accomplished the seemingly impossible: made Fox News's broadcast efforts appear credible by comparison. Needless to say, we never knew that reading *Mad* magazine needed to be part of our universities' core J-school curricula.

Here's a portion of what Roh submitted:

> "We're trying to get Comrade Kerry elected and get that capitalist enabler George Bush out of office," said seventeen-year-old Komoselutes Rob of Communists for Kerry.
>
> "Even though he, too, is a capitalist, he supports my socialist values more than President Bush," Rob said, before assuring FOXNews.com that his organization was not a parody group. When asked his thoughts on Washington's policy toward Communist holdout North Korea, Rob said: "The North Koreans are my comrades to a point, and I'm sure they support Comrade Kerry, too."

Now, for most of us, there's a point at which we progress from innocent, literal-minded babes to savvy observers of life capable of separating bullshit from reality. Usually, this gestalt shift arrives somewhere between our fifth and tenth birthdays. For Fox News's Jane Roh, it came shortly after she filed this report. After several critics jumped on Roh's story, Fox was forced to print a clarification:

> In a version of this article that was published earlier, the Communists for Kerry group was portrayed as an organization that was supporting John Kerry for president. FOXNews.com's reporter asked the group's representative several times whether the group was legitimate and supporting the Democratic candidate, and the spokesman insisted that it was. The Communists for Kerry group is, in fact, a parody organization.

Now, contrast this with the Dan Rather CBS Memogate

scandal, also from the fall of 2004. Certainly it differs in many important respects. Rather was CBS's signature star; Roh is a nobody. The memo story appeared on *60 Minutes Wednesday;* the Communists for Kerry story appeared on the Fox News Web site. The memo story accused a candidate himself of wrongdoing; the Kerry story merely advanced an unsavory association with a group that was beyond the candidate's control.

And though the consensus among Rather's critics was that Rather was so motivated to believe that the documents (which CBS obtained from former Texas Army National Guard officer Bill Burkett and which were supposedly written in the early seventies) were real that he didn't question them thoroughly enough, he did in fact have them vetted by experts. Roh and her editors, on the other hand, apparently so wanted to believe that communists really do support Kerry that none of them bothered to do a ten-second Google search or check out the satirical group's Web site.

But while the Rather documents have never been definitively authenticated or debunked, at least they were superficially plausible. The Roh story was so clearly false that you can't help but assume Fox was simply eager to report anything that might make Kerry look foolish. It would be as if Rather had insisted on using the Burkett memos even though they'd included frequent references to Mr. T and were printed on *A-Team* stationery.

Nice job, Jane Roh!

Say, we wonder why she never got around to interviewing the guys from NAMBLA for Bush.[1]

FOX TAKES ON FAT KIDS

SEPTEMBER 9, 2006, was not a slow news day. You had the release of a Senate intelligence report disclaiming alleged links between Al Qaeda and Iraq, the recovery of an Air Force officer who had gone missing in Kyrgyzstan, a space shuttle launch, a 15,000-acre forest fire raging forty miles north of Los Angeles, and a tropical storm near Bermuda that was threatening to develop into a hurricane.

Hell, it was just two days before the fifth anniversary of 9/11! No, there was definitely no need for filler on a day like this.

But on Fox's *Studio B Weekend*, host Trace Gallagher seemed more interested in imitating Bob Saget's evil twin than playing the part of a credible cable news anchor. With a knowing chuckle, Gallagher heavily promo'd a video that had recently been making its way around the Web:

> Caught on tape and put on the Net. This clip becoming an online favorite in what's supposed to be a fun day at the amusement park, but it scared the daylights out of this young roller-coaster rider and he may [be] pushed away for good. He practically slips through his harness there, and his pleas for somebody to stop the ride falling on his mother's deaf ears. She just keeps on laughing the whole time, but apparently all's well that ends well, I think. The car pulls to a stop with no injuries, although maybe having your video of your mother laughing all over the Internet might not be the best and happiest of endings.

Great. So now the lame-ass Internet forwards you get from idiots you barely know have become network news staples.

Now, plenty of news programs use light and humorous segments to inject a bit of fun into their newscasts. But these are usually along the lines of squirrels waterskiing or Willard Scott macking on centenarians.

This particular video showed a kid who, significantly, happened to be overweight, sitting next to a woman (presumably his mother, though the kid referred to her by her first name) who sat by and laughed maniacally while her boy screamed for his life. We took the liberty of transcribing the video. It's like classic George and Gracie:

TERRIFIED YOUNG BOY: Ahhhhh! Ahhhhh! Ahhhhhh! Ahhhhhh! Help me! Stop! Stop it! Stop it! Stop it! Stop it! Stop it! Stop it! Stop it! Stop it! Stop it! I'm falling . . . Janice. I'm falling . . . Janice. I'm stuck. Help me, Janice, I'm stuck. Ah! This hurts!

This hurts! This hurts! This hurts! Oh, this hurts! Oh, this hurts! It's not funny! This hurts! Ahh! Janice, it ain't funny. Ah!

JANICE: Ha ha ha ha ha ha ha, etc.

Remember when you were in college and that creepy guy in your chem lab kept inviting you over to his dorm to watch *Faces of Death?* Yeah, apparently he's now a producer for Fox News.

Now, we're still trying to figure out what Fox thought was so funny about this clip. Was it the kid's blood-curdling screams? The cackling woman? Or was it the fact that the kid was really fat? Somehow we get the feeling that if little Dakota Fanning had been strapped into a sketchy carnival ride and a videotape surfaced of her screaming at the top of her lungs while she hung onto her seat for her life, the reaction might have been a little different.

Oh, but the show was just getting underway.

After the roller-coaster clip, the network promoted a newly released Al Qaeda training video showing masked men with knives mimicking techniques for slitting people's throats. A bit sensational maybe, but certainly newsworthy. Well, just after that they showed another video of two kids playing soccer. In the latter clip, a child kicks a ball, which ricochets off a goalpost and smacks the goalie in the face.

These videos were promo'd back to back. In fact, the two were run together so often that at one point they mixed up the voice-overs that went with them, no doubt leading Fox reporter Jane Roh to conclude that Al Qaeda could very well be plotting a devastating game of smear the queer on American soil.

Of course, we all know that cable news is not held to the same standards as network news, but isn't all this just a little beyond the pale? It's like television for people who have outgrown blowing up frogs with firecrackers but are still too young to get drunk and pick fights with minorities.

Once again, can you imagine Lesley Stahl laughing at a video of an obese boy screaming for his life? Or Anderson Cooper yelling across the newsroom, "Get me that clip of the kid being smacked in the face!"?

Now let's take another look at the Geraldo quote that began this chapter:

> The history will be made by those who have affirmative thoughts, who make, you know, innovative suggestions in life and are inclusive.

You tell 'em, Maya Angelou. History will indeed be made by those with affirmative thoughts—or by those who publicly ridicule mortally endangered children. Either way.

FOX TAKES ON DEMOCRATS WHO HATE DEMOCRACY

IT CAN BE both amusing and infuriating when a new election cycle rears its head and candidates go to previously unimagined lengths to brand their opponents.

For instance, if a congressman votes against a budget that includes thousands of items, one of which just happens to be retinitis pigmentosa research, the candidate can pretty much expect an onslaught of ads accusing him of being Congress's number one proponent of degenerative eye disease.

If a candidate has never held elective office, he'll be called dangerously unqualified. If he's a longtime incumbent, he'll be labeled a Washington insider with Washington values who spends a suspicious amount of time in Washington doing whatever it is Washington people do in big, fancy cities like Washington.

If he supports the war in Iraq, he loves seeing kids come home in body bags. If he voted against any part of the War on Terror, well, he might as well just give Osama bin Laden a hand job and save his opponent the trouble of hiring a graphic artist.

It's pretty unseemly stuff, but then if politics doesn't make you at least a little queasy, you either have no brain, no soul, or no gag reflex.

So if you happen to be a hired political flack, you may be able feasibly to argue that you were just doing your job while you're playing badminton with Hitler and Joan Rivers's plastic surgeon fifty years or so from now. But if you're a reporter, you really have no excuse.

On August 8, 2006, Fox News anchor Gregg Jarrett was framing his candidate's opponent in the starkest possible terms. He kicked off an interview with Senator Christopher Dodd (D-Connecticut) with a broadside against Democratic senatorial candidate Ned Lamont, who was challenging fellow Democrat Joe Lieberman in the Connecticut primary:

> As the violence escalates in the Middle East, voters go to the polls in the state of Connecticut in what is widely seen as a referendum in the War on Terror. Senator Joe Lieberman facing stiff challenge from an antiwar candidate by the name of Ned Lamont. Lieberman's lost a lot of support because he supported democracy in Iraq. And if he loses, is that a bad sign for other candidates who support democracy in the Middle East? Will this issue drive moderate Dems to the left?

Okay, Jarrett might as well have said, "Lieberman's lost a lot of support because he does not crave the tender, savory flesh of missing and exploited toddlers."

Unless we missed something and Lamont ran on an explicit "no democracy in Iraq" platform, Jarrett's being just a little too sly here. Maybe Lieberman lost a lot of support—and ultimately lost the Democratic primary (before winning the general election as an independent)—because he backed a president who invaded a country that had no significant connection with 9/11 or Al Qaeda. Oh, but saying it that way might go against the script.

Later, Jarrett added that Lamont has done well, "because of his rather strident antiwar rhetoric. If that succeeds and more Democrats embrace that position, is it possible the Democrats could become the sort of modern-day George McGovern, who got really creamed politically for his antiwar stance?"

Wow, they're playing the McGovern card. That'll scare people.

You might as well bring up that story about Jimmy Carter and the killer rabbit.

But this is an interesting strategy, to be sure: take a deeply unpopular war and viciously characterize a candidate as an opponent of that war, then try to tie him to an eighty-four-year-old man who ran unsuccessfully for president three and a half decades ago.

After all, how could the good people of Connecticut vote for someone with whom they agree if they find out he superficially resembles George McGovern? They'd have to be out of their minds!

Later, Jarrett commiserated with Dodd over the direction of Dodd's party: "By opposing the war in Iraq, are you concerned that Lamont and other members of your party will get branded as soft on terror and weak on security?"

Just in case you didn't catch it, Fox was getting ready to brand Lamont as soft on terror and weak on security. Over and over. Usually in the form of a question.

Indeed, Jarrett was doing everything he could to discredit Lamont short of suggesting that Cindy Sheehan would be Lamont's chief of staff if he wins:

JARRETT: . . . there is a joke going around that Cindy Sheehan will be Lamont's chief of staff if he wins.

Throughout the program, Fox also showed a series of not-at-all-suggestive screen titles, including:

Is the Democratic Party soft on terror?

A Lamont win, bad news for democracy in Mideast?

And our favorite:

Have the Democrats forgotten the lessons of 9/11?

What were the lessons of 9/11 again? To brand as "soft on

terror" and "weak on security" candidates who for some reason prefer to actually go after the perpetrators of 9/11?

Finally, following an interview with a Republican and a Democratic strategist during which Jarrett quoted a *New York Post* editorial that—surprise, surprise[2]—compared a Lamont victory to the "George McGovern debacle in '72," Jarrett concluded the segment with this: "It looks like Lebanon and Israel are trying to get in their last licks. Coming up, fair and balanced coverage from both sides of the battlefield."

It really is like watching those guys on *To Catch a Predator* say they're just coming over to talk.

FOX TAKES ON MONTEAGLE STEARNS'S MOTHER

ON MARCH 29, 2005, the *Fox & Friends* gang weighed in on the controversial nomination of John Bolton for U.S. ambassador to the UN:

BRIAN KILMEADE: You know that guy John Bolton, who seems to speak his mind and that bothers a lot of people in the diplomatic world? Well, it bothers people so much that he is going to be the man nominated to be the next ambassador to the United Nations from the U.S. that fifty-nine former U.S. diplomats have signed a letter and given it to Senator Lugar and said, "Do me a favor, don't nominate this, don't confirm this guy. Just kick him out. We don't want him there."

Now *this* is news. Right. George W. Bush nominates a controversial figure to represent us at the United Nations and numerous diplomats sign onto a letter of protest. Yes, this is definitely an issue worthy of vigorous debate. No doubt *Fox & Friends*'s hosts will mount a robust and cogent defense of the Bolton nomination by drawing on the longtime public servant's deep experience and singular talents.

Here's what happened next:

E. D. HILL: Here's what struck me about that story. Here are a couple of the names of the diplomats who don't want John

Bolton to get the nomination: Princeton Lyman, Monteagle Stearns, and Spurgeon Keeny . . .

KILMEADE: Those guys again!

HILL: Just odd names.

KILMEADE: Who the heck are they?

HILL: You've got to have one of these funky names to be an ambassador. Who names their kid Spurgeon?

KILMEADE: But you know what, the coolest name in sports . . . you know what, sometimes you look at an infant and you think, "That's a Spurgeon."

HILL: Monteagle? Monteagle?

E. D. Hill was born Edith Ann Tarbox.
Glass houses, people.

NOTES

1. A nonexistent Republican PAC, as far as we know.
2. Coincidentally enough, Rupert Murdoch also owns the *New York Post*. Weird, huh?

5

FOX VERSUS BEVERLY . . . HILLS, THAT IS

SOMETIMES THE ONLY way to really understand Fox News is to imagine you're back in high school.

The jocks run the school, but they have to share the halls with an assortment of outsiders—academically ambitious grinds and science geeks, burnouts, bottom-feeders, loners, B-list wannabes, and French foreign exchange students.

Now, the community loves its school but resents the fact that it has to pay for the educations of kids who've never so much as gang-piled a pale asthmatic kid or offended a single Native American's sensibilities with papier-mâché. Indeed, when the townsfolk are not grossly overtipping Hooters waitresses or endlessly retelling the story about the time their cousin nearly won the Plinko game on *The Price Is Right*, they're living for Friday night football.

The jocks feed off this and seek to further amplify their importance by marginalizing everyone else. The burnouts, bottom-feeders, and loners are easy. They take themselves out of the game. Even if the nerds could get over their social retardation, they'd still be hated for blowing the curve on tests. No threat there. The wannabes are easy to co-opt, and the French kid is too busy trying to sell Cartier watches in defiance of the school boycott to care about much of anything else.

Indeed, the only real challenge to jock hegemony comes from the artsy students. They don't think or act like everyone else, yet they've carved out a niche. The more eccentric ones even have a certain countercultural cachet. By joining the drama club, they've gained proximity to pretty girls, which has terribly upset the established school hierarchy. And somehow the gay ones seem not to have noticed how unpopular they should be. It's as if they all lived in this parallel universe where their differences—which should make them dread outcasts—have actually enhanced their popularity.

Worse yet, many of them don't appear even to care about the football team. They think the captain is a self-absorbed prick who got his daddy's friends on the school board to make him quarter-back. It's almost as if they want the team to *lose*—like they hate the school or something! So as the artsy kids continually traverse this sort of tenuous wormhole between suspicion and popularity, they give the jocks fits.

And where does Fox News fit into all of this? They're the cheer-leaders, of course—chirpy, bright-eyed girls selected for their looks and pep, and can-do guys who don't want to get injured but would like to think they're somehow contributing to the school's victories by standing on the sidelines and staring up the skirts of their co-workers.

Now, some may object that we've stretched this analogy simply to paint Fox as a bunch of fatuous, nattering poseurs whose sense of patriotism is cravenly built on denigrating the patriotism of everyone else and whose masculinity is perversely—some might even say homoerotically—tied to the valor of others.

Yes, of course.

But the proof is in the lime Jell-O and creamed corn.

Indeed, Fox News is truly high school writ large. It hates the unpopular kids and fawns over the popular ones. And the popular ones who refuse to join their clique? They must be destroyed.

If you still don't believe us, take a look at the following transcript from the May 17, 2006, *Hannity & Colmes.* Without a doubt, it could have been lifted straight from any eighties or nineties high school cafeteria table in America. Really, we challenge you to find any difference. Substitute characters from your own adolescence for "Sean Hannity" and "Barbra Streisand," and we guarantee you'll be hypnotically doodling Journey logos on your pale-blue Trapper Keeper folders in no time. We join the conversation shortly after Sean Hannity has introduced former George H. W. Bush speechwriter Jennifer Grossman, who has some interesting gossip about a certain *some*one we all know!

HANNITY: All right. So you just happened to be on line, going to see *Mission: Impossible III,* Tom Cruise's big movie, that's supposed to be a blockbuster.

GROSSMAN: Yes. Right. Absolutely.

HANNITY: And then tell us what happened. What did you see?

GROSSMAN: Well, actually, the theater was not in Malibu. Malibu Theater burned down a couple of years ago so this is in the Valley. And I go there to try and meet a friend to go see a movie. There was a mix-up. We went to different Mann theaters. So we're both tapping our feet. Finally, I didn't have a phone, so I went to the customer service desk to ask to use their phone, figured it out and I'm figuring out, okay, which movie am I now going to see?

And I hear this couple talking next to me, saying, "Oh, we asked for you. It's been so long since we've seen you."

And this flustered young man says, "Oh, well, I got transferred, but of course you're welcome here. You're always welcome here. We'll take care of you." And I looked to my side and it's Barbra Streisand and her husband. And I see them waltz right through. And I think, well, what's that about?

So I had to wait because my girlfriend had to come over from the other theater. We had to wait for our next showing. And I go over to the ticket—the guy ripping the tickets, and I said, "Dude, did you just see that couple that waltzed in? Did they—did you rip their tickets?"

"No."

"Did they pay for tickets?"

"No. They asked to see the customer service manager."

So—and by the way, there wasn't any line to cut. This isn't New York. This isn't some, like, twenty-minute line around the block. There was no line. They asked to go in, to go and see the customer service manager and say, "Oh, so nice to see you."

HANNITY: Yes. Look, I've got to imagine, you know, and the ticket manager is admitting—I just got to imagine, and it's sort of bizarre that they're multimillionaires and they can't shell out, you know . . .

GROSSMAN: Twenty bucks.

HANNITY: What is it, ten dollars per ticket? Twenty dollars?

GROSSMAN: Yes, ten dollars per ticket, you know.

HANNITY: I have a hard time understanding why they would even ask for a ticket in that sense.

GROSSMAN: I was talking to the makeup artist right before coming on the show. And she has said that she is just—boy, it touched a nerve with her. She's seen so much of this.

AL HAIG, FORMER SECRETARY OF STATE: Oh my God, that is so totally queer. She, like, lives in a mansion, doesn't she?

HANNITY: Totally.

PEGGY NOONAN: Plus, she's not even that cute.

HANNITY: Not at *all!*

Okay, so we added that last bit, but you had to think about it for a second, didn't you?

Now, it's hardly fair to the rest of us mortals that Streisand should get into the movies for free, but we're guessing she's not the first celebrity to get comped by eager-to-please business interests. Chances are Hannity, O'Reilly, and the rest receive plenty of celebrity perks. It comes with the territory.

It sucks, but they're just movie tickets, for God's sake—and, frankly, a shrewd investment on the part of the theater manager. It's not like Streisand and James Brolin were seen speeding away from Washington in a pair of Bentley limos packed to the ceiling with U.S. Ag Department stationery and surplus government Brie.

So what exactly is Hannity trying to prove here? That liberals are irretrievably corrupt and venal? Or simply that the network's eyes and ears are everywhere, and no liberal sin, no matter how petty, will be overlooked by the intrepid night watchers on the right? Or maybe this is simply part of an orchestrated campaign to undercut anyone who openly dislikes George W. Bush.

Yeah. High school.

Geez, next they're going to tell us that Harry Belafonte and Vanessa Redgrave smuggled a box of Jujyfruits and a warm Ting into a matinee showing of *Click*.

That might finally be worthy of a Peabody.

FINALLY, SOMEONE IN THE MEDIA IS COVERING ANGELINA

IT TURNS OUT that Fox actually has a pretty serious problem when it comes to covering the entertainment industry.

While they understand the right-wing bona fides that can be earned by bashing Hollywood elites, they also know that celebrities are very popular among the general public.

So while at times they may run "hard news" segments that excoriate Hollywood's values and politics, at other times their reporting possesses all the depth of Mary Hart interviewing a drunk emu.

The truly special moments, though, are when they combine titillation and moral opprobrium with the grace and poise of a serial killer who specializes in prostitutes:

BILL O'REILLY: In the "Personal Story" segment tonight, this week Warren Buffett announced he was leaving billions to charity, and the new trend among America's rich and famous is to present themselves as humanitarians.

Angelina Jolie deflected bad publicity from intruding on the marriage of Jennifer Aniston and Brad Pitt by doing charity work for the UN, as you know.

Mr. Pitt himself is on the cover of *Newsweek* magazine, also as a humanitarian, gaining goodwill while dodging the bad fallout from his former marriage.

The question, is all this largesse from the powerful sincere or a calculated PR campaign? (*The O'Reilly Factor,* June 28, 2006)

Now, you can tell how desperately a network wants to cover Angelina Jolie when they use Warren Buffett as a news peg. They might as well say, "Newly appointed chairman Ben Bernanke has hinted that the Fed may raise a key interest rate, leading Wall Street investors to comment on the recent troubling inflation of both world commodity prices and *Mean Girls* star Lindsay Lohan's lovely jubblies. With us now is *Us Weekly* editor Janice Min . . ."

Of course, in the real world, causes tend to precede effects. Jolie started her UN humanitarian work in 2001. She didn't hook up with Pitt until 2004 or 2005. So if she actually was using her UN work to deflect criticism from her role in the Brad and Jen breakup, she's a friggin' genius who deserves not only Jennifer Aniston's husband but yours as well.

Also, not to be insulting, but people lining up for *Gone in Sixty Seconds* are not that hard to fool. Mutter something vaguely altruistic about the rain forest at the People's Choice Awards and you're pretty much good to go. Even among the publicity-hungry glitterati, filling your home to the rafters with Cambodian children is generally considered overkill.

Of course, Jolie, who refuses to come on O'Reilly's show for any reason, no matter how much he denigrates her UN charity work or rewinds portions of *Gia*, would not be let off the hook so easily.

O'REILLY: We did an investigation, Jeanne [Wolf, of Movies. com], as you might know, into Angelina Jolie, and we wanted to see if she has given all the money she said she has given, and she did. Absolutely has given a lot of money. She's adopting those children, and she's going to the countries and doing a lot of good.

Oh, what we wouldn't give to be flies on the wall during Fox News staff meetings: "Yeah, Bridget, something about this Angelina Jolie UN work doesn't smell right. Make some calls. Find out if she's making all of this up so people will go see *Shark Tale.*"

IS URKEL'S FOREIGN AID PACKAGE ENOUGH?

CLEARLY, THEN, EVEN when Hollywood celebrities' cynically self-serving multimillion-dollar donations and philanthropic work do check out, the ethical paragons over at Fox are loath to give them credit.

But what about when there's a crisis and celebrities *don't* publicize their giving?

On January 5, 2005, just ten days after the deadly Asian tsunami, Sean Hannity wondered why Hollywood hadn't done more to help.

HANNITY: The *Los Angeles Times* picked up today on a question that we were asking on last night's show. How come Hollywood stars have been so slow to respond to the tsunami tragedy with donations of their own?

Now, it seems to me they spent a lot of money to beat up on President Bush but they've been comparatively silent after this disaster.

Consider this: billionaire Bush basher George Soros spent at least twenty-seven million dollars to defeat George Bush, according to the *New York Times.* Well, that means he paid roughly a hundred and seven thousand dollars for each of the two hundred fifty-two electoral votes that John Kerry won. But to date we cannot find any public mention of him donating any-thing to the victims of the tsunami tragedy.

Yes, veteran Hollywood character actor George Soros. Say, didn't he play the guy who molested Arnold's friend Dudley on that very special episode of *Diff'rent Strokes?*

HANNITY: Now, Soros isn't exactly a Hollywood celebrity, but it does raise an important question: Where are these people's pri-orities? They lecture us all the time.

Oh, so he's *not* a Hollywood celebrity? Then why would Han-nity point to him as the exemplar of Hollywood stinginess? It would literally make more sense to mention how little Ralph Macchio has done to stop feline leukemia.

HANNITY: Joining us now, nationally syndicated radio talk show host and author of the best-selling book *Twice Adopted,* Michael Reagan is with us and Democratic strategist Kirsten Powers.
   By the way, Michael, I understand Jane Wyman, your mom, has a birthday today. I want to send out a special birthday.

MICHAEL REAGAN: Happy birthday to Mom. Yes.

HANNITY: Happy birthday, Mom.

Yes, happy birthday, Jane Wyman, you no-giving-to-indigenous-Papua-New-Guinea-tribal-schools-as-far-as-we-know *beeyotch.*

HANNITY: All right, Kirsten, let me—and by the way, Sandra Bullock deserves a lot of credit: second donation of one million dollars to the Red Cross by her. Even Leonardo DiCaprio, who I don't particularly love, he gave a donation.
   Here's the point: Where is all of Hollywood, the rest of Hol-lywood? Liberals that want higher taxes, want to elect politicians that want higher taxes, that want redistribution. You know, here they can put money where their mouths are. Where are they?

So the chick from *Miss Congeniality 2* gave nearly 7 percent of the amount President Bush originally pledged as America's entire public contribution? Are you sure you want to do this story, Sean?

Now, many celebrities eventually did pitch in to help the tsunami victims. For example, NBC televised a big benefit concert just ten days after *Hannity & Colmes* aired their story (which, to be fair, Alan Colmes mentioned when that thick-browed troglodyte Hannity finally stopped panting over Sandra Bullock). The *New York Times* called the show "celebrity-studded," which could be why Warren Buffett and George Soros were not allowed to sing "I Got You, Babe."

Further, a November 2006 Google search on "tsunami," "aid," and "celebrities" returned 943,000 hits—and though we didn't have time to examine all of them, we suspect very few involved Sean Hannity complaining about how little George Soros was doing to help.

Then again, we have a feeling this had more to do with grinding axes and deflecting attention from the president's clumsy response to the crisis than taking a fair look at tsunami aid. Or maybe that's just too cynical.

EVERY CELL IS SACRED

IF YOU'RE NOT a Republican, a Christian, or rich and you still want Fox to go to bat for you, your best bet is to be a frozen speck of undifferentiated human cells.

Yes, if there's anything Fox hates more than a celebrity who gets free movie tickets, it's a celebrity who wants an easy way out of his Parkinson's disease and doesn't care how many frosty fifty-celled bundles of joy he tramples along the way.

On the November 4, 2006, edition of Fox's *Weekend Live*, host Brian Wilson asked viewers to respond to the "e-mail question of the day": "Do you pay any attention to political endorsements made by celebrities?"

The question was an obvious allusion to actor Michael J. Fox's commercials in support of candidates who endorse embryonic stem cell research. Fox's Parkinson's had progressed to a point where its effects had become impossible to mask, and many conservatives thought it unfair that people might actually see what obstructing medical research does to people.

Wilson chuckled through the responses to the question, all of which had the same theme:

> I absolutely pay attention to whom celebrities endorse. They endorse, and then I vote for the opposite candidate. (Monika, Goldboro, NC)

> When a candidate seeks out a celebrity to gain support, I figure they are probably weak in presentation or position. (Bruce, St. Louis, MO)

> When I see a celebrity endorse a candidate, I just laugh. They have no idea how real people live. Their opinions mean nothing to me. (Lyn, Knoxville, TN)

> I refuse to take advice from people who rarely get out of bed before noon. (Scott, Jacksonville, FL)

> You're talking about a group of people who were until recently unemployed with random career stints in the service industry, i.e., waiters and waitresses. I think that explains their views pretty well. (Daniel, Sunland, CA)

> Yeah, we agree with Fox News viewers. It's about time Michael J. Fox keeps his mouth shut until he decides to get his ass out of bed before noon and see how real Americans live.

FOX DEFENDS A CELEBRITY . . . JEW HATER

AS EVERYONE REMEMBERS, in July of 2006, actor Mel Gibson was pulled over in Malibu, California, for drunk-driving his car at 87 miles an hour through a 45-mile-per-hour zone. It was soon revealed that Gibson had subsequently launched into a weird anti-Semitic tirade, allegedly saying that the Jews are responsible for all the wars in the world, claiming that he owned Malibu, and posing a somewhat vulgar rhetorical riddle to a female police officer.

Within days he had apologized to the public, the police, and Jews, though, as this book was going to press, he had yet to reach out to the sugar-titted community.

Naturally, there was a huge backlash in the media, and Fox could hardly ignore the story. But that didn't mean they couldn't do their darnedest to minimize it.

While its commentators took pains to point out that Gibson's behavior was over the line, just how far over was a matter of interpretation. After all, they had previously promoted him as one of Hollywood's few remaining good guys.

On his first night on the air after the story broke, Bill O'Reilly gave us the no-spin truth about Hollywood's latest fallen star—that is, Mel Gibson is just like Bill's grammy:

O'REILLY: Well, he made appropriate remarks all the time. He was hammered, and he was just speaking gibberish.

But here's—react to this. I think that people who do this are for two reasons, number one, fear. My grandmother used to say bad things about blacks, and I said to her one time, "Grandma, you never even met a black person in your life." But she was afraid, all right? And she wasn't well educated.

First of all, Gibson wasn't just speaking gibberish. Gibberish is more like, "Where the fuck is Tom Bosley's house, Aquaman? Mmmm, filo pastry. BADGERS!"

"The Jews are responsible for all the wars in the world" and "What do you think you're looking at, sugar tits?" is not gibberish. It's pretty clear.

Secondly, if Mel Gibson really is afraid of the Jews, it's worse than we thought. What could he possibly be afraid of? That they're direct descendants of Satan who control Hollywood, the banks, and the media? Bill, stay off his side, please.

Two days later, on *Hannity & Colmes,* Operation Scrub Mel's Image was entering its second spin cycle.

To bring some sorely needed perspective to the story, H 'n' C invited world-respected humanitarian, philosopher, and Holocaust survivor Elie Wiesel to the . . . or no, that's a typo. They had Ann Coulter.

Oh, it went a little something like this:

HANNITY: All right. Now I want to ask you, when Patrick Kennedy crashed his car into a barrier, saying to police at three in the morning he was going for a vote and was taken home by police, I said, "I want to get him help." I said, "But what he didn't do at the time was admit the truth."

COULTER: Right.

HANNITY: Gibson, I want him to get help.

COULTER: Right . . .

HANNITY: He's drinking. He says these things.

COULTER: Right.

HANNITY: But he came on and admitted it, profoundly apologized. After he gets help, he plans to make good. It seems it's not going to be accepted by people. Should it be?

COULTER: Sure. Of course. What people do when they're drunk, especially someone with a problem, as Gibson apparently has, I mean, obviously it's a different standard. He didn't, you know, drive a woman off a bridge and, you know, he's not trying to sit on the Senate Judiciary Committee either.

Now, anyone who drives impaired should be ashamed of himself. And Ted Kennedy certainly should have been raked over the coals for his role in Mary Jo Kopechne's death in the summer of 1969. But what does that have to do with Mel Gibson in 2006? That's like telling Coulter she can't criticize Bill Clinton because Warren G. Harding was so much worse.

And alcohol doesn't just magically alter people's personalities. Hitler didn't all of a sudden become a peace-loving hippie when he had a couple beers.

What Gibson did isn't really all that common, after all. As far as we know, drunken Jew-baiting is not an FBI Uniform Crime Report category, and to date, a LexisNexis search of "Jews" and "all the wars in the world" brings up only Gibson's name.

Of course, as any student of history knows, it's not enough to simply deflect blame when bad things happen. You gotta stick that blame on someone else:

O'REILLY: But here's the deal. And I think this is more important than—look, everybody can make up their own mind, as you said. And I agree with you a hundred percent, how you're going to look at Mel Gibson. Not my job to tell you. Not your job to tell. Everybody in America has a mind to make, their own mind up. Nobody can make an excuse for what he did. It's inexcusable, okay? No excuses made. That point is on the record. But there comes a point where the media and individual Americans start to enjoy the suffering of rich and powerful people.

GERALDO RIVERA, HOST, *GERALDO AT LARGE:* I agree.

O'REILLY: All right? They wallow in it. They can't get enough of it. They've got blood all over their mouth, these vampires, okay? They're in the media, these people. This is what they live for.

That's wrong. It's morally wrong. It's maybe not as bad as what Gibson did, but it's approaching that. Because there comes a point where every human being does stuff wrong. Everyone. We all do wrong things.

Weird, huh? Oh, but ya know Bill was just getting warmed up. Later in the interview, he said this:

O'REILLY: I'll tell you this. You need to think about it, and so does everybody else. These corporate masters that have allowed our society to degenerate into a society that rejoices when this stuff happens and makes money from it. These are the truly evil people.

So let's review.

Celebrities who get free movie tickets from theater managers: Bad.

Celebrities who give money to the Third World and publicize it: Bad.

Celebrities who *don't* give money to the Third World: Bad.

Celebrities who fight for disease cures at the expense of a handful of insentient cells: Bad.

Celebrities who get piss drunk, drive 42 miles an hour over the speed limit, resist arrest, claim they own their city of residence, tell the arresting officer that Jews are responsible for all the world's wars, and call a female cop "sugar tits": Similar to O'Reilly's grandmother.

Media who are still talking about the drunk-driving, vulgarly sexist, insanely megalomaniacal, Jew-baiting celebrity four days after the story breaks: Evil vampires with blood all over their mouths.

You know, sometimes it's hard to decide whether they're more fair or more balanced.

6

FOXXXY NEWS

THOSE WHO KNOW Fox News by reputation alone might assume the network is as conservative about sex as it is about everything else.

Oh, sweet Traci Lords, would they be wrong.

In reality, Fox looks pretty much like the Roman Catholic Church might if it had elected Rick James pope back in 1978 instead of John Paul II. The conservative doctrine may have survived reasonably intact, but Christmas mass at St. Peter's Basilica would have been changed forever.

Those who have studied Fox News closely know you'll find more blond bimbos, gratuitous skin, and inappropriate middle-aged banter on the network than anywhere outside of NFL Sunday at a Texas Hooters.

Indeed, when it comes to sex, Fox exhibits a bizarre mix of traditional Augustinian forbearance and winking, Austin Powers permissiveness.

For instance, while Bill O'Reilly is a genuine media scold, it's fair to say the man is obsessed with sex. Even if you discount the Andrea Mackris sexual harassment affidavit,[1] there's enough material in his books alone to confidently pin the dirty-old-man label on him.

His novel *Those Who Trespass* is about what you'd get if you forced Roger Mudd and Jackie Collins to write a term paper together. And his political nonfiction books include so many creepy sexual land mines that it's only a matter of time before Amazon.com starts suggesting you buy them together with Dramamine.

Contrast that with O'Reilly's reaction to the infamous Janet Jackson Super Bowl appearance, which included a harsh rebuke of media commentators such as CBS's Andy Rooney, who thought it was all much ado about nothing: "The reason the culture is in such trouble is that elites like Rooney, network news in general, liberal pundits, and cowardly politicians have all failed to make judgments about obvious bad behavior encouraged by the media," said O'Reilly. "So we have now a culture that drowns children with sex and violence and a society that largely looks the other way."

Quick reader quiz: Which book is the following a passage from, Bill O'Reilly's *Those Who Trespass* or Andy Rooney's *A Few Minutes with Andy Rooney?*

Suddenly another sensation intruded. Ashley felt two large hands wrap themselves around her breasts and hot breath on the back of her neck. She opened her eyes wide and giggled. "I thought you drowned out there snorkel man."

Tommy O'Malley was naked and at attention. "Drowning is not an option," he said, "unless, of course, you beg me to perform unnatural acts right here in this shower."

Answer: it's from the O'Reilly book. How do we know? There's no folksy bit about how hard it is to open condom wrappers, and Rooney is even older than Bill, so *his* sexy dialogue would have been even more out-of-touch and wooden (probably something along the lines of: "Drowning is not a foreseen contingency, unless irregular means of gratification are indicated—and by that I mean cunnilingus.").

Indeed, the strangest thing about both O'Reilly's and Fox's abundant sexual perversity is how out in the open it is.

First of all, the network's female anchors and guests invariably tend toward the—how shall we put it?—superfly. Sure, most networks take physical appearance into account when hiring on-air personalities, but Fox is the only one that seems continually on the verge of publishing a calendar. On the other hand, for some reason the network's stable of male anchors looks disturbingly like the people you'd find sitting around at 2 AM on a Wednesday at a Vegas sportsbook.

Second, they never miss a chance to titillate, even as they bemoan the rampant sexualization of the culture and the media.[2]

Maybe they have an only-Nixon-can-go-to-China arrogance about their conservative bona fides that makes them think no one will notice how odd it is to show a giggling Victoria's Secret model expounding on her latest photo shoot just minutes after a sober, policy-laden segment on how the Democrats are ruining the economy.

Or maybe they're so friggin' horny they just don't give a rip.

VICTORIA'S SECRET IS THAT NEIL CAVUTO IS A PERV

Fox News touts *Your World with Neil Cavuto* as the "number one business show on cable."

But along with news on finance, trade, and fiscal policy, the program features more T&A than a sweeps-week episode of *Charlie's Angels.*

Cavuto is the Hugh Hefner of cable news. We figure it's only a matter of time before he starts wearing a smoking jacket on the air. Indeed, by our best estimate, Neil is about eight months away from installing a grotto in his studio.

If there's ever an opportunity to have a hot chick on his show, Neil is all over it. Sure, the business tie-in is usually pretty loose. But you have at least to admire Cavuto's talent for digging up stories with which he can run video of women in their underwear.

A typical Cavuto lead-in might be something like: "Southern cotton growers are facing tough economic times as commodity prices lag for a second consecutive quarter. And you know what's made of cotton? Panties! Here are two young ladies to update us on the latest developments."

Well, you get the idea.

Newshounds.us, a Web-based Fox News watchdog, noticed the same pattern we did and compiled a list of the best examples of Cavuto's boobie fixation from January through June of 2005.

We picked up on their research, tweaked it a bit, and added our own thoughts. Because we didn't want to spark a world pulp shortage, we decided to focus on just a month's worth of Neil's exploits (edited, incredibly enough, for brevity).

(Thanks to News Hounds' Melanie for doing the considerable legwork for us on this one.)

January 11, 2005

Cavuto features the new Victoria's Secret 2005 Swim Book catalog. During the segment, he shows pictures of Victoria's Secret models in revealing swimwear.

As you'll soon see, this is typical Cavuto. Think Neil does this for all catalog releases? No. No, he doesn't. Hey, isn't there a new Montgomery Ward catalog coming out soon? Do you figure Neil will feature it? Well, perhaps just the pages with brassieres on them.

Cavuto teases an upcoming segment with "You think only babes can sell Snapple?" The tease is accompanied by video of hot babes. The segment being teased is an interview with Snapple spokeswoman Wendy Kaufman.

First of all, this is just insulting. The zaftig Kaufman was a Snapple employee who took it upon herself to answer the company's fan mail—a task that ultimately led to a featured role on the company's television commercials.

It's a charming story of an ordinary woman who, through

chutzpah and personality, became a minor media sensation. So why lead with an insult? Everyone can see she's a large woman. Is it necessary to point out that modern society might not consider her the physical ideal? And what newsman says "babes" in the first place?

We took an informal survey of several episodes of PBS's *Wall Street Week* to see how many references there were to "babes." Know how many? *None!* You know why? Because it's an unwritten rule of financial news that you don't talk about chicks you think are hot during the friggin' broadcast!

January 19, 2005

Cavuto runs tape of Victoria's Secret models in bras and panties while reporting, "Limited brands *shaking things up.*"

(Yes, he really did stress that last part.)

Cavuto reports that Limited Brands, which owns Victoria's Secret, is being split into three business groups: "One will focus on lingerie, another on apparel, and a third on beauty and personal care."

Of course, Limited Brands also owns retailers such as The Limited, Express, C.O. Bigelow, and Henri Bendel. But none of these brands feature boobies and therefore don't make for great video.

February 4, 2005

Cavuto airs a portion of the Super Bowl ad for GoDaddy.com, featuring a large-breasted woman. In the same show, he interviews two women who are scheduled to compete in that weekend's Lingerie Bowl, a pay-per-view event that airs during the Super Bowl, featuring scantily clad women playing football.

Just prior to those segments, Cavuto interviews Focus on the Family's Dr. James Dobson, who complains that "popular culture is at war with parents today" and "pornography is everywhere, as you know."

We don't know if Dobson said that because he was sharing the green room with Cavuto's Lingerie Bowl guests (who were bedecked in lace-up bras), but we're guessing it was just a coincidence.

We should also note that the Lingerie Bowl participants were shown opposite Cavuto on split screen, and were strategically positioning their bosoms with their upper arms to maximize their assets. (Although it was a close finish, Neil clearly won the contest for biggest boob.)

February 11, 2005

In his Biz Blast segment, Cavuto reports on Jennifer Lopez's new clothing line. He airs video of Lopez looking sexy along with video featuring panty- and bra-clad models.

Since when is Cavuto a fashion maven? When was the last time he interviewed Donna Karan or Isaac Mizrahi about their new spring lines? Yet whenever there's the remotest justification for showing a gyrating singer or a female underwear model, Neil's all over it.

February 14, 2005

Cavuto reports on the $12 million Victoria's Secret bra, which is still on the market. During the segment, he runs video of Victoria's Secret models in bras and panties.

Okay, the bra in question was first offered in 1996. It's not really much of a story anymore. Every year they haul the thing out, dust it off, and slap it on the new "it girl." Then Cavuto gets a chub and runs another story on it.

Yeah, we're starting to understand why he's beating Wolf Blitzer in the ratings.

Of course, Cavuto's business coverage is not just drenched with enough sex to repel your average thirteen-year-old boy or prison inmate. He also loves the sly double entendre.

For instance, on May 26, 2005, while promoting a segment on the private charter service Hooters Air, Cavuto said Hooters' owners were "milking the concept big time" and that Fox was "abreast" of it.

Later, Cavuto promo'd the story again and announced that Hooters was "shaking up the industry."

Well, at least we know what the *Three's Company* writers are up to these days. Seriously, we half expected Mr. Roper to burst through the door and accuse Cavuto of gettin' it on with Janet and Chrissy.

Really now, are they trying to compete with CNN or with Cinemax?

SEX WITH TEACHERS: IT'S NOT JUST FOR PRINCIPALS ANYMORE

IF THERE'S ONE thing Fox hates it's child predators. For example, O'Reilly champions Jessica's Law, which calls for harsh minimum penalties for child sex offenders.

Indeed, this seems to be one area where Fox serves as a genuine and impassioned advocate. That is, unless the predator is a really good-looking woman. Then they all think it's kinda hot.

During an April 13, 2006, My Word segment on the notorious Pamela Rogers case, titled—we are absolutely not making this up—"Hot for Teacher," John Gibson asked, "What's with the hot babe teachers trying to seduce underage boys?"

Now, this is a curious title for a segment on child predators, since it implies that it's the child who's the aggressor. But maybe you can chalk that one up to an insane intern or a disgruntled producer. Let's let Gibson explain it himself: "She even put pictures of herself in a bikini on the Web site to make sure the boy was hooked. You can see why he would be. She's hot. Very hot. He's young, probably thinks this isn't such a bad deal."

Is this about child predators or John Gibson's fantasies? Why is it that CNN, MSNBC, NBC, CBS, and ABC can all air programs about child predators and not get sexually excited, whereas Fox anchors appear incapable of muzzling their penises?

A few weeks later, Sean Hannity and Alan Colmes grabbed the pervert baton from Gibson and ran it to the finish line.

On the May 3, 2006, edition of *Hannity & Colmes*, Hannity puzzled over the Rogers story, which included revelations that Rogers had sent her victim a video of her doing a striptease: "Finally tonight, Tennessee prosecutors allege that Pamela Rogers, a twenty-eight-year-old elementary school teacher and coach, sent this racy cell phone video to a thirteen-year-old former student."

Hannity later added, "You know what's amazing? I don't understand this. It seems if you're good-looking, if you're attractive, if you're blond, and it's a female versus a male, you get leniency."

And still later, "This is a child. We're talking about kids here."

Colmes added, "It's unfortunate, and there is a double standard. You're absolutely right."

Bravo! Here was a concise, strongly worded condemnation of what was clearly illegal and inappropriate conduct on the part of a woman who was entrusted with the care and learning of children and who subsequently violated that trust. Sean and Alan certainly weren't mincing words or winking their approval.

Just one problem. During each promo for the segment, they showed the video on a loop not once, not twice, but five times. The clip was edited to show the most titillating moments and was accompanied by Van Halen's "Hot for Teacher."

Somehow, a song that includes the lyric "Got it bad, got it bad, got it bad, I'm hot for teacher" doesn't seem like the most appropriate backdrop for a story about pedophilia.

Now, if this all somehow seems like picayune, blue-nosed Puritanism on our part, ask yourself this: despite their laments about double standards, do you think Hannity and Colmes would have ever cleared the use of "Hot for Teacher" for a story about a twenty-eight-year-old man having sex with a thirteen-year-old girl?

Of course not.

They'd probably play "Sometimes When We Touch."

BIKINI BEACH PARTY SERIAL KILLER

FOX CAN INCORPORATE sex into pretty much anything. Just name it. We've already seen how they make world finance and pedophilia look hot, but can they find the sexy side of . . . murder?

On March 23, 2006, *Fox News Live's* Martha MacCallum reported on a developing story in Florida:

> Daytona Beach, a popular destination for college students of course on their spring break, but this year there's a bit more to worry about there than a bad case of sunburn. A serial killer is on the loose in the Daytona area. So far it's been three prostitutes who have been the targets of this guy.

Fox invited crime analyst Rod Wheeler on to discuss the killings and showed two inset screens: One pictured Wheeler and the other showed footage from Daytona.

Here's a rough blow-by-blow:

WHEELER: The first victim was actually killed about three months ago . . .

(Video: Woman on a stage in a bikini dancing and shaking her breasts.)

WHEELER: . . . but what's really important in this case . . .

(Video: Woman turns to show her backside and shakes her butt while the camera zooms in to the point where the inset screen, which is twice the size of the screen showing the guest, is completely filled with the girl's bikini-bottomed butt.)

WHEELER: . . . the suspect has used a handgun, from what I understand, and has shot the victims . . .

(Video: A large group of people, with two women in the foreground—one in a black bikini, the other in a purple bikini.)

WHEELER: So anytime, Martha, you have a rapist on the loose, and a rapist who likes to commit murder, that is not a good thing in any community.

(Video: A bikini contest.)

Soon Wheeler's inset was pulled completely away and the entire screen was cleared to accommodate the contest, which featured five girls onstage with close-up shots of the contestants' breasts.

When the small inset with Wheeler returned, the large inset showed the butts of the bikini contestants . . .

Cue First Horseman of the Apocalypse.

Now, if this serial killer had been targeting kids on spring break, all this video would have merely been gratuitous and in poor taste. But the fact that the murderer was after prostitutes made it irrelevant and completely inane.

It would be like doing a story on trade policy with Thailand and showing video of O'Reilly at that live sex show he told Andrea Mackris about.[3]

PORN STARS AND THE REPUBLICANS WHO LOVE THEM

ON MARCH 16, 2006, Neil Cavuto interviewed former California gubernatorial candidate Mary Carey about her plans to make a second run for governor.

Sounds reasonable. The previous California governor's election led to a big media frenzy, resulting in the election of the guy from *Kindergarten Cop*. And Governor Schwarzenegger has certainly endured some rough patches during his term, making him vulnerable to criticism from former challengers.

Of course, of the 135 people who ran for governor in the 2003 recall election, Cavuto decided to interview the only one (as far as we know) who gives blow jobs for money. Yes, that's right, kids. Another porn star on Fox News.

Before the interview, Cavuto aired video of candidate Carey dressed in a French maid's outfit while she performed *la danse du poteau*. (Okay, so we're trying to make "pole dance" sound a little more sophisticated.)

Here's how Neil sold the story:

We have a lot more coming up for you in the next half-hour. Her political platform included taxing breast implants and making lap dances tax deductible. But before you laugh at porn star Mary Carey, remember this: She placed tenth of a hundred thirty-five candidates running for California governor. Wait till you hear what she's up to now. Meet her, next.

It's really sad that the mainstream liberal media are missing out on these stories. They could learn something from Fox. Why isn't Katie Couric interviewing Chinese prostitutes about Sino-American relations? Why doesn't Matt Lauer ask gay-for-pay porn stars about their feelings on a constitutional amendment defining marriage? And why, oh why, won't Stone Phillips ask Thai sex-show performers about U.S.-Asian trade imbalances? What if they hold all the answers?

We should note that Ms. Carey is not a *retired* porn star. Her official campaign Web site showed her topless—a brilliant tactic that her challengers in the 2003 recall election, with the possible exception of Peter Ueberroth, must have felt helpless to counter in kind.

When the interview began, Neil took up the cudgel on behalf of Fox's loyal conservative Christian viewers and zinged Carey with hard-hitting questions such as, "So, you're serious about this?" "You're still doing the porn thing?" and "You have a boyfriend, don't you?"

But Cavuto summed it up best when he said, "You know, there are going to be purists who are going to say, Mary, that you shouldn't be running for a high political office, that we should have standards."

Well, Neil, some think the news media should have standards, too. Some old-school journalists might think twice about dedicating an entire segment to a woman who flaunts her breasts on TV for votes—unless it's in that cute, conservative Republican way that Katherine Harris does it.

Later in the interview, Cavuto melted down like a sixteen-year-old boy who'd just seen his first naked lady. Neil and Mary resumed their Socratic dialogue as Neil's once-melancholy sperm danced a lively Scottish reel.

Opined Carey: "I mean, doing a couple movies a year, that is just providing entertainment. It's no different than, you know, Arnold Schwarzenegger doing movies where he kills people. I think mine is—you know, mine is promoting love, not, you know, violence and war."

Carey later added, "I don't ever kill anybody," to which Cavuto responded, "Better than kill them. Well, that's actually a good point."

No, Neil, it's actually not a good point. First of all, *5 Guy Cream Pie* didn't promote love. Secondly, while there are few universal axioms, one of them just happens to be, "the governor of the largest state in the union can't be the lead in *Boobsville Sorority Girls*."

Later, while informing Neil how she scored a ticket to the National Republican Congressional Committee dinner, Carey said, "the women were kind of snobby with me on the phone," and then added, "but the guys from the NRCC are very, very nice."

We have no doubt, Mary.

NOTES

1. Which you shouldn't. Here's the link: www.thesmokinggun.com/archive/1013043mackris1.html.
2. As in a November 10, 2005, *The Big Story* segment where John Gibson led a discussion on a Kaiser Family Foundation study that noted a sharp spike in sex scenes on TV. Fox correspondent Alisyn Camerota remarked, "Seventy-seven percent of all shows have some sexual content. Even the History Channel is doing the history of sex. And, you know, furthermore, I mean, kids don't want to watch C-SPAN all day long, so they are going to get an eyeful whenever they turn on the TV." For the record, Alisyn Camerota is also very hot.
3. Seriously, you must check out the link: www.thesmokinggun.com/archive/1013043mackris1.html.

THE SHOWS

▼

7

SWEET JESUS, WE STILL HATE BILL O'REILLY

WHEN BILL O'REILLY'S charming, statuesque wife approached us one memorable night two summers ago, her rain-swept tears melting away a night's-worth of hard drinking, her timid, quavering, red-glossed lips finally forming the words she'd longed for years to say—"please, please, guys, help me save my crazy-ass husband"—we, of course, were moved.

A liberating heart-to-heart, three pots of hot coffee, and two gentle kisses on the forehead later, we knew what we had to do. And we knew how we'd have to do it—balls out.

The intervention wouldn't work, she warned us, unless it was dramatic—a rhetorical blow to the solar plexus that brought the Spin King finally, abjectly, to his knees. Years of half-measures and gentle coaxing had only emboldened her husband, she told us. "You gotta knock him on his ass," she offered, with uncharacteristic coarseness for such a lovely lady.[1]

Our response, crafted with love for Bill and his family—but

especially for Maureen—was *Sweet Jesus, I Hate Bill O'Reilly*, a bracing book-length psychological inventory of its titular inspiration.

Well, honey, you gotta make your husband read the damn thing!

Despite great feedback from readers and enthusiastic accolades from fellow Bill interveners Al Franken and Keith Olbermann, our book sadly failed to effect change in the one man who needed it most—O'Reilly himself.

Indeed, since the publication of *SJIHBO*, Bill's condition has, if anything, worsened. His leaps of logic have become more acrobatic. His enemies list has swelled beyond Nixonian proportions. And as for his megalomania—well, on a scale of one to ten, with one being George W. Bush and ten being Caligula near the end of a six-day palace bender, Bill is about a thirty-seven.

For instance, in a letter to his fans to announce the release of his book *Culture Warrior* (which, to be frank, is about what you'd get if you gave a book deal to Jesse Helms and assigned Charo to be his ghostwriter) O'Reilly wrote, "This book could very well change the direction of the country. In fact, I can almost guarantee it will."

Okay, Witchie-poo. Good luck with that, then.

So, needless to say, in the year since we published our last book, O'Reilly stories have been accumulating in our files like *Boy Meets World* slash fiction on Mark Foley's hard drive.

Following are just a few of our favorites.

THE EQUAL AND OPPOSITE WORLDS OF HITLER AND DREW BARRYMORE

O'REILLY HAS ALWAYS presented himself as a fair-and-balanced arbiter, lambasting ideologues on both the far left and far right.

Indeed, he once told *Factor* viewers, "As you may know, I have a big problem with both the far left and the far right in America. I believe extremists hurt this country and should be scorned."

Of course, we always suspected that Bill was scorning one side a bit more than the other, but we didn't realize just how skewed his perceptions were until, acting on information in his

Wikipedia.com entry, we did our own meticulous search of *O'Reilly Factor* transcripts from January 1999 (the earliest dates available on LexisNexis) to November 2006.

It placed Bill squarely in the "far-gone" camp.

Here's the list of people and organizations Bill considers "far right."

Nazis	American militia groups
The Ku Klux Klan	Former KKK Grand Wizard
Rush Limbaugh	David Duke
Michael Savage	G. Gordon Liddy
Ayn Rand Institute	Jerry Falwell
Ann Coulter	Pat Buchanan
Pat Robertson	Bob Jones University
Dan Quayle	

It should be noted that Ann Coulter has been one of Bill's favorite guests and that *The Factor* once referred to her in a tagline as "No Spin Ann." O'Reilly has also said that Ann is "as far right as she is funny" and "entertaining."

Also, G. Gordon Liddy became an enemy of *The Factor* only after he said O'Reilly's ratings weren't that great. We also find it odd that poor Dan Quayle is lumped in with Nazis.

The far-left list is a little longer (apologies to anyone we may have inadvertently excluded):

Jodie Foster	Meg Ryan
Drew Barrymore	Danny DeVito
The Osbornes	Ellen Degeneres
Matthew Perry	Billy Crystal
Sharon Stone	Bill Maher
Susan Sarandon	Russ Feingold
Barbara Boxer	*Slate* magazine
Pinch Sulzberger	Ned Lamont
Cindy Sheehan	Ted Kennedy
Bruce Springsteen	Bill Moyers
Harry Belafonte	Howard Dean
The Dixie Chicks	Al Franken
George Clooney	Barbra Streisand
Media Matters for America	ACLU
Air America Radio	MoveOn.org

New York Times
Paul Krugman
The World Can't Wait
Amnesty International
Peter Lewis
Rob Glaser
Anthony Romero
Boston Globe
The German media
St. Petersburg Times
Think Progress
Robert Scheer
Brattleboro Reformer
Michael Kinsley
Capital Times
Lynn Woolsey
David Cole
Bob Herbert
Bob Garfield
Minneapolis Star-Tribune
Gavin Newsom
Katrina vanden Heuvel
San Francisco
Baltimore Sun
Citizens for Responsibility
    and Ethics
The Sundance Channel
MSNBC
Federal judge Anna Diggs Taylor
The Daily Kos
The Democracy Alliance
Sarasota Herald
Alessandra Stanley
Tim Rutten
Keith Watenpaugh of the Center
    for Peace and Global Studies
Walter Cronkite
Rob Stein
Human Rights Watch
Rick Kaplan
Rainbow/PUSH
Jimmy Breslin
James Carroll
Fenton Communications
L.A. Times

Atlanta Journal-Constitution
Campaign for America's Future
Andres Oppenheimer
George Soros
Natalie Maines
Planned Parenthood
Michael Moore
The French media
San Francisco Chronicle
Sheldon Silver
David Corn
Richard Cohen
Cynthia Tucker
Frank Rich
People for the American Way
Barbara Lee
Molly Ivins
Ray McGovern
Nicholas Lemann
San Francisco board of
    supervisors
Jay Bennish
London *Guardian*
Ninth Circuit Court of Appeals
Secular progressive movement
Nancy Pelosi
Noam Chomsky
Robert Siegel
Lynn Samuels
Peter Ames Carlin
Tim Gill
A. O. Scott
Manhattan district represented
    by Assemblyman Sheldon
    Silver
ACLU scholarship recipients
    Shannon Baldon and
    Elizabeth Lipschultz
Ford Foundation
Rob Reiner
Andrew Rappaport
Joel Stein
John Carroll
Robert Greenwald
Nikki Finke

Danny Glover
Joanne Ostrow
Unbrand America
Heather Mallick
Arianna Huffington
Lehigh University
James Brolin
Sean Penn
Kevin Bacon
Ed Asner
Martin Sheen
Robert Reich
Woody Harrelson
Ellen Goodman
Phil Donahue
Jerrold Nadler
Rosie O'Donnell
Fordham professor Bruce Andrews
Al Sharpton
The Oregonian

Ben Cohen of Ben & Jerry's
Judge Greg Mathis
Norman Mailer
Ward Churchill
Tides Foundation
Ted Rall
Toronto Globe & Mail
Larry David
London mayor Ken Livingstone
Judy Davis
Tim Robbins
National Public Radio
Angela Davis
TomPaine.com
Northwest Immigrant
   Rights Project
Angela Oh
Alan Dershowitz
Fairness and Accuracy
   in Reporting

You know who's fucking up this country? Meg Ryan. And you know who's ignoring it? The far-left media. Those bastards!

Keep in mind, this list includes only people and organizations that Bill has specifically referred to as "far left"—not left, loony left, crazy left, fanatical left, radical left, left-wing nuts, off-the-chart left, hard left, ultra left, or anything else. It might have been fun to include those as well, but our publisher told us they're not in the habit of installing hard drives in their spring releases.

So apparently, as Al Franken pointed out when we brought these lists to his attention, if you bisect the distance between Nazis and Meg Ryan, you arrive precisely at O'Reilly.

Hmmm, sounds about right.

Speaking of Franken, wherever you'd like to place him on the political spectrum (he's admitted to being a liberal, though we prefer to categorize him as "just to the left of Noam Chomsky and just to the right of Kevin Bacon") it would seem a stretch to refer to him as the liberal Ann Coulter.

But on the June 8, 2006, installment of *The O'Reilly Factor,* O'Reilly was doing just that—though he made one critical distinction: "Here's the difference between Franken and Coulter . . . Coulter doesn't lie. Coulter doesn't lie.[2] I mean, she's over the top in my opinion, and I don't like her tactics at all, and I think they diminish her."

Earlier that day on *The Radio Factor,* O'Reilly scolded Coulter about the dangers of calling some of the 9/11 widows "the witches of East Brunswick" who are enjoying their husbands' deaths.

Here's how O'Reilly took down this far-right character: "You don't have to do that . . . because you're going to be demonized as some far-right kook, who all she wants to do is be mean, and that's what the *New York Daily News* did to you yesterday."

Now, let's put it in perspective for you. When anyone in the media simply mentions O'Reilly's sexual harassment scandal (which was in the public record, by the way), he calls them smear merchants and character assassins. But when Coulter says the Jersey Girls are enjoying their husbands' deaths, O'Reilly merely warns her that she's in danger of being demonized (while implying that others are out to smear *her*), but takes care to note that she "doesn't lie."

After reading that, you almost wonder what Bill would have said to Hitler: Those Waffen-SS uniforms are a bit on the drab side?

BILL TEACHES US ABOUT THE WORLD WIDE INTERWEB

WHEN YOUR POLITICAL outlook is as skewed as Bill's is, it's easy to ascribe sinister motives to ordinary liberals that one would never think of attributing to right-wingers.

Indeed, in order to prove to himself that he occupies true north on the political compass, O'Reilly has consistently shown himself willing to plot map points that simply aren't there.

In his August 8, 2006, Talking Points Memo, Bill went after what he called "anti-Semitic stuff directed at Joe Lieberman":

As you may know, some radical left Americans have been vilifying Lieberman for his support of the Iraq War. The usual suspects on the Net have smeared the man, and now Lieberman's campaign is accusing radical bloggers of hacking into their Web site and damaging it.[3]

But far worse are the anti-Semitic rants. This was posted on the far-left Daily Kos Web site, quote, "as everybody knows, Jews *only* care about the welfare of other Jews. . . . We might better ignore all that Jewish propaganda about participating in the Civil Rights movement."

And this was allowed on the Huffington blog, quote, "Leiberman [*sic*] cannot escape the religious bond he represents. Hell, his wife's name is Haggadah or Muffeletta or Diaspora or something you eat at Passover."

Nice. But the media has generally ignored the far-left hatred directed towards the senator and his family. I wonder how Mel Gibson feels about that.

Apparently, Bill has no clue how a blog works. And we're guessing that the majority of his viewers, many of whom had their first sexual experience in the backseat of a stagecoach, don't either.

As most people with Internet connections know, a blog consists of a series of posts generated by the blogger on which readers are invited to comment. The comments are usually posted automatically right after they're made. It's a pure form of reader participation, and it's not always pretty.

O'Reilly's not quoting posts here, but comments by readers. He might as well do a searing exposé on what's written on the bathroom stalls at his local Arby's. (Actually, that would be a lot easier than scouring the hundreds of reader comments Daily Kos and the Huffington Post get every day. As News Hounds pointed out, the comment O'Reilly plucked from The Daily Kos—which on closer inspection appears to be a sarcastic [i.e., *not* anti-Semitic] response to an earlier comment—was made on December 7, 2005, so he must have gone through thousands of comments to find something offensive enough to air.)

O'Reilly continued:

The far left in America is dominated by haters, people who despise their own country and want to injure those with whom they disagree.

The smear merchants are now all over the mainstream media and have spread like lice on the Net. They are truly misguided and, in some cases, emotionally disturbed human beings.

Really?

On BillOReilly.com, we came across a posting about a crocodile that was found in the Rio Grande in October of 2006. Here are some of the reader comments that were allowed on Bill's message board (remember, these are by people who've paid a premium to be members of BillOReilly.com, not just random trolls):

Hummmmm not a bad idea. Crocs in the river. Free food for the crocs and no waste after. (09 Oct 2006; 7:09 AM PT)

Maybe some loyal American planted it there. We'll rename the Rio Grande the North American Moat. "Cross at your own risk." (09 Oct 2006; 11:45 AM PT)

CrockPot River . . . Hot Tamales . . . Twist and Turn . . . Rest in peace . . . Amen. (09 Oct 2006; 12:15 PM PT)

How about importing some piranhas from the Amazon? (10 Oct 2006; 4:19 PM PT)

Damn you mainstream media for ignoring the posts on Bill's message boards!

Luckily, though, Bill is giving us the tools to fight the haters on the Web: "So, how do you combat them? Exposition is the best way. My upcoming book, *Culture Warrior*, does that. It documents who these people are and what they're doing behind the scenes."

We'll give it to Bill. He knows how to make a buck off anything.

HIGH SCHOOL HONOR STUDENTS GONE WILD!

WHEN BILL DOESN'T have the country's random blog posters on the run, he's fearlessly taking on high school kids who hold opinions he doesn't like.

In his May 15, 2006, Most Ridiculous Item of the Day, Bill called out a pair of students who were being honored by the ACLU:

> The ACLU, which is opposing troops on the border—of course they are—also announced today it is giving scholarships to worthy students. The criteria? Being a far-left kid.
>
> For example, Shannon Baldon of Louisville, Kentucky, is getting a scholarship for refusing to stand for the Pledge of Allegiance. Very nice. Elizabeth Lipschultz from New Jersey is being honored for trying to convince students not to cooperate with military recruiters.
>
> There's no truth to the rumor that the ACLU students will be matriculating in Iran, but anything could happen. It might also be ridiculous.

You can be sure there's a special place in hell for O'Reilly.

What Bill *didn't* report is that Shannon Baldon played a key role in starting the ACLU chapter at her predominantly African-American high school in Louisville, Kentucky. She plans on attending Harvard University and eventually law school.

In her scholarship essay, Baldon wrote:

> I never doubt my ability to do something, but at times I question how well I can do it. Becoming the President of the Student Chapter of the American Civil Liberties Union was a blessing in disguise. I may not always be the most talkative person, but I am in a position to give a voice to those who do not. Having this position is going to help prepare me for the future and test my loyalty to my future career plans as an attorney. It is good that I start speaking up more for myself now, because I will be doing a whole lot more of it in the future. My

plan is to become an assertive activist, but in a different way. I will help those who need help being heard and educate others on the rights and liberties that they have.

What a disgusting far-left kid. She should be at home watching MTV's *My Super Sweet 16* and reruns of *The Simple Life*.

Writing in Louisville's *Courier-Journal*, columnist David Hawpe noted that Baldon received her scholarship for helping start the ACLU chapter at her school and serving as its president, and for tackling a range of civil liberties issues, including, according to the ACLU, "the requirement to stand for the Pledge of Allegiance, the confiscation of certain books and the right to form a Gay-Straight Alliance."

Hawpe interviewed Beth Wilson of the Kentucky ACLU, who called O'Reilly's characterization a "blatant lie," and said Baldon was getting a scholarship "for attempting to protect the rights of students, for starting an ACLU chapter and for taking a leading role in holding a youth rights leadership conference," adding, "Whether Shannon stands for the Pledge or not I don't even know, but she certainly stands for the right of students to make that decision for themselves."

Hawpe also interviewed the girl's parents:

> Shannon's mother, Camilla Conley, said O'Reilly was "taking a cheap shot at the ACLU and using a child to do it." . . .
>
> Shannon's father, Virgil Baldon, who works in TV production, said he wasn't surprised, "because I know what Fox's bent is," but he added that he's disappointed that "they would use a high school student, particularly my daughter, in this way."

Really, Mr. Baldon? You didn't think O'Reilly would use your young daughter for personal gain? Well, just be glad she doesn't work for him.

BILL DOESN'T UNDERSTAND WHY
VERMONT TEDDY BEARS ARE ANGRY

ON JANUARY 13, 2006, Bill began his program talking about Edward Cashman, the Vermont judge who handed a sixty-day prison sentence to a child rapist.

While we weren't in chambers during the judge's deliberation, we have to agree that the sentence does seem pretty friggin' light. But somehow even we underestimated the depths of Bill's outrage. In his Talking Points Memo, O'Reilly put the heat on the Vermont government, asking his viewers whether the whole state should have to stay after school for the actions of a few: "As for Governor Jim Douglas, a Republican, he's dodging our calls, he's MIA. So we now must send the governor a message as well: The new BillOReilly.com poll question is, if Judge Cashman is not removed from the criminal court, will you boycott Vermont?"

Okay, half the population of Burlington just spat out their maple syrup. Jesus, even when Bill has a point, he can't resist taking an unscheduled detour to Loopy Town. Assume for a moment that despite O'Reilly's pitiful track record, he had somehow motivated his viewers to boycott Vermont, the movement had snowballed, and it became a resounding success. We'd have undermined the economy of an entire U.S. state. And a tiny one at that.

Still, we seriously doubt Bill's Svengali-like hold on his viewers would have ever led to any measurable downturn in the fortunes of Vermont ski resorts as Fox fans abruptly changed their vacation plans and furiously booked flights to Gstaad. More likely, millions of Sam's Club shoppers would have started reading those Mrs. Butterworth's labels with just a bit more scrutiny.

Still, Bill is an influential guy, no question about it. The man is to broadcast news what Tony Orlando and Dawn were to seventies-era musical variety shows. But these days he sounds more like Yahweh after the Israelites' little gold cow gaffe than a workaday cable news pundit.

While interviewing Vermont state representative Michael Kainen three days later about the ongoing controversy, Bill announced his viewers' plans to pour figurative salt on Vermont's once-fertile soils: "The state of Vermont's never going to recover from this, ever, unless Cashman is removed. People will not go there, they will not buy your products, they will turn their back, and your state will have a stigma forever. People will remember. This isn't going away."

Now, again, we don't have any sympathy for Cashman. Sixty days in prison for raping a child is just nuts. But face it, there's a reason you didn't go down to IHOP this morning and pour real Nevada syrup on your freedom toast. Bill's just not that powerful.

But even if he were, "forever" is a pretty long time. Come on, sixty years ago Germany was systematically gassing people to death, and now you can't swing a dead dachshund without hitting an aging boomer in a Beetle.

But according to Bill, Vermont is destined to become the Chernobyl of New England because it let a misguided judge keep his job a little too long.

But then O'Reilly is hardly one to admit when one of his nutty boycotts doesn't go as planned. Remember Bill's reference to the *Paris Business Review* and his claims about the billions of dollars France has lost in trade with the United States?

Later, in his column on BillOReilly.com, Bill wrote, "They say the skiing is great this winter in Vermont. But I'm not going. There's something in the air there that I cannot abide."

Now, it's clear that Bill is a man of moral fortitude. When he sees injustice, he stands behind his convictions. And he expects the people of Vermont to take a stand against this injustice as well or face both his and his viewers' wrath. Nothing will change this. He is a man of principle.

He knows full well that statewide industries could be affected by his bold and uncompromising words, but if the people of Vermont take action they can be forgiven.

This isn't about politics, it's about children. And Bill O'Reilly will do anything to protect children, regardless of how it might affect the economy of one of our smallest states. He will not be moved.

Unfortunately, by January 19, Bill had apparently gotten

busted by one of his advertisers and issued this statement on Bill OReilly.com:

No Vermont Boycott

To be clear, *The Factor* is not calling for a boycott of Vermont or Vermont's products. We're even encouraging viewers and listeners to buy Vermont Teddy Bears, because that company's support for us allows us to campaign for justice.

Apparently all it takes for O'Reilly to cave on an issue as important as the molestation of children is a single phone call from a random advertiser. Bill's strong sense of morality seems a bit more malleable when it affects his pocketbook.

Still, O'Reilly wasn't done. Now that it was no longer safe to hector the entire state of Vermont, he had to look for another villain.

On the January 27, 2006, *O'Reilly Factor*, a picture of Cashman was displayed next to a picture of Bill's bête noire, billionaire George Soros. The words "Shocking Connection" appeared on the screen.

O'Reilly firmly stated: "Ahead on the rundown, we found a connection between far-left radical George Soros and Vermont judge Edward Cashman."

Now, we'll be honest and admit that we were very curious about what this shocking connection might be. Perhaps an old campaign contribution? Oh, that would be good. Had they met at a party and posed for a photo with Jane Fonda and John Kerry? We could only be so lucky.

O'Reilly loves a lame connection and would be the first to parade his discovery around like he was Howard Friggin' Carter. But "shocking connections" are hard to come by. O'Reilly had to have something meaty. Did they kill that Aruba chick? Did they date in college? We expected something good, to be sure.

As the segment began, Soros's and Cashman's headshots again appeared onscreen, this time with the word "Connection!"

Ooooh, Bill had added an exclamation point. Then he revealed the nature of their unseemly confederation: "*The Factor* has learned that Cashman is a believer in the restorative justice theory that is also embraced by far-left radical George Soros."

If you're waiting for more, you're not going to get it. That was it. O'Reilly is a moron.

For the record, that's not a connection. It's a commonality at best. A lame commonality. That's what should have been on the screen: Soros's photo, Cashman's photo, and the words "Lame Commonality."

Bill's guest, Joshua Marquis, a member of the board of directors of the National District Attorney's Association, was then brought on to strengthen the sleeper hold that O'Reilly had put on both Cashman and Soros. Certainly he would thoroughly expose the cancerous ideology both men had naively signed onto. Obviously this man would illustrate how Cashman was a rogue judge who adopted some loony theory and subsequently pushed its radical, dangerous, and unproven tenets on the people of Vermont. Marquis went in for the kill: "Restorative justice is the official policy in Vermont since 2000."

Why is O'Reilly on the air? Restorative justice is the *official policy* of Vermont! Cashman is a judge in Vermont. Ergo, his sentencing is likely to follow said policy.

So what's the story here? Two guys O'Reilly doesn't like believe basically the same thing. But sharing an ideology is not a "shocking connection." For all we know, they've never met. For all we know, they hate each other.

Incidentally, here are some other "shocking connections" we've unearthed between Edward Cashman and George Soros:

1. George Soros is Hungarian. Cashman is a fan of Hungarian actress Eva Gabor.
2. Both like *Designing Women* reruns (but not after Delta Burke left the show).
3. Both prefer Bosco to Ovaltine.
4. Neither has ever gone parasailing in Haiti.
5. Both liked Dick York better than Dick Sargent.

O'Reilly ended the segment with the following: "George Soros. Edward Cashman. Restorative Justice."

Bill O'Reilly. Pedophile priests. Catholicism.

Thank you very much.

MEN WHO DRESS AS NUNS AND THE EIGHTH-DISTRICT CONGRESSWOMEN WHO LOVE THEM

WHILE VERMONT IS a liberal state to be sure, nothing gets the O'Reilly Nation going like a good old-fashioned Left Coast progressive.

On Thursday, October 12, 2006, Bill was spooking his traditionalist zombie horde with the specter of a U.S. Congress ruled by a wacky witch from the S-P (Bill's abbreviation of "secular progressive") capital of the world, San Francisco:

> A new Fox News poll out today says fifty percent of Americans will vote Democrat, forty-one percent Republican, in the congressional elections next month. President Bush's approval rating is forty percent, fifty-six percent disapprove. So the smart money believes that Democrats will make solid gains in the upcoming vote, but here is something interesting.
>
> If the Dems win the House, Nancy Pelosi will become Speaker. However, according to the Fox poll, forty-three percent of Americans have never heard of Congresswoman Pelosi. They know nothing about her. So the country is facing a possible big change, and almost half of us have no idea what the change might be.

Remember where you were when you found out that Tip O'Neill was going to be Speaker of the House? Wow, that takes you back, huh? Remember how the *CBS Evening News* told the country that we'd all be ale-besotted Irish Catholics and whiny Red Sox fans in no time? Don't you wish you'd heeded that warning?

Nancy Pelosi is a committed secular progressive who embraces San Francisco values. Those are: a massive federal government that dispenses entitlements paid for primarily by affluent Americans. That is called income redistribution, or the shorthand: "tax the rich." San Francisco values also seek to exclude spirituality from the public square but embrace displays like the Bay City's gay pride parade, where Christianity is often mocked and demeaned.

This is where O'Reilly shows video of a man dressed up like Jesus surrounded by drag-queen nuns. What exactly does this have to do with Nancy Pelosi and the midterm elections?

Of course, the tax structure O'Reilly implies could be just around the corner if Pelosi is elected—as well as the estate tax he hates so much—actually has a long history. According to the fabulously gay Web site www.ustreas.gov:

> The entry of the United States into World War I greatly increased the need for revenue and Congress responded by passing the 1916 Revenue Act. The 1916 Act raised the lowest tax rate from 1 percent to 2 percent and raised the top rate to 15 percent on taxpayers with incomes in excess of $1.5 million. The 1916 Act also imposed taxes on estates and excess business profits.

Granted, there was no federal program to help low-income gays purchase Ben Wa balls, as there no doubt will be now that Nancy Pelosi is Speaker, but the point is that a certain level of income redistribution actually reflects long-standing *American* values.

Regardless, what the hell do drag queens have to do with local congressional races anyway? Watch O'Reilly spin: "Now, I'm not saying Congresswoman Pelosi is on board with that, but I am saying her district wants to ban military recruiting while setting up citywide pot shops, and that San Francisco is now perhaps the most far-left city the United States has ever seen."

So O'Reilly shows some men dressed up as nuns and then tries to cover his ass with "I'm not saying Congresswoman Pelosi

is on board with that." Oh yeah? Then why the hell are you
showing it?

Obviously, Bill wants to draw a clear association between homos
in habits and a House controlled by Democrats. Yes, gay pride
parades down Pennsylvania Avenue will no doubt become an
almost daily occurrence now that the Dems control Congress. Oh,
and the pot shops sprouting up in your downtown? You thought
there were too many Starbucks? Hang onto your bong, Millie.

Ah, but here's where Bill gets all fair and balanced on your ass:

> On the other side, forty-four percent of Americans have never
> heard of Speaker Dennis Hastert. And those who have over-
> whelmingly believe he was not proactive in the Foley scandal.
>
> Add to that the Iraq mess. More than sixty percent of Amer-
> icans believe the war is not going well. And you have a very dif-
> ficult choice this November: Should Americans vote for San
> Francisco values or perceived failure overseas?

So the nation-destroying San Francisco values are a given, but
the foreign-policy failure is only "perceived." You can almost hear
Factor viewers scratching their heads in unison as they try to make
up their minds.

> Now, at this point, the Fox News poll indicates that many folks
> feel change is necessary, and that's good news for the Demo-
> crats. Remember, not every Dem is a hyperpartisan S-P like
> Nancy Pelosi and Howard Dean. But any increase in their
> power is troubling if you are a traditionalist.

Wow, so the Republican Party controlled the Senate, the
House, and the presidency, but it was troubling to O'Reilly that
the Democrats might get more power. Could he possibly believe
any of this?

> Talking Points believes the left is more energized right now,
> and therefore the Dems have a big advantage. The illegal

immigration mess, big spending by the Bush administration, Foley—all have angered conservatives, and many indicate they'll stay home on election day.

So that's the current picture. It could change, but with Iran and North Korea doing everything they can to make Mr. Bush look weak, the GOP is really up against it. We may indeed be saying "hello" to San Francisco values.

Yes, if North Korea and Iran get their way, we'll have gay pride parades in Lubbock and hash brownies at every bake sale.

Maybe we could even make Rip Taylor secretary of state. Come on, everyone loves confetti!

IF O'REILLY WERE KING

FOR SOMEONE WITH no military background, O'Reilly sure likes to talk tough.

For instance, in the aftermath of Hurricane Katrina, he suggested that authorities should "shoot looters on sight."

After his famous imbroglio with Al Franken on BookTV, he said that had they been in the Old West and had a shootout, he would have shot Franken "between the head."

And on his radio show he once said, "I'll tell you what. I've been in combat. I've seen it, I've been close to it, and if my unit is in danger, and I've got a captured guy, and the guy knows where the enemy is, and I'm looking him in the eye, the guy better tell me. . . . That's all I'm gonna tell you. If it's life or death, he's going first."

Needless to say, O'Reilly's never "been in combat." He was a journalist in a war zone. Not quite the same thing.

So maybe it wasn't all that surprising when O'Reilly told *The Radio Factor* listeners how he would rule Iraq if he were in charge—that is, like a power-mad Irishman with a bad TV show:

Now, to me, they're not fighting it hard enough. See, if I'm president, I got probably another fifty, sixty thousand with orders to shoot on sight anybody violating curfews. Shoot them on sight. That's me. President O'Reilly. Curfew in Ramadi, seven o'clock at night. You're on the street? You're dead. I shoot you right between the eyes. Okay? That's how I run that country. Just like Saddam ran it. Saddam didn't have explosions—he didn't have bombers. Did he? Because if you got out of line, you're dead.

Now, is that the kind of country I want for Iraq? No. But you have to have that for a few months to stabilize the situation so the Iraqi government can get organized, can get security in place and get the structure going.

Now, it goes without saying that if we'd wanted someone to run the country like Saddam ran it, our government could have saved a shitload on Apache helicopter fuel, and Fox itself could have cut Geraldo's moustache maintenance budget at least in half.

Of course, Bill is not a complete ogre. While he's also known for his tough talk on immigration, on May 2, 2006, he had a more humane solution to the crisis—demand that Mexico become a wealthy nation: "If Mexicans can demonstrate in Los Angeles and other American cities, why can't they demand action in their own country? Surely that's the long-term solution to illegal immigration. Have Mexico become as prosperous as Canada. There is no reason that should not happen."

A few weeks earlier Bill had invited an activist from the American Friends Service Committee on his show. The guy tried several times to explain some of the poorly understood global forces that combine to keep ordinary Mexicans in poverty. Unfortunately, they're still poorly understood, because Bill wouldn't let him talk.

So the many complex reasons a peasant farmer in Mexico might figure it's better to get a meatpacking job in Iowa than try to compete on the open market with Cargill were once again brushed over by Bill's little kindergarten paint kit.

But maybe we really do need more commonsense thinkers like

O'Reilly to provide balance to all the pinheaded intellectuals out there. The world could be a better place in, say, two or three days. Here's how:

1. Force all Muslims to convert to Judaism, or vice versa.
2. Install Arnold Schwarzenegger as president of Iraq. Tell people that he's a Shiite, but Maria's a Sunni.
3. Show Kim Jong Il Madden 2007 on the PlayStation 3. Let him know that's just one small example of what capitalism can do for him.
4. Tell Darfur enough with the horseplay already.
5. Tell Afghanistan to get a job.

See, it's really all quite simple. Why the hell hasn't Bill run for office yet?

BILL DOESN'T UNDERSTAND HIS JOB

OF COURSE, WHILE Bill is always eager to stick it to high school honor students, bloggers who don't have time to scour their Web sites for random comments from knuckleheads, Meg Ryan, innocent Iraqis we're trying to help, entire U.S. cities, and each and every resident of the state of Vermont, he takes a somewhat gentler approach when it comes to Republican politicians.

On May 18, 2006, Bill ran an interview with Secretary of Defense Donald Rumsfeld. At one point during the discussion, he made a feeble attempt to get to the bottom of allegations that U.S. Marines may have murdered up to twenty-four innocent civilians in Iraq.

Since it was a criminal proceeding, Rumsfeld wasn't at liberty to discuss the case in depth, and Bill knew this. Still, O'Reilly was apparently eager to comment on what he perceived as overzealousness on the part of some in the media:

O'REILLY: All right, I need you to do me a favor. Right after this interview tonight, we're going to run a story on this investigation, all right, a separate story apart from you and I conversing. If there is nothing to this, I don't want to do that story. I don't want to besmirch the U.S. Marine Corps if this is bull.

RUMSFELD: Yeah. And the answer is that the only people who know that answer are the people in that process, and ultimately it will be adjudicated, and you and I will not know actually what took place until that's been concluded.

So if the secretary of defense had said there was nothing to a story that could potentially embarrass the administration and our military, Bill would have simply dropped it?

Way to go, Mike Wallace!

Seriously, would he give this wide a berth to a member of a Democratic president's cabinet? He can't even be bothered to double-check his smears of high school kids yet he appears willing to spike a story on military misconduct based on the word of one of the handful of men in the country who would end up taking the most heat from it.

Of course, O'Reilly is quick to claim that he doesn't shy away from criticizing the Bush administration. But one of the key issues he points to is the president's reluctance to secure the Mexican-American border. In other words, he likes to criticize Bush when he isn't *conservative* enough.

Oh, and for the record, Bill did run a segment on the alleged murders by Marines that night. It was an interview with Oliver North.

Nice.

As far-left kingpin Matthew Perry might say: Could Bill *be* anymore fair and balanced?

BILL O'REILLY AND MARK FOLEY: CULTURE WARRIORS

ON SEPTEMBER 29, 2006, Bill waited until relatively late in the program to discuss the unfolding Mark Foley scandal. That quintessential O'Reilly outrage had somehow faded into the night, and we were left with a rather subdued Bill:

In the Impact Segment tonight, a very disturbing story. Republican congressman Mark Foley of Florida has resigned for sending a series of e-mails to a sixteen-year-old former congressional page.

Foley was a strong advocate of Jessica's Law and protecting children from predators, now finds himself having to explain his relationship with a young boy.

O'Reilly later explained that "Mark Foley is the co-chairman of the House Missing and Exploited Children Caucus. He's been on this program many times on Fox News Channel, often talking about protecting the kids."

We were still waiting for O'Reilly to go ballistic. After all, how would he have reacted if Howard Dean had been caught up in such a thing? O'Reilly spelled it out to Fox News reporter Major Garrett: "Yes. You know, a real tragedy here, Major. I know you're just reporting and you don't comment as a reporter. But the real tragedy is that Foley did some good work, you know, getting the database up, the federal database to track child predators."

Sadly, Bill feels the real tragedy is that he has had Foley on the program multiple times and has propped him up as a fine example of a child protector, and now it turns out his fellow culture warrior may very well be whacking off to Garanimals ads. As for Foley's database, it's a fine idea, but you're not supposed to treat it like your own personal eHarmony.com.

"And now it's all gone. And there's deep suspicion on the part of a lot of people about politicians in Washington, even when they try to help the kids. I mean, that's the tragedy of this whole thing."

He concluded, "Yes. It is a depressing situation."

What the hell is O'Reilly talking about? We've never seen him go this easy on a newspaper publisher who declines to censure an editorial writer who defends a judge who gives a pedophile less than forty years breaking rocks in Guantanamo Bay. But now the best he can muster is, "It is a depressing situation."

Could it be that Bill so effortlessly groups people into insipid

ing the S-P fanatics on the June 23, 2003, edition of *The Factor:*

> **O'REILLY:** In the Impact Segment tonight, a *Time* magazine article spotlighted a Florida camp for kids that does not require clothing that has led to some controversy.

Joining us now from Washington, Congressman Mark Foley is running for Senate in Florida. Mr. Foley is the co-chairman of the Congressional Missing and Exploited Children's Caucus.

> **FOLEY:** Well Bill, we're talking about kids, impressionable young kids that are being put together in camps that I think are not only degrading to them but dangerous to their well-being. People that are working around these camps, people that are peering through the fences can have significant ill intent. And so this is like putting a match next to a gas can. It's sooner or later going to explode and there'll be real dangerous consequences.

Foley later added, "Kids deserve protection. People that are under the age of eighteen need supervision by someone who will look out for them."

You know, Foley's right. Kids under eighteen do need supervision. We thought we'd look at his particular brand of child protection by reviewing some of the instant messages Foley sent to an underage male page, also in 2003. Let's just see how he looks out for the kids:

> did you spank it this weekend yourself?

Here the Republican from the great state of Florida seeks to build a rapport with the boy by discussing his weekend activities. Showing an interest in the boy is a key part of providing much-needed supervision.

where do you unload it

Again, Foley shows an interest in the boy. By asking questions, he can really build that mentor relationship that is so important between members of the House of Representatives and their pages.

cute butt bouncing in the air

Building up the self-esteem of the minor is very important. Foley understands this. By complimenting the boy's ass, Foley shows that he appreciates him as a person.

i always use lotion and the hand

Now we start to see the mentorship aspect of the relationship. Now the boy can take some of what Foley has learned and apply it to his own circumstances, perhaps avoiding some of life's great pitfalls . . . like chafing.

and (grab) the one-eyed snake

Gross. Seriously.

On the night after this interview aired, O'Reilly read a letter from one of his viewers: "Nancy Williamson, Naples, Florida: 'I was recently at a nude camp. The youth were well supervised, well mannered, and comfortable with the environment. I challenge Congressman Foley to visit.'"

Nancy, we believe Congressman Foley will accept your challenge.

Incidentally, on October 2, the Monday after the story broke, Bill decided to lead off his program with the Foley scandal, using it as a springboard to remind his viewers of how far-left Howard Dean and Nancy Pelosi are.

Oh, dear Bill. Please get better. Soon.

NOTES

1. This is a dramatization based on what we think probably would have happened at any moment had we not announced the release of *Sweet Jesus, I Hate Bill O'Reilly* when we did. We gratefully acknowledge Maureen's tacit endorsement, however, and send her our love. And sympathy, of course.
2. If you're interested, a quick Google search of "Ann Coulter" and "lies" might be enlightening—and kind of fun, too.
3. After the Lieberman campaign attributed its Web site problems to "dirty politics" and "Rovian tactics," several bloggers jumped on the story, noting that it may have actually been the Lieberman team's cluelessness that led to the trouble. A story in the online *New Haven Independent* offered at least one explanation for the crash of the Lieberman site:

> Lamont's campaign and sympathetic bloggers raced to work trying to figure out why Lieberman's site was down, since the Lieberman camp itself had no explanation.
>
> By the time the polls closed, Lamont's top staff blogger, Tim Tagris . . . reported that the Lieberman camp had messed up in how it set up its site. The site couldn't handle the increased election-day traffic.
>
> "They use a shared server with 72 other sites. They pay their server $15 a month for 10 gigabytes. We've gone through more than 10 gigabytes in the last 24 hours," Tagris reported. The Lamont campaign pays $1,500 a month for Web service.

8

HANNITIZATION: IT'S LIKE A FLU SHOT FOR STUPID PEOPLE

L ET'S GET ON the record right away and say we believe Sean Hannity to be a real human being.

His elocution and body movements are very authentic; his official Fox News bio includes no patently false or implausible information; and his Social Security number and high school transcripts basically check out.

That said, he often appears to us as some sort of Republican Talking Points Doll—a slightly better mannered, somewhat more refined Chucky singularly devoted to reciting GOP propaganda as if it were the opinion of an actual person.

So, as instructive as it may be to think of Hannity as an evil, possessed string puppet, we have no actual evidence that he's anything but carbon-based.

But whereas Hannity may be fiendishly partisan in his attacks on liberals, at least he's not Alan Colmes.

While Colmes is officially given second billing on the duo's eponymous prime-time political affairs show, a better title might be *Hannity & Republican Guest & Other Republican Guest & Ann Coulter & Liberal Guest with Premature Baldness and Speech Impediment & Guy from a Right-Wing Think Tank Nobody's Ever Heard of &, if There's Still Time, Maybe Colmes.*

We're not saying that Colmes doesn't have a role on the show. He most certainly does. Unfortunately, it's about as meaningful as Teen Girl Number Four in any random *Friday the 13th* sequel. (Sure, he is learning to run faster, but that doesn't mean he's not getting killed.)

So, as there's currently about as much footage of Colmes on Fox as there is of the second gunman on the Zapruder film, this chapter will focus primarily on Hannity and his techniques (read: childish bullying) for exposing liberal legerdemain.

JUST GIVE ME THE ANSWER I WANT MY VIEWERS TO HEAR

USUALLY FOX NEWS'S bookers are pretty good at screening their guests. Their ideal liberal candidate is someone who is superficially knowledgeable, awkward in delivery, and has an impressive-sounding title but little actual influence.

If he appears to represent an entire group but comes off like he just finished his first debating class at the Learning Annex, he's likely to get fast-tracked onto prime time.

But every once in a while they screw up and book someone who's studied the network's tactics and knows how to roll with the punches.

It's these exceptions to the rule that act as the perfect radioactive dye for examining Fox's well-worn debating techniques.

As we saw in Chapter 2, Sean Hannity just loves to use guilt by association, especially when he gets to do the associating. In truth, it's hard to muster sympathy for the clueless liberals who fall for it. It's like watching the nerdy kid on the playground who gets beat up every day but never really sticks up for himself. You want to help him, but you can't completely hide your contempt either.

But on September 26, 2005, Ted Lewis, human rights director for Global Exchange, a San Francisco–based advocacy group, was ready. He had participated in a series of protest rallies the previous weekend that Hannity wanted to slam, and evidently he was either familiar with Fox's tactics or too savvy to fall victim to them.

God, Hannity hates it when his guests don't fall through the trapdoor.

HANNITY: Here to tell us about what happened, one of the participants in this weekend's protest rallies, human rights director of Global Exchange Ted Lewis.

All right, Ted. You know what? I just think it makes Alan's [Colmes] side look better and better every time they open their mouths. Calling the president fascist, the Führer, a liar, a murderer, a terrorist.

Well, that's pretty much what Cindy Sheehan has been saying: America is not worth dying for, that it's been taken over by thugs. . . . Are you willing to align yourself with all of that radical extremism?

Now, you might think from this line of questioning that Lewis himself had been making such statements. That would be reason enough to have him on the program. In reality, Lewis was merely at a rally where there was a wide variety of signs and banners on display—some of which veered toward the radical.

As with any free and open democracy, there's bound to be a range of opinion expressed at this kind of event. And if you attended such a rally, it could hardly be assumed that you stood behind every person in attendance, much less their statements.

It's like assuming everyone at a Pet Shop Boys concert is automatically a fan of *Absolutely Fabulous*. (Okay, that's probably a 95 percent crossover, so maybe it's not such a good example.)

To his credit, Lewis refused to take the bait:

LEWIS: Good evening, Sean. You know, I saw a different protest out there. There were a lot of things going on. It really affected me to see so many Iraq veterans out there marching in front of the White House, talking about their experiences and why they are disillusioned with this policy.

Touché, Mr. Lewis. But we should warn you: Monsieur Hannity prefers when his fencing partners stand motionless, cow-eyed, and mute. Your insolence will not be tolerated. These little matches are well-planned in Sean's mind and he doesn't like it when his foils go off script.

HANNITY: I'm not really—I don't care about your thoughts. You can tell them to Alan. I'm not asking you. I'm asking you this. Cindy Sheehan said George Bush is the biggest terrorist in the world. Cindy Sheehan said America is not worth dying for. Cindy Sheehan called the president a lying bastard, a filth spewer, a warmonger, and an evil maniac. Do you support those radical statements, sir?

Again, this is not designed to shed light on Lewis's beliefs or the goals of Global Exchange. Lewis could have just as easily asked Hannity if he agrees with some Republicans that Israel must regain control of the Temple Mount in Jerusalem by any means necessary so Jesus can return there as prophesied in scripture.

LEWIS: I think Cindy Sheehan has done a great job of waking up a lot of people around America.

HANNITY: You support those statements? You agree with those statements? You want to call the president of the United States a terrorist, the world's biggest terrorist?

Yeah, we're not really sure why Hannity has guests on his program. We get the feeling that if Sean invited Jack Hanna on his show, he'd ask the ring-tailed lemur if *it* supported Cindy Sheehan.

LEWIS: Look, if Cindy Sheehan said certain things, I think what we need to listen to is the heart of her message. The heart of her message is . . .

HANNITY: With all due respect, I'm not looking at the heart of her message. I'm asking you a specific question. Do you think America is worth dying for? Do you think she's right to call the president of the United States the world's biggest terrorist? Please stop distracting yourself. Answer the question. Do you believe that or not? Is that the right thing to say or not?

LEWIS: Sean, I wouldn't have said those things.

HANNITY: You wouldn't have said them.

LEWIS: I think—I think that there is a better way to talk about these issues.

HANNITY: Finally.

LEWIS: And to look clearly at the fact that this war has become a disaster for America. I don't think we should distract ourselves with these kinds of arguments.

HANNITY: That's what was said all weekend. This president was called every name in the book from a terrorist to the Führer to, you know—they want to castrate Dick Cheney. All these signs I see. And this was your march; these were your people there. This is your left-wing radical taking over the Democratic Party. And people like you, if you really believe what you're saying, need to distance yourself from the extremists that were running this thing.

This is the sort of thing you'll hear frequently on both *Hannity & Colmes* and *The O'Reilly Factor.* The suggestion is that the guy with the "Bush is a Nazi" poster and the chick who flips off the camera will soon be, if they aren't already, delegates at the Democratic National Convention. Not only are telecasts searched to find these folks, but they're immediately propped up as generic representatives of the left. Never mind that Bill O'Reilly frequently compares people to Nazis, fascists, and communists, or that you can find random conservatives wearing equally provocative T-shirts with slogans such as "Why's *Our* Oil Under Their Soil?" and "Liberals of the World Ignite."

These are supporters of the president, Sean. Do you agree with your party that our country has a proprietary claim on Arab oil and that liberals should be immolated? Come on! Yes or no?

Then again, maybe true believers on both the left and right are merely exaggerating for comic effect or are simply blowing off steam. And maybe Ted Lewis of Global Exchange couldn't care less what they say because he's too busy doing his job.

> **LEWIS:** Sean, I think in a democracy, a lot of things get said. But the heart of the issue here is that the Iraq War is a disaster for our country. That too many people have died and that we need to pull our country together and find a way out of this situation.

Well said. Of course, Hannity had to have the last word. After Colmes questioned Lewis, Sean ended the interview with this: "When the dictator is dead and the world is better off, whether you guys agree or not. Thanks for being here. Appreciate your time."

Gracious to the end. Honestly, what kind of interviewing technique is that? That's like Jay Leno inviting Tom Cruise on *The Tonight Show* to plug his latest movie and ending the broadcast with, "Yeah, well, *Days of Thunder* sucked. Thanks for stoppin' by."

WHY DO YOU HATE THE AMBER WAVES OF GRAIN?

WHILE HANNITY'S LITTLE "yes or no" waltz has become as trite and predictable as a seventies sitcom catchphrase, he will occasionally enhance its effect with "the ole' switcheroo."

This allows him to ascribe thoughts and beliefs about America to a guest that the guest never actually expressed.

For instance, in his August 24, 2006, interview with Democratic strategist Michael Brown, Hannity questioned his guest about the opinions of two high-profile members of Brown's party:

> **HANNITY:** Let me go to Michael Brown. Michael, I want to ask you two yes or no questions. Yes, do you agree with Howard Dean, the leader of your party, that Ned Lamont is the future of your party? Do you agree with that statement, yes or no?

BROWN: Well, clearly, as . . .

HANNITY: Yes or no?

BROWN: Yes, I know you . . .

HANNITY: Question two. Here we go. I want to know if you agree with John Murtha, the number one campaigner now for the Democratic Party, your guy. John Murtha said that, instead of deterring terrorism, American policies are fostering it. Do you agree with that, yes or no?

We figure Hannity is just a blast at parties: "Do you have Tostitos brand tortilla chips? Yes or no?! Are these beverages chilled? Yes or no?! Do you agree with your caterer—your guy—that these cucumber sandwiches and this Brie wheel with water crackers were the best choice for finger food? Yes or no? YES OR NO?!?"

Of course, it's perfectly legitimate to think that we've done little more than stir up a hornet's nest in Iraq and that the war there might have served as a lightning rod for anti-American sentiment. So it's fair to ask whether the decision by the current administration to invade that country, which was sold as a way to defeat terrorism, may have actually increased it.

BROWN: Absolutely yes. And, frankly, for the end of Ann's (Coulter) question that she had, clearly the Republicans in the Bush administration have not been able to sell that the Iraqi war is connected with the war on terror.

HANNITY: Wait a minute. Let's get to the . . .

BROWN: The American people are speaking, and they're going to speak in November.

HANNITY: You are saying—wait a minute. Let's put emphasis on this.

BROWN: I said absolutely yes.

HANNITY: You are telling America tonight that America . . .

BROWN: You don't have to repeat the question. I said absolutely yes.

HANNITY: . . . is causing terrorism. That's what it said.

Ah, did you see what happened there? Hannity reframed a partisan critique of the Bush administration's war on terrorism and the war in Iraq as an anti-American screed by a shiftless traitor.

What his guest actually said was that the policies of the *Bush administration* were counterproductive. But in Hannity's mind, Brown was accusing America itself of causing terrorism—something that is sure to sound unforgivably unpatriotic to his viewers.

But this was no mere slip of the tongue. No, Sean chose his words the way Ted Haggard chooses a masseuse. By claiming that his guest is accusing *America* of midwifing terrorists, Hannity insures that his flock is likely to brook no further discussion of the Bush administration's policies. Clever boy.

Of course, Hannity was never shy about criticizing Bill Clinton's actions while he was president. Fox News couldn't get enough of the Monica Lewinsky scandal, for example.

Sean, were you telling us that America was getting fellatio while eating pizza and talking to a congressman in the Oval Office? You heard it. Hannity is telling America that America got a blow job from an intern. That's what he said.

To his credit, Brown was quicker than most and saw through Sean's cynical wordplay:

BROWN: Not America. Not America. The Bush policies. The Republican Bush policies, not America.

HANNITY: So did we cause what happened in Spain and Bali? Did we cause what happened in Russia? Did we cause the first Trade Center attack? Did we cause the embassy bombings? Did we cause the Khobar Towers?

BROWN: No, no, clearly everything is not done in a vacuum. You can go back in time all that we want. We can go back to the Reagan administration, too. The question is: What's happening today in the world, and what have our policies done to foster that hatred toward our country?

HANNITY: You know something, Ann Coulter . . .

BROWN: There are more countries now that hate the United States than ever before in the history of our . . .

HANNITY: Go ahead. You blame America. This is . . .

Again, Hannity won't even discuss the issue on the table. Clearly, the point of *Hannity & Colmes* is not to debate but to bait and trap. The mantra "you blame America" plays perfectly into Hannity's viewers' simplistic take on foreign policy.

BROWN: I'm not blaming America. I'm blaming the Bush policies and what they have done to this government.

HANNITY: You are saying that we—our policies foster—Ann Coulter, this is the problem. The party that's weak on national defense . . .

We should mention that Ann Coulter was also on the program via live remote. Otherwise it might sound like he's trying to summon her supernaturally like Major Nelson in *I Dream of Jeannie*. (Frankly, we're a little surprised that's not already a regular feature of the show.)

BROWN: We're not weak. We're weak because we disagree with the policies?

HANNITY: Excuse me—Michael, Michael, wait a minute. Ann Coulter, the party that's weak on national defense, that doesn't want the PATRIOT Act, the NSA program, the data-mining program, that wants to confer rights on enemy combatants, the party that's always been weak on defense . . .

No doubt Brown would have loved to take each of these arguments apart, but that's not the format of *Hannity & Colmes*. It's a show that makes the postmatch commentaries on *WWE Smack-Down!* look erudite by comparison.

The PATRIOT Act? One might argue that some of its provisions were overdue while others overreached.

NSA spying? Democratic—and Republican—objections were confined to *warrantless* wiretaps.

Data mining? What some see as a key antiterrorism tool others may see as an invasion of privacy and a clear violation of the Fourth Amendment.

Oh, and if you don't believe in torture, you're a member in good standing of the Pussy Party.

BROWN: Sean, that's just wrong. It's not . . .

HANNITY: . . . now blames America for the series of attacks that's taken place around the world. That should be the issue of this campaign.

Yes, Sean, saying that someone blames America when he just told you numerous times that he faults not the country but specific policies of the Bush administration—that's quite a campaign issue.

Then again, what else should we expect from Fox? Its debates are nothing more than a series of word-twisting chutes and talking-points ladders. The goal is not to debate but to attack.

Going on *Hannity & Colmes* is like calling Dr. Laura to discuss your extramarital affair.

With a student.

Who's fifteen.

SOME PEOPLE SAY YOU WERE KISSING BIN LADEN UNDER THE BLEACHERS

Also coming up tonight: If the Democrats win—if they win in November, is it a victory for the terrorists? Some people are saying that. And a new poll could mean some very good news for Republicans. We'll share that with you.

—*Sean Hannity, August 22, 2006*

IN HIS FILM *Outfoxed: Rupert Murdoch's War on Journalism*, director Robert Greenwald highlighted Fox's frequent use of the phrase "some people say." It's a tactic that leads viewers to the conclusion that narrow personal views are actually part of a broader trend of opinion or that they can be attributed to knowledgeable authorities.

Well, Sean Hannity is a regular "some people say" sensei.

On December 6, 2006, Hannity ran a clip of Democratic National Committee chair Howard Dean making this statement: "The idea that we're going to win this war is an idea that, unfortunately, is just plain wrong. And I've seen this before in my life, and it cost us 25,000 brave American soldiers in Vietnam. I don't want to go down that road again."

Hannity responded: "Republican National Committee and the Speaker of the House, and many others have now criticized Dean's comments. Some people are even accusing the good doctor of treason."

Gosh, who are these "some people"? The president? The Supreme Court? The FBI director? A sizable portion of the voting population? Oprah?

Turns out, the "some people" in this instance was primarily Hannity's guest for that segment, right-wing talk-show host Michael Reagan. (Hannity could have also thrown in right-wing talk-show host Mancow, whose rabid attack on Dean in response to the same quote is featured in Chapter 1 of this book.)[1]

Here was Hannity's and Reagan's most illuminating exchange:

HANNITY: Michael Reagan, I'm listening to the modern liberal Democratic Party. They have called this president a liar, said he's hyped, misled. They have undermined him basically every step of the way.

When you heard Howard Dean yesterday, you said he should be arrested and hung for treason. And you also said—or put in a hole until the end of the Iraq War. Do you really mean that? Is that the appropriate response to them being irresponsible?

REAGAN: I think it's time that people stand up and call a spade a spade. I mean, here's a man, just through a statement that he made yesterday on WOAI, how many deaths are going to be caused by that statement, by giving aid and comfort to the enemy, the Zarqawis of the world, who are going to believe that we are folding our tent, and going to go home, and give them just another push for another day to kill more innocent people there in Iraq, and kill our military there, to help Iraq become a democracy in that area of the world?

How many deaths are going to occur because of that statement that he made?

Of course, there was hardly a groundswell of opinion in this country in favor of hanging Howard Dean for treason, so the "some people" attribution was at the very least misleading. We think a better intro would have been, "Our next guest is even accusing the good doctor of treason" or "Mancow and Ronald Reagan's son, who's clearly out of his fucking mind, are even accusing the good doctor of treason." But then we might be a little biased.

Still, if you do insist on using the weaselly "some people say" line over and over, there's an honest and a dishonest way to do it. This is the honest way:

Some people say Sean Hannity is guilty of the second-degree intentional homicide of an underaged male Thai prostitute from whom some people say he contracted a raging case of herpes.[2]

ALAN GROWS A PAIR

WE KID ALAN Colmes. He's not a bad guy overall, and he has a tough row to hoe as one of the few outspoken nonconservatives at Fox.

Trying to get a word in edgewise with Hannity in the room can't be easy, after all.

Indeed, some people say[3] that each *Hannity & Colmes* broadcast is like a Harlem Globetrotters game. Sean shoves the key argument down his pants while Alan is left standing there bewildered and scratching his head. It's actually more theater than competition, and the outcome is always predetermined.

Still, every once in a while Colmes stands up and attempts to fight to the end (the end being when Hannity admits he's full of crap, which never really happens).

On December 5, 2005, Karl Rove pulled Hannity's string, and Baby Squawks-A-Lot took to toeing the company line:

HANNITY: The leaders of Alan's party, the Democratic Party, saying they want to cut and run, saying that our Army is failing, saying that, you know, all the things that Kerry said and Dean said, it's unbelievable—that we're not going to win? What do the troops think of that?

Later in the conversation, Colmes took Hannity to task for echoing the "cut and run" meme:

COLMES: By the way, he didn't put down the troops. And I haven't heard any Democrats say "cut and run." And General Sanchez . . .

HANNITY: Murtha . . .

COLMES: He didn't say cut and run. Murtha didn't say cut and run. He said . . .

HANNITY: He said redeploy and pull them out.

COLMES: He said at the most appropriate time. He didn't say cut and run.

HANNITY: Pull them out. Yes, he did.

COLMES: No, he did not. He did not. We disagreed about that.

HANNITY: He said redeploy.

COLMES: That's not cut and run.

HANNITY: Take them out.

Of course, "cut and run" is a well-worn Republican mantra—a

cynical attempt to craft language so that any discussion of changing the president's Iraq policy will be seen as weak-kneed appeasement.

So for a pundit ever to use the phrase is hackery. The way Hannity leans on it here, you'd think it's the Nicene Creed.

By the summer of 2006, even Republican Senator Chuck Hagel had had enough of the phrase. During a June 21 Senate debate, Hagel said in so many words that "cut and run" was as played as "you go, girl" or "talk to the hand":

> The American people want to see serious debate about serious issues from serious leaders. They deserve more than a political debate. This debate should transcend cynical attempts to turn public frustration with the war in Iraq into an electoral advantage. It should be taken more seriously than to simply retreat into focus-group-tested buzzwords and phrases like "cut and run." Catchy political slogans debase the seriousness of war.

Of course, Hagel is right. And avoiding serious debate is exactly what Hannity was trying to do. If Congressman John Murtha could be marginalized as a cowardly cut-and-runner, there would be no need to discuss his plan.

For the record, here's what Murtha, a highly decorated combat veteran, was actually calling for:

- Immediately redeploy U.S. troops consistent with the safety of U.S. forces.
- Create a quick reaction force in the region.
- Create an over-the-horizon presence of Marines.
- Diplomatically pursue security and stability in Iraq.

Unfortunately, you can't really capture that in a catchphrase, which is presumably why we have nationally broadcast political talk shows that focus on the issues.

But, again, it's not really the purpose of *Hannity & Colmes* to inform or enlighten. It's to parrot talking points and outtalk and degrade one's opponent.

CNN's *Crossfire* used the same conservative-versus-liberal format to somewhat more civilized effect. But it still came off as shallow.

As *The Daily Show*'s Jon Stewart famously told *Crossfire* hosts Tucker Carlson and Paul Begala during an appearance on their show: "You're doing theater, when you should be doing debate, which would be great."

We couldn't agree more. But if *Crossfire* was theater, then *Hannity & Colmes* is dinner theater. In Alabama. And the play is *Waiting for Godot*. And it stars Jimmie "J. J." Walker.

BUT AT LEAST THEY HAVE A LIBERAL ON THE PROGRAM

OF COURSE, FOX often argues that the presence of liberal voices on the network confirms the legitimacy of its "fair and balanced" slogan.

We find these voices to be few and far between, typically more centrist than liberal, and often oddly apologetic about their views.

But Colmes isn't a hard-line conservative, and we trust that he is paid—though we're guessing not as much as Hannity.

Still, at least there's Alan: "Welcome back to *Hannity & Colmes*. I'm Alan Colmes. Coming up, New Jersey Republicans are charging Democrats with playing politics with homeland security. We'll tell you why some people say it's actually putting lives at risk."

Et tu, Alan? Et tu?

NOTES

1. Indeed, the echo chamber was just gearing up. A day later, Rupert Murdoch's *New York Post* called Dean "the sedition-mongering former governor of Vermont" and claimed he "now is working overtime for a terrorist victory in Iraq."
2. Joseph Minton Amann and Tom Breuer, *Fair and Balanced, My Ass!*, page 127 (and some people say we'd be lying).
3. Pretty much just Al Franken and liberal media watchdog group Fairness and Accuracy in Reporting (FAIR). See how easy this is?

9

THE ABOMINABLE ALBINO
NEWSCREATURE

LET'S JUST DEAL with the big white elephant in the living room first.

John Gibson is, in a word, white.

Actually, "white" is far too impoverished an adjective to be useful here. Milk has often been described as white, as have laser printer paper, pearl earrings, the pope's miter, Elmer's glue, and Fiona Apple.

These things might more properly be considered off-white.

But John Gibson is *white*.

Those of you who have seen his show, *The Big Story* (and those of you who have subsequently taken megadoses of potassium iodide as a precaution to protect your thyroids) know that we're referring not just to Gibson's cultural leanings but to his peculiar "glow" as well.

Seriously, he looks like the unholy result of a tryst between an anemic marine biologist and a preteen beluga whale.

Now, dwelling on other people's appearances, may seem horribly petty—and it is. A cable news anchor's decision to appear on television without the basic courtesy of a lens covering fashioned from Vaseline, thick gauze, and No. 14 welder's glass is his and his alone. But we bring it up for a reason.

You see, John isn't just *white* white. He's Caucasian to the extreme. T.G.I. Friday's and Applebee's spring up around his feet like mushrooms on a wet log. We're guessing his most culturally adventurous moment was when he did the Macarena after two Corona Lights near the end of the Cinco de Mayo celebration at his local Bennigan's.

And being as white as he is, he's naturally worried about remaining true to his, well, ideology.

Indeed, here he is during the May 11, 2006, edition of *The Big Story,* imploring the Aryan-American community to work to increase their numbers:

> Now it's time for My Word. Do your duty. Make more babies. That's a lesson drawn out of two interesting stories over the last couple of days.
>
> First, a story yesterday that half of the kids in this country under five years old are minorities. By far the greatest number are Hispanic. You know what that means? Twenty-five years, and the majority of the population is Hispanic. Why is that? Well, Hispanics are having more kids than others. Notably, the ones Hispanics call gabachos—white people—are having fewer.

Apparently John's producer cut him off before he could pull out his phrenology charts or unveil his secret plan for annexing the Rhineland, but his point was made: the fondue in our melting pot could use a little less queso fresco and a little more Velveeta. (We'll just leave aside for the moment that John apparently believes everyone who watches his show is, in fact, white. We're not saying he's wrong; we just find it odd that he assumes it.)

Of course, none of this is a coincidence. Indeed, we believe Gibson's sublime paleness is both a cause and a result of what he's become. It is his Alpha and his Omega.

You see, John Gibson is on the Fox News B-list. He's second

string, if you will. Indeed, if Bill O'Reilly is the dashing JFK of Fox, Gibson is at best a Skakel. While O'Reilly gets invited to all the gala events (Republican National Convention), freaky John is left toiling back at the manse. O'Reilly gets the sit-down with President Bush, the big press, and, most likely, the hottest interns. Gibson gets an exclusive interview with seventies TV star Robert Conrad. They might as well make him scrub toilets.

Make no mistake about it—all this makes John Gibson one pissed-off albino.

Now, Gibson may or may not be the craziest man at Fox News (though he certainly gives O'Reilly a run for his money). But we are convinced he's the most hateful and irresponsible. It's as if the world has shunned him for his appearance and, instead of using his limited gifts to foster understanding between his kind and humanity, he's turned into a cheesy comic book villain.

Now, far be it from us to compare anyone unfavorably to Bill O'Reilly. But we get the feeling that while Bill found something of a niche during his formative years, running with his loutish Levittown cronies before eventually parlaying his limited athletic talents into a modicum of mainstream popularity, Gibson has been wholly shaped by his perpetual, joyless banishment to the D clique.

Yes, we're guessing that Gibson was an odd child—probably because he was pushed out of a cetacean womb. One never recovers from that.

KNOW WHAT'S REALLY HILARIOUS? TERRORISM!

JOHN GIBSON IS a conservative. That's not really our problem with him. There are many thoughtful conservative pundits out there—people who present fair, well-reasoned commentary with intelligence and panache. Gibson simply ain't one of them.

The man lives in a black-and-white world. (Insert your own albino joke here; we're spent.) But worst of all, he's reckless. When it comes to measured, insightful political analysis, the guy has more in common with Bill Bixby Jr. than Bill Buckley Jr.

But there are a lot of reckless, hate-filled commentators out there. That most of them ply their trade atop barstools while marinating in Pilsner is a refreshing comment on the forbearance of most mainstream newspapers and news networks. Unfortunately, Fox has no such hang-ups.

On July 6, 2005, while guest-hosting Bill O'Reilly's *The Radio Factor*, Gibson was apparently brimming with post–Independence Day patriotic euphoria when he said this:

> By the way, just wanted to tell you people, we missed—the International Olympic Committee missed a golden opportunity today. If they had picked France, if they had picked France instead of London to hold the Olympics, it would have been the one time we could look forward to where we didn't worry about terrorism. They'd blow up Paris, and who cares?

Now most people, having heard the words "London" and "terrorism" coming out of their heads (while at the same time suggesting that a terrorist attack in the capital of a major Western ally was no big deal) would have been horrified upon opening the paper the next day to discover that in fact a major suicide bombing undertaken by Islamic fanatics had caused dozens of deaths and hundreds of injuries in, of all places, London.

Indeed, most commentators would have said something like, "Oh my God! I hope no one remembers that tasteless joke I made yesterday. I must sound like some kind of drunk ogre! Well, with any luck it'll just blow over."

But not Gibson. The next day on *The Big Story*, the man was braying like Jeane Dixon after a blueberry and Sodium Pentothal smoothie: "The bombings in London: This is why I thought the Brits should have let the French have the Olympics—let somebody else be worried about guys with backpack bombs for a while."

Oh, John. You are the funniest man in any room that does not also include Danny Gans, Heinrich Himmler's cremains, or Dick Cheney's frozen organ-donor clone.

It should by now be evident that possum huntin' and critter trappin' have long since replaced France bashing as the favorite pastime of John Gibson fans. But it's one thing to stuff your pasty, iron-deficient head with freedom fries and quite another to titter over the prospect of women and children getting their arms and legs blown off by terrorist bombs in Parisian cafes because they didn't buy into your president's ultimately unprovable case for war.

Now imagine for a moment that some fly-by-night commentator in France had joked about an unsuccessful U.S. Olympic bid, remarking that it was too bad because it might have been kind of cool to see New York get blown off the map.

You can just imagine it. The outrage would have begun and ended with Fox, and Gibson would have been among those screeching the loudest.

Then again, the French support their own cabinet-level culture ministry, whereas Fox News's parent company produces shows in which former athletes muse over how they might have killed their ex-wives and men challenge bears to hot-dog-eating contests. It shouldn't be that surprising, then, that Fox News is spared much of the critical analysis to which other news media—and other human beings—are subjected. Fox is like the undisciplined kid who the teacher simply hopes will make it through the school year while creating as little disruption as possible. He's not held to the same standard, but he's not held back either. Truth is, he's a little slow.

HIS WISDOM FLOWS LIKE MANNA FROM HIS BUTT

ONE'S WORLDVIEW IS a complex and ever-evolving internal essay on how one views oneself and humankind. It is global, quite literally, in its scope.

At its noblest, it is a dynamic, organic system of beliefs that reflects what we want the world to be at a given moment and how we'd like to leave it when we die.

When John Gibson weighed in on the controversial nomination of John Bolton as U.S. ambassador to the UN, he gave us a little window into how he sees the world:

He's going there to give the 190 other nations in the UN a dose of reality, which goes like this:

We're sick of this organization operating as an anti-American one-upmanship club.

We're sick of paying the bills and getting trashed by every tin-pot dictator the UN can invite into its midst.

We're sick of the UN acting as if the world or the UN can get along without the U.S.

And we're sick of all of you working against good ideas just because they come from the U.S. or President Bush.

The list of "we're sick ofs" could go on and on, but I'll stop there. Somebody's got to tell them, because the Brits won't, the French won't, because they're the worst offenders, and that vast collection of fat kleptocrats, so-called diplomats from the Third World won't either. That latter group includes a huge number of so-called nations, little more than spots on the map that would get invaded, taken over, subsumed, eliminated, except no one wants to get stuck with their problems of poverty and disease and corruption. So, by benefit of their sorry state, they get to maintain their independence and membership in the UN and the right to complain, endlessly, about the U.S.

It's a motley crew that is largely meaningless in terms of how the world is run, or how things turn out, but they want respect, they want to be a voice in big decisions, and they want people like George Bush and John Bolton to notice them. They would be better appreciated and noticed if they made less noise.

Bolton needs to tell them that even if they don't want to hear it, and oh, just by the way, five former United States secretaries of state have now written a letter to the Senate recommending John Bolton be confirmed as the UN ambassador. That is My Word.

And that, ladies and gentlemen, is why Fox is the Number One Name in News.

While Gibson was ostensibly speaking for himself, his commentary here is really emblematic of a pervasive philosophy at Fox.

Indeed, we're waiting for the Fox News gift shop to start peddling bumper stickers featuring a crude drawing of John Gibson peeing on Kofi Annan.[1]

But however one views the minutiae of Gibson's argument, as a whole it goes to the broader issue of how Fox sees the United States and its role in the world. We mock those smaller and less fortunate. Were the world a playground, Gibson and Fox would be kicking out the crutch of the one-legged boy, laughing at the underprivileged girl's clothes, and sticking magnets on every scoliosis brace within reach.

But the utter contempt shown for nations less fortunate than ours is as much a reflection of Fox's audience as of its analysts. Fox viewers are largely a paranoid lot that see any erosion of American power as a slippery slope leading to secular humanism, one-world government, and the rise of an army of UN-trained vegan lesbians who force the nation's children into reeducation camps to teach them why Jeff Foxworthy isn't funny.

Now, thanks largely to the popularity of the *Left Behind* novels and movies, there is a handful of modern-day Christians who, relying on a loose reading of Scripture and some half-baked theories about Israel, are convinced that the UN is a sinister organization bent on coaxing the planet to the precipice of destruction, spurred on by an as-yet-unnamed Antichrist who will deceive the world into a great tribulation and bring about the ultimate battle of good versus evil. This will culminate in a global conflagration that will either plunge you into eternal, soul-searing torment or elevate you to sublime, everlasting bliss, depending on whether you found Jack Van Impe convincing.

Of course, Fox News viewers are more inclined than other Americans to accept this narrative as the most plausible interpretation of the biblical book of Revelation. And Fox, through overcooked rhetoric like Gibson's, has, wittingly or not, positioned itself as the go-to outlet for these loons.

But such theories can cut several ways. Indeed, what do folks such as Gibson see as the preeminent force on this planet—the one entity capable of and poised to bend all other nations to its will? Who, according to this view, should exercise cultural hegemony and regard its own opinions as sacrosanct and above reproach? The United States, of course.

And what high-profile personalities scream the loudest about their dedication to God while most frequently contradicting the scriptural admonitions to work for peace and comfort the poor?

What are we getting at? A very simple proposition, really:

John Gibson could very well be the Antichrist.

Let's face it. If anyone looks the part, it's Gibson. He may not have seven heads and ten horns, but otherwise he's spot on. If anyone on this planet has a time-share on the lake of fire, it's ole' Gibby. Is it that much of a leap, then, to say that he sits at the right hand of his dark prince, Satan, bound to do his master's bidding until the hosts of heaven and hell gather for a final, decisive battle upon the fields of Armageddon?

Of course not.

Consider, for example, this verse, from the apocalyptic book of Daniel:

> He said: "I am going to tell you what will happen later in the time of wrath, because the vision concerns the appointed time of the end. The two-horned ram that you saw represents the kings of Media and Persia." (Daniel 8:19–20)

King of Media? Fox? Sound familiar? And how grateful is Iran (Persia) that Gibson and his Fox cronies successfully brokered war between the United States and Persia's chief enemy, Iraq, ultimately setting the stage for a Shia takeover of Babylon?

Now, only time will tell if John Gibson is actually the Antichrist. After all, you'd think the Devil would be far too savvy to send someone so unappealing. More likely Gibson's some escaped incubus from the Lower East Side of Hades.

And that mark on Gibson's belly could just as easily be a 999, depending on whether you view it standing upright or hanging upside down in his secret underground blood-harvesting chamber.

So this is all just speculation. Scripturally sound, intuitively credible speculation, but speculation nonetheless.

Then again, he could be just another hick paranoiac flag-waver from the sticks who somehow got on TV. Perhaps we'll give him the benefit of the doubt for now.

LAW & ORDER: ALBINO NIGHTS

IN SPRING OF 2005, as some prominent Christian leaders fought to keep Terri Schiavo's immortal soul trapped in its corporeal prison rather than allow her to go to heaven, the leading lights at Fox were working themselves into a good old-fashioned lather.

But while Bill O'Reilly, Sean Hannity, and others at the network all stepped up to express their righteous indignation, it was John Gibson who raced to the head of the pack of crazy wolves.

During his My Word commentary on March 24, Gibson had this to say:

> Just to burnish my reputation as a bomb thrower, I think Jeb Bush should give serious thought to storming the Bastille. By that I mean he should think about telling his cops to go over to Terri Schiavo's hospice, go inside, put her on a gurney, load her into an ambulance, take her to a hospital, revive her, and reattach her feeding tube.

We don't know what's scarier: that a prominent Fox anchor would suggest the governor of one of our largest states defy the considered opinions of state and federal courts, the majority of the populace, and the wishes of a persistently vegetative patient and her next of kin, or that one of his primary ethical touchstones is apparently *Weekend at Bernie's*.

Of course, Gibson's use of metaphor here is likely no accident. It's not that he thinks eighteenth-century French prisons are analogous to modern-day Florida hospices. No, he just wanted to associate the Schiavo tragedy with something French-sounding. He might as well have said, "Jeb Bush should give serious thought to storming the Bastille and knocking the *pain au chocolat* right out of the hands of those Bordeaux-swilling bastards who are trying to kill Terri Schiavo."

But there can be little doubt that Gibson's well-muscled rhetoric on Schiavo's behalf was simply another in a series of cynical rallying cries to ramp up Fox's culture war, or else he'd have been urging Jeb Bush to storm into Florida homes to force free medical care on uninsured children.

But this was a lot more fun. Just in time for Easter, liberal judges were trying to murder a suburban white girl. Alas, if only some brave Fox News commentator had come along in time to save her.

RUH-ROVE

ON JULY 12, 2005, John Gibson got up on his demented little soapbox and let loose a rant that was so inane it made Anna Nicole Smith's drunken awards show presentations look like a series of David Brinkley commentaries. Here was his take on the ongoing Valerie Plame affair:

> I say give Karl Rove a medal, even if Bush has to fire him. Why? Because Valerie Plame should have been outed by somebody. And nobody else has the cojones to do it. I'm glad Rove did, if he did do it. And he still says he didn't.
>
> Why should she have been outed? Well, despite her husband's repeated denials, even in the face of a pile of evidence, and conclusions from a joint investigation of Congress, it appears all evidence points to Joe Wilson's wife, spy Valerie Plame, as the one who recommended him for the job of going to Niger to discover if Saddam was trying to buy nuke bomb materials.
>
> Why is this important? Because Wilson was opposed to the war in Iraq, opposed Bush policy, and pointedly and loudly said so. Consequently, it was [of] some interest how he got chosen for this sensitive job, which people at the time might have

thought would be a fulcrum point for a decision about the war. You wouldn't send a peacenik to see if we should go to war, if we need to go to war, now would you?

Hmmm, give the president's top political operative a medal for outing an undercover CIA agent? Of course, we had a lengthy, droll, and trenchant response all ready to go here, but it's really best we move on. You start to argue too much with these people and you run the risk of sounding childish.

So all we have to say is this: when God was handing out brains, John thought he said "skin pigment," and he said, "I don't want any."

NOTES

1. To be sold in conjunction with the reclining–Katherine Harris mud flaps.

THE COST OF A SOUL

One of the greatest pieces of economic wisdom is to know what you do not know.

—*John Kenneth Galbraith (attributed)*

Blame Liberals for High Oil and Gas Prices!

—*Fox News*

THE ECONOMY IS a pretty wild and woolly animal. It's not easily brought to heel, no matter what your political stripe.

It's been robust under Democratic presidents, anemic under Republicans, and vice versa.

Because the economy's so unpredictable, then, it's fairly easy to cherry-pick information and harness preconceptions to suggest that one major party is an economic disaster and the other is a boon for the country.

For instance, if you wanted to prove the economy performs better on Democrats' watch, you'd probably reference Michael Kinsley's preelection August 2004 *Washington Post* story that tracked forty-three years of data showing that Democratic administrations have brought higher growth, lower unemployment, lower inflation, and lower deficits as a percent of Gross Domestic Product.

Or you might follow stock market performance under Republican and Democratic administrations, as University of Pennsylvania economist Jeremy Siegel did in a March 2006 online column, noting that annualized stock returns for the past fifty-eight years have averaged 15.26 percent under Democratic administrations and just 9.53 percent under Republican administrations.[1]

If, on the other hand, you wanted to prove that Republicans are better stewards of the economy, you'd likely undertake a comprehensive meta-analysis of Fox News story promos.

You know, like these:

The Tax Hike about to Crush the Housing Market.
Blame Liberals for High Oil and Gas Prices!
Did President Bush Save the Stock Market?
Liberals on Iraq: Bad for America & Stocks?

Now, we know what you're thinking. This could hardly be more embarrassing for the Democrats. After all, one party's foreign policy is clearly providing you and your family meaningful and lasting economic security, whereas the other party's constant pacifist sniping is threatening to marginally devalue your $32 million in Halliburton and Carlyle Group stock.

But then you probably knew that already. Come on, they're Democrats! They want America to fail!

Of course, while few subjects are as vulnerable to rhetorical mischief as economics, it still may surprise some readers to know that Fox News's Saturday block of business shows, titled "The Cost of Freedom" (yeah, um, we're not kidding), is arguably the most agenda-driven programming on the network.

The lineup includes *Bulls & Bears, Cashin' In, Cavuto on Business,* and *Forbes on Fox.* In addition, on weekdays, Neil Cavuto hosts *Your World*—a show that, as we've seen, gives a wrap-up of the day's financial stories along with the not-infrequent T&A shot.

EARN TWICE AS MUCH DURING NUCLEAR HOLOCAUST AS YOU DID AT YOUR OLD JOB

FOX NEWS BUSINESS teasers usually include a bit of spin, a dash of propaganda, and a hearty dig at just about anyone who's left of center. Indeed, you could make a four-piece bongo set and a back-yard trampoline out of the skin left over from Greta Van Susteren's face-lift if you could do to it what Fox's business mavens routinely do to reality.

Virtually any story is subject to the artful manipulations of Fox's financial analysts and anchors. And this usually means that Republicans and conservatives carry the day while liberals and Democrats take a serious beating.

For example, on April 12, 2006, Fox aired this promo for its Saturday-morning business programs:

Saturday. All the business news you need is on the Cost of Freedom.

Iran's nuke program progresses. Could their military strengthen our economy? Surprising answers.

Then, some say Dems are trying to sabotage the markets to get votes. What have they done? How far will they go?

Plus, gas prices put the pinch on Americans. Could a new tax plan put us on the road to recovery?

The smart money with answers! Saturday! Watch the most powerful business block on cable news. The Cost of Freedom starts at 10 AM.

Now, it would be naïve to pretend that world events don't significantly affect nations' economies. Indeed, America's fortunes didn't really turn around following the 1929 stock market crash until the government ramped up war spending more than a decade later.

But last time we checked, horrifying centuries-long nuclear winters had an overall *negative* impact on most economic sectors. Unless your portfolio is heavily tilted toward hazmat and mutant control stocks, chances are your inflation-adjusted income will actually fall somewhat under such a scenario.

Now, Fox isn't actually saying they want Iran to possess nukes, but they don't want you to miss the silver lining in that mushroom cloud either. You should be prepared:

Look into companies heavily invested in remote eugenics labs carved into the sides of volcanoes. Note that energy stocks are likely to plummet as the atmosphere is initially suffused with a blast of searing thermal radiation but will recover nicely as the Earth is shrouded in light-reflecting dust and debris obliterating 98 percent of all animal and plant life. You might also consider selling off that time-share on St. Barts.

Of course, through its promo, Fox had already helpfully provided the "what" (Iran's nuke program and military may help our economy), so we were all anxiously awaiting the "why," "when," "where," and "what the Jesus H. Christ?" The answers arrived as promised on April 15, 2006, courtesy of Quentin Hardy, *Forbes on Fox's* Silicon Valley bureau chief:

> The more we press Iran, the more they have to build up their military. And all Iran has is oil. So the more you cut off aid and back them into a corner, the more they have to pump oil to help pay for it all. The more they pump, the more supply there is, and then prices drop. They say they can survive an embargo, but they can't. Iran has forty percent of its population below the poverty line and has sixteen percent inflation.

So pressuring Iran to build up their military capabilities will cause gas prices to drop? Did he really just say that?

Okay, so let's say oil prices do drop. Before long, forgetful Americans will give up on conservation and abandon hybrid cars in favor of rugged new SUVs that can tow Coast Guard cutters.

Meanwhile, we continue to "press Iran" (and you know how Iranians love to be pressed) and they continue to build up their military and nuclear program. So when they finally do nuke us off the face of the earth, at least we'll be groovin' to *Bob Seger's Greatest Hits* in kickass SUVs on our way to relaxing weekend getaways in Tahoe.

Yeah, that's great. Sounds sort of like trying to negotiate a better rate for your one-night stay at the Bates Motel.

WHAT COLOR IS THE SKY IN
YOUR WORLD WITH NEIL CAVUTO?

ON APRIL 14, 2006, Neil Cavuto led a discussion on people who withhold part of their federal taxes in protest of American military spending.

Now, you could argue that such token gestures are silly and ineffective and therefore far less worthy than simply organizing politically or crafting unique media campaigns that resonate with the public.

After all, there's always going to be stuff in the budget that individual taxpayers have a problem with. A lot of conservatives chafe at tax dollars buying food stamps for able-bodied adults, liberals hate the bloated Pentagon budget, and certainly most Americans must resent paying for Secret Service protection for Dick Cheney when he is quite obviously the Penguin.

But when you live in a society as complex and politically pluralistic as ours, there's no getting around certain realities, and one of those is that your taxes will eventually be used to pay for something you don't like.

Okay, so you could almost argue that Fox has a winning issue here. No doubt these tax resisters are simply following their consciences such as they are, but it still seems a fairly naïve approach to national security.

Oh, but it's not enough for Fox simply to knock down a straw man. They have to emotionally abuse it, too.

Before long, the Fox panelists were comparing the war protesters to the Unabomber, who, ironically, had no qualms about blowing people up.

Now, as the kids at Fox know, these people have about as much chance of their protests being upheld by our courts as we have of being hired as *O'Reilly Factor* interns. And, anyway, we doubt if the amount these folks are withholding from the government would be enough to pay for the rubber bullets they'll eventually be shot with. In the grand scheme of things, this isn't really that important, no matter which side you come down on.

But Terry Keenan of *Cashin' In* apparently saw it differently: "There are tens of millions of Americans, and that's probably not too big a number, who are cheating on their taxes, and if there was compliance and if they were made to stick to the laws, we wouldn't have a budget deficit right now."

Whodawhadda? Is Keenan really implying that war protestors are causing the budget deficit? If not, why is she bringing this up in the middle of this discussion?

Or is she saying that the tens of millions of Americans who cheat on their taxes are really secretly war protestors?

Call us crazy, but we're guessing there are relatively few war tax resisters who have recently incorporated in the Cayman Islands.

Yeah, the deficit couldn't have anything to do with that billionaire tax relief or those gaping tax loopholes that are big enough to drive a Carver Yacht through. Must be all that undeclared patchouli revenue.

THERE'S A PRICE ROLLBACK ON BYPASSES IN THE CARDIOLOGY DEPARTMENT

TO MANY CONSERVATIVES, business is really a religion. It's as if Adam Smith's invisible hand is some sort of literally existing avatar and everything in heaven and on earth is subject to its wrath and beneficence.

Indeed, if Jesus hadn't run around in hippie sandals and said so many mysterious, borderline-commie-sounding things, he would have long ago been remade into a hotshot broker who can both raise the dead and set them up with a nice high-performing, low-risk mutual fund.

On the February 4, 2006, edition of *Cavuto on Business*, Neil wondered if that invisible hand that had been jerking Wal-Mart's competitors around for four decades might also be able to magically heal them:

Does Wal-Mart have the answer to America's health care crisis?
Memo to health insurers: the competition just got a lot tougher!

Wal-Mart's now selling health insurance to small businesses through its Sam's Club stores. Can Wal-Mart do for health care what it did for TVs, toasters, and groceries? Bring costs way down?

Memo to Wal-Mart: physician, heal thyself. Asking Wal-Mart to provide good, affordable health care to everyone else is a little like asking McDonald's to host seminars on heart-healthy cuisine.

Of course, the reason Wal-Mart can sell toasters so cheaply is that they pay a substandard wage to their employees and have so much produced overseas. This may work with a Hamilton Beach four-slice with darkness control, but it's not exactly scalable to neurosurgery.

Low-wage doctors and sweatshop-made pacemakers are probably not the answer to the health care crisis in this country. And we don't think it's too much to ask that the person performing our angioplasty be able to spell angioplasty.

But this is the gospel according to Fox News. If big business can figure out how to sell gallon jars of Vlasic pickles for less than three bucks, certainly they can apply the same principles to prenatal heart surgery.

But why stop at health care? Might big business also have an answer to the centuries-old conflict between security and liberty that has bedeviled even our greatest social philosophers?

Of course it might.

On the same day Cavuto wondered if Sam's Club's health insurance program might be history's turning point on wellness, he also said this: "The controversy over wiretapping without warrants: Does Wall Street have a rooting interest? Terror attacks shatter lives and sink our economy and stock market. The president says his wiretapping policy will help prevent another 9/11. So is this a policy Wall Street endorses?"

With all due respect, who the hell cares what Wall Street thinks? If warrantless wiretapping is illegal or unconstitutional, it should be stopped, regardless of how it affects Merrill Lynch's year-end bonus structure.

Cavuto talks as if we should be able to sell off our inalienable rights like some sort of commodity or as if maybe corporations should have some sort of interpretive role when it comes to the Constitution. Neil, it just doesn't work that way. When James Madison penned the Fourth Amendment, he didn't write in an exception for Toys "R" Us.

God forbid Cavuto's world actually does become your world. You'd be besieged with headlines like "PepsiCo's board is meeting today on whether it will endorse freedom of the press for the next fiscal quarter" and "Archer Daniels Midland has already ruled that their press releases provide plenty of good stories."

DO YOU BLAME JED CLAMPETT? MR. DRYSDALE? HOW ABOUT THE DEMOCRATS?

THERE ARE FEW subjects that get politicized as much as gas prices. It's easy to see why. People want to be at Taco Bell. They want to arrive there in a vehicle that could transport a Marine battalion across the Mekong Delta. And they certainly don't want to pay any more than they've been paying for the last twenty years.

Solve that problem, bitch!

So when prices do go up—which they have to eventually because we've wisely expended over a span of about a hundred years (and show no signs of stopping) energy that took millions of years to collect in the form of fossil fuels—people go a little nuts. Oh, who knows? They may even start looking for someone to blame.

That's when the fun begins.

In the fourth quarter of 2005, ExxonMobil posted a $10.71 billion profit. It was the highest profit ever recorded for a company in the United States. Around the same time, Americans were being hit with record gas prices.

On February 3, 2006, Fox News aired a promo for *Forbes on Fox* headlined, "Want Lower Gas Prices? Cut Taxes on Big Oil!"

The following day, Mike Ozanian, senior editor of *Forbes* magazine, visited *Forbes on Fox* and had this to say:

Oil companies are under siege! They pay a much higher tax rate than most companies. Their profit margins are narrower than most companies. We have to level the playing field and lower the tax rate for oil companies so they'll have higher profits. Higher profits will give them more incentive to get the oil out of the ground and get it to the customers. That will create more supply, lower gas prices, and a stronger economy.

Now that's an interesting take. Why not give the most profitable company in the history of our country a tax break so they can lower prices to consumers?

It's almost sickening the way we attack big oil by buying as much of their product as they can produce at whatever price the market will bear.

Clearly they're being harassed by excessive government regulation and confiscatory tax laws. They need more incentive. Look at their feeble business model: Drill for oil. Refine it. Sell it. Post record profits. If only there were a way to convince them to keep doing it!

But it can't just be high taxes keeping gas prices up. Democrats also stand in the way of civilization's progress, don't they?

Here is the fair-and-balanced question that was thrown out to the Trading Pit panel on the April 29, 2006, edition of *Bulls & Bears:* "For decades, Democrats have fought against drilling in ANWR in Alaska and against proposals to build more refineries. Either one would have helped to keep gas prices lower. If you want less pain at the pump, should you vote against Democrats in the midterm elections?

There you go. Don't let those pussy conservationists off the hook.

Now, the truth is, ANWR has always been pretty much a red herring. Hearing the Republicans and Democrats argue over whether we should drill there is about as interesting as listening to Strom Thurmond's doctors discuss the setting on his morphine drip. The big, overlooked energy story is that we're going to have to adjust our thinking sooner or later because oil is a finite resource, so we need to start talking about alternatives.

So blaming Democrats and caribou for high gas prices completely misses the point. ANWR is one small factor among many that could marginally affect fuel prices. You might as well blame the nation's bed-and-breakfasts for being so far to drive to yet so irresistibly charming at the same time.

A 2004 study by the Energy Information Administration, a branch of the Department of Energy, estimated that drilling in ANWR might lower world oil prices (that's oil, not gas, prices) by 30 to 50 cents a barrel,[2] though it noted that this was hardly a sure thing because "assuming that world oil markets continue to work as they do today, the Organization of Petroleum Exporting Countries could countermand any potential price impact of ANWR coastal plain production by reducing its exports by an equal amount."

So drilling in ANWR might, initially at least, have zero effect on gas prices. But what will almost certainly have an effect on gas prices now and in the long run is driving your kid to twelve soccer practices a week in a Bradley Fighting Vehicle. And drilling like mad to keep the price down is just going to make the oil run out faster—thus putting further upward pressure on price.

Anyway, when, if ever, would it be okay with the economic geniuses at Fox to conserve a natural resource? In ten years are we going to be arguing about selling off Sequoia National Park to The Home Depot?

Yeah, something tells us we will.

A MINI-CASE STUDY (JUST IN CASE YOU WERE STILL WONDERING ABOUT THAT "HIDDEN" AGENDA)

Program: *Cashin' In*
Host: Terry Keenan
Airdate: January 7, 2006
Headline before segment: Are the Dems rooting against the economy?
Teaser for the segment: Are the Democrats rooting for the economy to tank? Well, someone here says they're playing a dangerous political game with your money.

Tagline during segment: DEMS V$ THE ECONOMY?

Tagline 2 during segment: Are the Democrats rooting against America's economy?

Best quote: "It's almost as if Democrats have disdain for anybody who actually works for a living or doesn't want government handouts for everybody." (Jonathan Hoenig, managing member of a private investment partnership)

Yes, we know. *Wall $treet Week* it ain't.

NOTES

1. Details are available at http://finance.yahoo.com/columnist/article/futureinvest/3022. The highest average return, 19 percent, was achieved under Bill Clinton's watch, and the lowest, -1.32 percent, occurred under Richard Nixon. But George W. Bush wasn't far off the pace—Nixon's pace, anyway. He clocked in at -0.92 percent as of February 2006. To be fair, that was more than a year ago, and he had to cope with the fallout of 9/11, whereas Clinton mainly just had to deal with the startling collapse of Pets.com.
2. The EIA said this was "relative to a projected 2025 world oil price of $27 per barrel (2002 dollars)," which shows you how reliable anything having to do with oil is these days.

11

TWO GUYS, A GIRL, AND A CRAZY PLACE

WEEKDAY **MORNING NEWS** programs are not exactly meetings of the Algonquin Roundtable.

Put it this way. If you were boarding a space pod as the world was coming to an end and you were scrambling to find a journalist to chronicle our final, fateful decades on our home planet, you'd have a hard time choosing between Matt Lauer and the guy who writes *TV Guide*'s Cheers & Jeers column.

Now, that's not necessarily all Lauer's fault. Morning network television isn't exactly designed to stimulate the intellect. The format pretty much consists of five minutes of hard news followed by light banter, pointless national weather updates, and seemingly endless segments featuring veteran journalists promoting Tyra Banks's latest project while trying not to swallow their own tongues.

But while the big three networks' morning shows may occasionally make you want to gouge your eyes out with your own thumbs, Fox News's morning installment, *Fox & Friends,* will make you want to toss those suckers in the nearest Osterizer and hit "frappe."

Yes, Fox has taken the candy-apple sensibilities of morning television and added those missing magic ingredients we never even knew we wanted: reactionary politics and ape-shit-hysterical xenophobia.

Now, we could give you dozens of examples of *Fox & Friends*'s odd pastiche of avuncular chitchat and right-wing agitprop, but, frankly, the show's just too weird to look at for any length of time. Indeed, tuning in to Fox on any random morning can feel a little like watching the birthday clown you hired for your kid's party hand out John Birch Society literature between hugs and balloon animals.

One minute they're laughing and talking about the weather and the next minute they're giving us the latest far-right Republican talking points. Of course, if you have a liberal-bashing cookbook and you want to push it while people are at home enjoying their Folgers Crystals, *Fox & Friends* is known to be an easy lay. But it represents a challenge for those of us who are to the left of G. Gordon Liddy.

Honestly, it's gruesomely surreal.

So please forgive us if the following comes off as a little more slice-of-life than comprehensive. It could have very well been slice-of-wrists, believe us.

THE KIDS ARE ALL LEFT

AS YOU MAY have figured out by now, Fox really hates protesters. Whether it's a protest at a Republican Party rally, a proenvironment march, a candlelight vigil for the victims of war, or a silent protest to protect our civil liberties, Fox treats them all with equal contempt.

In January of 2006, the network unleashed its big dogs on those civil liberties wackos. Yes, Brian Kilmeade, Steve Doocy, and E. D. Hill, who for many years were the liquid flavor burst at the center of each *Fox & Friends* broadcast (Hill moved to *Fox News*

Live in September 2006 and was replaced by fellow robo-blonde and former Miss America Gretchen Carlson), clamped onto the legs of a few extreme left-wing Constitution-huggers and refused to let go:

DOOCY: There are a lot of parents who may be sending their kids to Georgetown University in Washington, D.C. They're spending forty-five thousand dollars a year to send them to that place and they might have actually wound up on television on Tuesday (January 24, 2006).

KILMEADE: Because speaking there was the attorney general, Alberto Gonzales, and in the audience . . .

HILL: Talking about the surveillance program.

KILMEADE: Right. And in the audience, people who don't, I guess, like him . . .

DOOCY: Yeah.

KILMEADE: . . . or the surveillance.

DOOCY: More than two dozen students turned their backs and stood during the entire Gonzales half-hour speech. Five pro-testers, as you can see right there, were wearing black hoods with a banner—see, it obscured the television camera view—the banner said, "Those Who Would Sacrifice Liberty for Security Deserve . . ."

HILL: "*Ni*-ther"

DOOCY: "*Nee*-ther."

HILL: Yeah. Benjamin Franklin. Everybody's sort of passin' that one around.

Everybody's sort of passin' that one around? It's a quote from one of the greatest men in our nation's history, yet Hill talks about it like it's "Where's the Beef?" or "Whatchu talkin' 'bout, Willis?"

But Franklin's quote, which goes to the heart of our Founding Fathers' antityrannical ideals, stands in stark contrast to Fox News's philosophy: Give up your personal freedoms. Don't ask questions. Nothing bad will happen if you simply trust your leaders. Let them monitor your communications, look at your bank records, and hold suspects indefinitely. Hey, it's only a police state if Hillary's trying to keep you from loading up on Stinger missiles at the arena gun show.

DOOCY: So, anyway, for the proud parents of those kids . . .

HILL: Well, that's why they had the hoods on, so their parents wouldn't know who they were!

DOOCY: Yeah, maybe.

HILL: Get that chucklehead back home!

DOOCY: Well, freedom of expression.

HILL: Absolutely!

DOOCY: But in a lot of places they—the organizers would not allow them to continue to stand for the entire half an hour because it's disruptive to the people . . .

HILL: Right!

KILMEADE: Who are there.

DOOCY: . . . who can't see through the poster!

HILL: Well, it's—you know, you want to make this statement, you absolutely should be—you know, should have the right to do that, but I think they should do it outside, so that the people who are there who want to listen . . .

DOOCY: Sure.

Now, it's nice to see that the inalienable rights that were endorsed by our Founding Fathers, guaranteed by our Constitution, defended by the blood of thousands of soldiers, and secured by more than two hundred years of legal precedent are pretty much okay with E. D. Hill—that is, as long as no one sees people exercising them.

Of course, as host of the Gonzales speech, Georgetown would have had every right to limit the protests. Apparently, they chose not to, so Hill, bizarrely, condemned the students for not conducting a protest that was a bit more low-key.

> **HILL:** . . . to, you know, and watch, because you go there and, you know, you could sit at home, if you wanted just simply to listen to it, you could sit at home and, you know, listen on something else.
>
> **DOOCY:** Uh-huh.
>
> **HILL:** But they want to be there, watching and listening, and clearly these kids decided, well, they would take it into their own hands to determine who got to see it and who got blocked by them and their sign, so they stood up.
>
> **KILMEADE:** Yeah, so they stood up, they turned their backs and they stood there the whole entire time.
>
> **HILL:** Kinda rude!
>
> **KILMEADE:** More than kinda rude! Greg Kelly, who's . . .

Yeah, the last thing you want to do while protesting the gradual erosion of our nation's founding principles is be rude. Because everyone knows how much more effective courteous political activism is.

No doubt Hill and Kilmeade would have liked the Boston Tea Party much better if it had actually been a bunch of Loyalists sitting around the governor's house drinking tea.

> **DOOCY:** Yeah, but what did the black hoods symbolize? Was that an Abu Ghraib thing?

HILL: No, I think that was so their parents wouldn't know.

DOOCY: You could have done that with a ski mask!

HILL: You kidding? If you saw your kid . . .

DOOCY: I'll bet it was an Abu Ghraib thing!

HILL: Eh. I think it's just because they didn't want their parents to know.

KILMEADE: Hey, Greg.

HILL: That's my guess.

Yes, E. D., they didn't want their parents to know. Which is much the same reason the famous Sons of Liberty who organized the Boston Tea Party dressed as Indians, and why we tried, unsuccessfully it turns out, to publish this book under the cryptic pen names Phineas T. Smartybritches and Vidal Sassoon.

KILMEADE: Greg Kelly, by the way, is at the White House and, Greg, what's the last time you protested something? Do you remember the last time you held up a sign and just picketed?

GREG KELLY: Let's just say we all have regrets from college, okay?

KILMEADE: Oh, you do!

DOOCY: I have a few!

KELLY: Not necessarily protests but other incidents. Good morning, guys.

DOOCY: Streaking?

KELLY: No. No. Nothing. I didn't go to college in the sixties like you, Steve.

KILMEADE: Oh, my goodness! That's so wrong!

So, showing all the subtlety of a freshman at his first fraternity rush party, the brilliant Fox morning crew has equated several students' stand against what they see as the overzealous aims of the current administration with running nude through a football stadium and whatever you imagine Greg Kelly might have done in his college dorm. (Whatever that was, we're guessing he didn't want his parents to know.)

But there's an implicit warning here as well. Be careful what college you send your kids to or they may just come back knowing what's written in the Constitution.

TEX-MEX? BUT IT WORKS SO WELL FOR RESTAURANTS!

As a RATINGS-DRIVEN business, journalism often shifts rather abruptly from the sublime to the silly.

One of the most infuriating things about news outlets is their tendency to tout rare, poorly understood, and highly sensational dangers while ignoring more common, less murky threats.

For instance, while serious child abductions by strangers—what government statistics refer to as "stereotypical kidnappings"—are relatively rare compared to, say, deaths of children on roads and highways, abductions almost always draw greater media attention.

While one might argue that the public good would be better served, then, by giving more exposure to traffic deaths than abductions, one can at least understand the temptation to follow distressed parents around with boom mikes and cameras.

After all, serious child kidnappings *are* a genuine threat. According to the Department of Justice, somewhere between 60 and 170 occur every year.

So while it's extremely unlikely, it's at least possible that a child you know will be kidnapped this year. The danger is real, even if remote, and so it's not completely out of bounds to give substantial coverage to such incidents.

So your kid being nabbed? Possible, if highly unlikely. The state of California being kidnapped? That's another story.

Of course, that didn't stop Kilmeade et al. from planting that very fear in the minds of their viewers on the May 4, 2006, edition of *Fox & Friends*. Fox News contributor Michelle Malkin joined the gang to discuss an obscure concept called *reconquista* that is supposedly sweeping across the American South like hordes of Africanized killer bees:

DOOCY: Some Mexicans say that they deserve an open border because they claim that the United States took their land and the Mexicans want it back. This movement is called—I'm not making it up—it's called *reconquista*.

KILMEADE: And someone who knows you're not making it up is Michelle Malkin. She talks about this crusade and she is a Fox News contributor with a heck of a blog and a heck of a Web site. Michelle, now, first off, tell me about this movement and is it just a—is it just a niche group or a bunch of people who don't want to let go of something?

MALKIN: Well, a lot of people have been under the impression that this *reconquista* is a fringe intellectual fantasy, but they've been around for a long time, for decades actually, and in a lot of community colleges and universities, there are professors who have been plying this idea that the Southwest was stolen from Mexico and that Mexicans ought to rightly, rightfully, reclaim it. For a long time there were a lot of chapters of a student group called MEChA who believe this, and I debated one of these young students just the other day and it's as fresh as it was in the 1960s, and the indignance and the extreme nature of it has not died down and we saw that Monday at the May Day rally even though the mainstream media didn't want to show it.

Now, when Michelle Malkin says something is not a fringe intellectual fantasy, you can be pretty sure it's a fringe intellectual fantasy.

Of course, being that it's fringe, you've probably never heard of it. So unless you regularly watch Fox News or have a loose-lipped housekeeper, here's one definition of *reconquista,* from the online encyclopedia Wikipedia.com:

Reconquista was coined as a facetious term, popularized by Mexican writers Carlos Fuentes and Elena Poniatowska, to describe the demographic and cultural reemergence of Mexicans in the American Southwest. It was originally a jocular analogy to the Spanish Reconquista of Moorish Iberia, since the areas of greatest Mexican immigration and cultural diffusion are conterminous with northern New Spain and former Mexican territories. Since then, the term has been adopted by anti-immigration, anti-illegal immigration, and nativist groups who use it to imply a deliberate effort to retake the American Southwest by Mexicans.

The concept has also been advanced by Chicano nationalists to describe plans to restore the mythical Aztlán, though these groups do not generally use the word "reconquista."

Now, a quick Google search of "reconquista" soon confirms what this encyclopedia entry merely hints at—that it's primarily a right-wing obsession, not a Mexican one.

So, unless we're reading this wrong, *reconquista* started off as a joke but is now used primarily by far-right conservatives and anti-immigration groups to advance an agenda—much like Malkin herself.

Nancy Drew and the Case of the Missing Sovereignty would later continue:

HILL: But, second, if they want to reclaim this land, then why are they here in America, where they want our benefits and our jobs, yet they want to take the land and put it back to Mexico and then, what, sneak into Idaho?

MALKIN: The whole thing is absurd, E. D., and you point out a lot of the historical ridiculousness of it because a lot of the people that adhere to this idea of Aztlán, which is what they consider their territory . . .

HILL: Yeah.

MALKIN: . . . skip over the fact, you know . . .

HILL: It wasn't theirs.

MALKIN: . . . that they did sign a treaty. It was called the Treaty of Guadalupe Hidalgo, and Mexico received millions of dollars in settlement money for this so the history is ridiculous, but also just the ramifications of it, I think, are really serious. They consider this not a country. They do not respect our sovereignty, and the ultimate agenda of a lot of these pro-illegal-alien advocates, who are now pushing for amnesty, is to obliterate our border and, in many cases, if you think about it, they have succeeded.

Okay, we really have no idea how many of the millions of Mexicans who are in this country are here illegally because they have lingering contempt for the Treaty of Guadalupe Hidalgo, but let's just say it's all of them.

Let's assume they're in cafes and cantinas all over the Southwest United States going on and on about it: "Oh, señor, I had a good job back in Mexico, but I could not let stand for one more day the outrage that is the Treaty of Guadalupe Hidalgo!"

Fine. Malkin wins that one. Whatever.

The question is: What difference does it make? There's no fucking way we're giving California back to Mexico. SeaWorld is there. And the San Diego Chargers. So that's a red herring.

The only other possible danger is that the *reconquista* movement becomes a rationale for Mexicans to cross the border or for American policy-makers to cut them some slack.

But Mexicans hardly need more incentive to come here.

They need jobs. America has jobs. They come. It's hardly a mystery.

Now, if Malkin can produce one Mexican immigrant who has ever stopped at the border and stared wistfully over the Rio Grande while wrestling with his conscience over the moral implications of violating the Treaty of Guadalupe Hidalgo, we'll apologize. But to us it looks pretty much like a nonissue.

As for American policy, other factors are in play.

Business wants cheap labor; unions don't. Conservatives fear the "browning" of America; liberals less so. If, during a Senate debate, someone mentions that part of the United States used to belong to Mexico, well, that's the price of having an educated populace. But at most it will be a footnote in a much larger debate.

So, clearly, this is all just a big bowl of nothing.

But as Malkin droned on about the well-crafted conspiracy to turn a chunk of the United States into Mexico, the *Fox & Friends* gang listened on like a roomful of children hearing about unicorns for the first time.

Sure, they asked a couple skeptical questions, but for the most part they were buying the whole enchilada.

Ah, but what happens when your fear of foreigners runs smack up against your love of the president? You go even farther down the rabbit hole, that's what.

ANY PORT IN A POLITICAL STORM

IN FEBRUARY OF 2006, controversy swirled around George W. Bush after his administration approved the transfer of management contracts for six major U.S. ports to Dubai Ports World, which had purchased the British firm that held the contracts.

President Bush defended the transaction, insisting the United Arab Emirates, where DP World is based, was an important ally in the war on terror.

But the controversy created strange bedfellows, with several Republicans breaking ranks to oppose the deal.

It was also a challenge for the public to get consistent answers. An early *Washington Post* story on the transaction was typical of the mixed signals that were being sent:

> The State Department describes the UAE as a vital partner in the fight against terrorism. But the UAE, a loose federation of seven emirates on the Saudi peninsula, was an important operational and financial base for the hijackers who carried out the attacks against the World Trade Center and the Pentagon, the FBI concluded.

So at the very least the deal was suspect. After all, we were putting port management in the hands of people with clearer, more substantial ties to 9/11 than Saddam Hussein had. If Bill Clinton had waved through such a deal, he would have been reimpeached.

Now it goes without saying that Fox News is generally, um, suspicious of Arabs. Indeed, you could make a pretty strong argument that the Iraq War, for which they endlessly shilled, drew substantial rhetorical fuel from a general distrust of Arabs among Middle Americans.

So it's fair to say that if you'd been watching Fox News up until February 21, 2006, you might have developed a reason to fear management of our ports by a company based in a country that "was an important operational and financial base for the hijackers who carried out the attacks against the World Trade Center and the Pentagon."

But the president supported the deal, which must have meant it was okay.

KILMEADE: People get on the president and they say it's not a black-and-white issue. It should be a nuanced issue. For example, you like the leadership, help them out a little bit. And if you come down and rip this contract away, diplomatically it's a disaster.

LAUREN GREEN, NEWS UPDATE ANCHOR FOR *FOX & FRIENDS:* And, bringing up the other side of that, the issue, is that, you know, who better to vet really the terrorist organizations or elements in Saudi Arabia or in that area but a company who's based in there?

KILMEADE: Sure.

This is coming from the same network that would eventually entertain discussion about separate lines for Muslims in airports.

Of course, when you've just spent four years exploiting anti-Arab xenophobia to get the public to sign onto the president's war plans, you probably need a better argument than "if you want to stop Arab terrorism, hire an Arab." You need a thorough, unflinching analysis of the competing points of view wholly divorced from cheap demagoguery and partisanship:

KILMEADE: Everyone in the administration, big shots.

HILL: Big shots. And they have all looked at this deal and they all say it's okay. And you wonder would they do something to make their own jobs more difficult? Homeland Security's even on this.

Wow, we had no idea that the administration had brought in big shots. Never mind then. What more does the public need to know?

Maybe they can use this argument to quell every controversy. Warrantless wiretapping? Approved by big shots. Border security? The big shots say it's all good. Go back to sleep, Winifred.

Of course, it's nice to see that Fox can find nuance in a story like this and not just cynically portray it as America versus the Islamic world. Maybe they're not the hacks we thought they were. For example, if Hillary Clinton had backed the deal and the Bush administration hadn't, we're certain *Fox & Friends* would have stood their ground and fully supported the junior senator from New York.

HEY, ISN'T PAULA ABDUL A LEBANESE-AMERICAN?

SO WHAT DO we know so far? Americans who stand up for American values are an embarrassment to their parents. Foreigners who want to live in America and perhaps become Americans want America to be Mexico. Foreigners whose country had ties to 9/11 are looking out for American interests and are nothing to worry about.

But what about Americans who live in foreign lands and suddenly, through no fault of their own, find themselves war refugees?

Wait for it . . .

On July 20, 2006, during a quiet little chitchat about Americans fleeing war-torn Lebanon, the *Fox & Friends* crew had this to say:

DOOCY: The U.S. Department of Health and Human Services says its refugee resettlement program will provide assistance to evacuees up to ninety days after they return to the United States. Remember, a lot of them got on the plane after being on the boat, didn't have anything with them.

HILL: Uh . . .

DOOCY: . . . and so now the U.S. government is going to give them some assistance for up to ninety days.

HILL: Yeah, well . . .

KILMEADE: And they waived the hundred-fifty-dollar fee that was normally required for that.

HILL: I, I, okay.

DOOCY: As stated by law since 1956—that's the law. If you have to be evacuated out of a war area, you should be responsible for whatever costs are incurred. That's, that's the law.

HILL: Of a commercial ticket. So why aren't we following the law? And why, if we're evacuating Americans, would they need housing and financial assistance for ninety days, if they're, if we already paid taxpayer funds to get them back to America?

KILMEADE: We don't know. I mean, maybe some of those people lived in Lebanon and haven't been here in a long time.

Ah, therein lies the rub. Leave it to Brian Kilmeade to show his cards first. If they're such good Americans, why aren't they living in America? They're kinda traitors when you think about it. Who lives in Lebanon? The whole thing sounds awful fishy to the *Fox & Friends* gang.

DOOCY: In the meantime, a number of Americans who were in the Middle East are now in Baltimore-Washington International Airport. . . . The resettlement staff apparently is there on site. They're gonna provide mental health crisis counseling.

They're gonna arrange transportation for the travelers to their home states. That's a great deal.

HILL: Sure is.

Okay, okay, we get it. Americans being evacuated from Lebanon are being treated like the Queen of Sheba when they should all just be making a swim for it. Would they make the same argument if we were evacuating Americans living in England? Doubtful.

Later, the exchange got more bizarre:

DOOCY: A lot of them are there in Cyprus. Every hotel room on the island has been booked. Also, United States government, I understand, has contracted with a local convention center that does have AC. They've got tents up. They're trying to make people as comfortable as possible.

KILMEADE: Well, Cyprus is nice. I mean, this is not like a run-down community.

DOOCY: It's beautiful.

KILMEADE: So you could go in there, you got a credit card, then you're okay. And, if you're in Lebanon, more than likely you have some financial wherewithal, wouldn't you think, if you could travel to Lebanon on vacation?

HILL: One would think.

KILMEADE: Because that's not cheap.

HILL: One would think that.

KILMEADE: Right. So, and just have a ship pick you up. I mean, that must be a great feeling.

DOOCY: To get out!

KILMEADE: Because Senator Harry Reid yesterday was trying to make this political when he came out and said this was a mini-Katrina, because he felt as if the evacuation process was too slow.

This is coming from the same network that let Bill O'Reilly call the murder of a suburban woman by an illegal immigrant a micro-9/11. Yeah, let's not politicize.

Later in the interview came the coup de grace:

HILL: If they were concerned about where they were going to sleep, and I would imagine you would be, if you're being evacuated, why not bring a pillow and a blanket? I mean, stop complaining!

KILMEADE: And if you live in a Middle East country, at least bring the saltines. They're free and they come with the soup.

DOOCY: You know what? I bet folks there on Omni International wound up with some salty cashews for the long flight home.

So that's how the situation looked from Fox's Manhattan studios. What about from the actual battle zone? A little later the gang interviewed Sandy Choucair, whose husband had been visiting his mother in Lebanon when hostilities broke out:

DOOCY: Sandy, are you pleased with the way the State Department and the federal government handled the evacuation?

CHOUCAIR: No, not at all. I think they took too long. There was a lot of unnecessary things that happened that I think personally could have been avoided. Everybody else in the world was evacuating their citizens except us, and I think they took way too long, and my husband, like everybody else, went through a lot of unnecessary circumstances that, that didn't have to happen.

HILL: Like what?

CHOUCAIR: So I'm not, I'm not pleased.

HILL: Like what?

CHOUCAIR: Like, like living on the street for several days, going to the American embassy and asking for help and being told at the gate that you need to go home and listen to the news. But if he had a home, he would listen to the news. And he was turned away.

Yes, but did he get cashews?

We suppose the lesson to take from all this is that if you do find yourself stuck in a foreign country as a war is raging, the *Fox & Friends* crew will have your back right up to the point where the government starts trying to save your life.

The other lesson is that Matt Lauer, Meredith Vieira, and Al Roker suddenly look like Isaac Newton, Albert Einstein, and Stephen Hawking.

Okay, that's stretching it. More like Niels Bohr, J. Robert Oppenheimer, and Willard Scott.

12

A VERY SPECIAL EPISODE

To some degree, every media outlet panders to its core demographic.

Indeed, media are generally well aware of who's reading, watching, and listening and they're loath to alienate their most loyal consumers.

That's why *Barron's* has never run investment tips from the cast of *The O.C.* and why former GE chairman Jack Welch has yet to appear on the cover of *CosmoGIRL*—not even in an inset photo.

Now that sounds like a joke, but, as you'll see, it actually speaks volumes about Fox News's boundless dishonesty. The network knows the game as well as or better than anyone else, yet in its unambiguously titled *A Special for Young People* it looked as though the network was breaking new—some might even say monumentally insane—ground. Here's how it promoted the special on its Web site:

From a captain of industry (Jack Welch) to an Oscar-winning actress (Olympia Dukakis), a legendary heart surgeon (Dr.

Michael Debakey) to a World War II hero (Louis Zamperini), "A Special for Young People" presents unforgettable stories and life lessons the whole family will want to hear.

Yeah, we know what you're thinking. It's already hard enough to get your kids to do their homework, and now Fox is dangling geriatric war heroes in front of them. Then again, this *is* educational television. We can almost hear it: "Hey Brandon and Brittany! Come downstairs! The old lady from *Moonstruck* is on Fox News, and she has some pearls of wisdom for you!"

Of course, what might seem crazy and counterintuitive could actually be part of a well-honed strategy. It reminded us of Bill O'Reilly's top-selling borefest for teens, *The O'Reilly Factor for Kids*.

This was a book written for kids that contained more tips on how to avoid cataracts (again, this is not a joke) than the rest of his catalog combined.

Clearly, he wasn't going after the children's market. He was angling for a sweet slice of that holiday sock-and-dreidel budget. No one under fifty bought that book, and no one under fifteen read it.

So even for Fox, whose definition of a young person is someone who shipped out to Normandy a little late in the game, this was all just a little disingenuous.

But it would get even more tantalizing for the preteen set. The promo continued: "How is Jack LaLanne, at age 92, still able to meet a schedule that would leave men half his age panting for air?"

Yeah, there's nothing like a sweaty nonagenarian in a polyester jumpsuit to give you that whole Mountain Dew vibe.

Combine that with their other guests, and you've got a program specially designed to tap into that lucrative preteen MedicAlert market.

So, clearly, this was not a "Special for Young People." It was a special way to *torture* young people who were stupid enough to make eye contact with their grandparents while it was airing.

But, hey, if the real target audience could accept the premise of Jack Welch headlining a special for ten-year-olds, is there any wolf in sheep's clothing egregious enough to raise red flags for them?

Indeed, if we can learn anything from Fox's intermittent specials, it's that the network has taken preaching to the choir—and its own incestuous propaganda—to a previously unimagined level.

EVERYTHING'S COMIN' UP RUMSFELD

OF COURSE, IT'S difficult to pick a favorite Fox special because they're a bit like your Great-Aunt Fanny's annual Christmas card—they come on numerous occasions every year and make less sense each time.

For example, *Winning Iraq: The Untold Story* gave us all the proof we needed that the Iraq War was going gangbusters. This fair-and-balanced report included "interviews with grateful Iraqis," "a vibrant Iraq economy," and our favorite, "reports about peaceful vacation spots."

Now, you can arguably point to newly built schools as a genuine sign of improvement in Iraq, but vacation spots? We're guessing even the Baghdad Chamber of Commerce is having a tough time with this one. "Come to Iraq! It's like Branson if Andy Williams were lobbing ordnance at you. Remember to bring your Kevlar swimsuit, 'cause it's hot and shrapnelly out by the pool!"

Then there were *Religion in America: Church and State, Who is Jesus?, The Birth of Jesus,* and *Can We Live Without God?* Of course, the question isn't whether "we" can live without God, but whether Fox can live without selling God as a product.

Finally, five weeks before the midterm elections, we were treated to *Why He Fights,* a special about then–Secretary of Defense Donald Rumsfeld. In its promotion, Fox announced, "We'll break down the success of Operation Iraqi Freedom, the ongoing battle to rebuild a nation that toiled for years under a brutal regime, and why Rumsfeld faces heavy fire at home."

Oh, it was a jaunty little infomercial and, once again, Rummy's smoldering constipated squint melted the hearts of Fox viewers—but it still wasn't enough to save his job. He was cast off like a strip-club patron with a maxed-out Visa shortly after the Dems swept to power.

Of course, these remain some of our favorite Fox specials. But just before the 2006 midterm elections, the network threw out any semblance of objectivity with an hour-long propaganda-fest titled *Hannity on America.* 'Twas a beautiful thing.

And guess what? It appears Sean doesn't like Nancy Pelosi all that much.

WHAT THE HELL IS A PELOSI?

YOU GOT A sense of where *Hannity on America* was going near the top of the show, when Sean ran a teaser for an upcoming segment featuring people on the street telling him what they thought of him.

First, he showed a statuesque blond woman who was so pretty, she'd be at home in a Victoria's Secret catalog:

HOT BLOND: I think he's great. I love listening to his commentary.

Then he showed a squirrelly red-haired guy who looked like he may have made his home out of some Sears catalogs.

Not only was he not hot or blond, he looked like a cross between Ted Kaczynski and Beaker from *The Muppet Show:*

WEIRD RED-HEADED MAN: I just don't care for the guy.

And from there, the Hannity Propaganda Express departed the depot on its way to Republican Town.

Item one on the agenda was an interview with then-Speaker Dennis Hastert. Guess what? Hastert doesn't like Nancy Pelosi all that much.

But first, Hannity had to let his viewers know that Pelosi was not going to get a free pass—no, not in this politically motivated preelection TV special:

Here's the state of America the way I see it. Here we are five years after the worst attack in American history. We're nine days before the midterm elections. These are very consequential times. So what do Americans know about the woman who says she'd like to be the next Speaker of the House? Well, I don't think anyone knows how she's voted in the past and I don't think anyone knows where she'd want to take us in the future. And as we'll show you later, some people do not even know who she is.

Yes, indeed, we fear what we don't understand. Unfortunately, Alan Colmes was not there to act as a speed bump, and so Sean barreled ahead into his interview:

HANNITY: Mr. Speaker, there's Nancy Pelosi. She'll tell anybody who listens that she's gonna be the next Speaker of the House. Matter of fact, the quote is, Mr. Speaker, she can have any suite she wants. I assume tonight you're gonna take issue with that.

HASTERT: Well, I think she's trying to measure the curtains already, but, you know, we have a good story to tell and I think when American voters really focus in on what this election in Congress is all about, it's about lifestyle. It's about being able to keep a little bit more of your own money in your pocket rather than . . . losing the tax cuts that Republicans have brought forward in the last five years. You know, in the last five years we've created an economy where we've—6.3 million people have more jobs, new jobs in this country. . . . More people own their own homes than ever before in the history of the country, more minorities own their own homes than ever before in the history of the country, the stock markets hit a record high, we've had nineteen consecutive months of good economic growth in this country, and it's because we cut taxes when it was tough to do that back in 2001 and 2002, to get the economy going again, get people back to work, to get people to invest in America. We've been able to do that.

Of course, economics is a murky field. If you want a different perspective on these numbers—which, when more closely examined, translate into "please don't pay attention to any of our scandals or the war in Iraq"—a good starting point would be the Center on Budget and Policy Priorities at www.cbpp.org. To pick on just one Hastert factoid, when this interview aired, the Dow was actually well below its Clinton-era high after adjusting for inflation.

Then again, if Hastert's economic analysis is as sharp as his political prognostications, it's no wonder he's back sitting at the congressional kids' table:

HANNITY: . . . is the message on the economy that you're talking about, the job creation issue, home ownership issue, interest rates, inflation. Is that message getting out? And if you listen to just about anybody who's writing, any pundit, they all say Republicans are going to lose seats, it's a matter of how many. Do you expect Republicans will lose seats?

HASTERT: I think we could lose some seats. We could pick a seat up. But I think the pundits are looking at this as a national election. This election is district by district. It's about members of Congress getting out and talking to their constituents about what they've been able to accomplish. How we've made a better life for America in this country, and how we've kept this country safe from terrorists in the last five years, nobody talks about that.

HANNITY: Have you examined this issue in terms of the House races? Have you examined it district by district so you know, you're confident what the results will be on Election Day?

HASTERT: Well, you know, you're never confident, and the American people will make that final decision. But if you look district by district, the Democrats would have to come in and take fifteen Republican seats away from Republican districts. I just don't think that's going to happen.

Of course, hindsight is twenty-twenty, and in October 2006 it may very well have looked like the Republicans had a chance to "pick up a seat." But in the interest of fairness, we think Democrats should have been given a chance to respond or at the very least contribute a laugh track.

> **HANNITY:** Let's talk a little bit about the woman that would like to have your job a week from this Wednesday, and that's Nancy Pelosi. Now, she's referred to for example the president of the United States as mentally unstable. She says about Republicans in the Congress, they're immoral, they're corrupt, that they're running a criminal investigation [*sic*]. She's obviously talking about you. She says she could say much worse if she wants to. And then on the other hand she says she would like to restore civility. So here's the question. Does Nancy Pelosi in your view, would she have the temperament to be Speaker of the House of Representatives?

Note: if these questions had gotten any more solicitous he'd have had to offer Hastert a complimentary pedicure and facial.

> **HASTERT:** Well, you know, my experience is that working with Nancy it's been all politics all the time. And there's a lot of things that we could work together with in Congress that Republicans ultimately got done by themselves and we had to do it the hard way. But she would just turn off and say no, we're not going to help you, we're not going to work with you.

> **HANNITY:** Yeah.

> **HASTERT:** And last, two years ago she made a decision that the only way that they could get their message out was to trash the president and to trash Republicans.

Note: The day after this special aired, George W. Bush essentially told a Texas crowd that a vote for the Democrats was a vote for the terrorists: "However they put it, the Democrat approach in Iraq comes down to this: the terrorists win and America loses."

(Sure, one man's trash is another man's treasure, but it's a bit much for Hastert to pretend his party is the innocent victim of ruthless politicking.)

Finally, Hannity polished off that old chestnut about the Democrats being weak on homeland security because they object to the parts of the terror war that are blatantly unconstitutional. (Of course, Sean managed to talk about it without mentioning the constitutional dilemmas.)

Just in case you didn't get the subtle message that a vote for Democrats would be a vote for a terrorist in every garage, after the Hastert interview Hannity ended the segment wondering whether people really knew what they were getting into if they voted Democratic. Did people even know who this crazy obstructionist was?

"And with just nine days before this important election, does anyone know who Nancy Pelosi is?" asked Sean. "I took to the street to find out."

Surprise, surprise. The average person didn't know. Shocking.

Yes, we are too dumb to govern ourselves, Sean. Let's just vote for the status quo.

Of course, we wonder whom exactly Sean was asking. A *Newsweek* poll conducted shortly after the election was over showed that 34 percent had a favorable opinion of Pelosi, compared to 20 percent unfavorable. Seventeen percent had never heard of her, and 29 percent were unsure. So Sean's poll appears to have a sampling error of plus or minus 54 percent.

Then again, since Sean conducted *his* poll himself, maybe it's simply the case that stupid is drawn to stupid. Or maybe the problem was that he wasn't going by name recognition at all but by whether people could identify her picture.

THERE'S A STRANGER IN THE HOT SEAT?

DID WE MENTION that Sean Hannity doesn't like Nancy Pelosi all that much?

After promoting his new segment "The Hannity Hot Seat" a

couple times by showing an unknown woman sitting in shadow, it was at last time for the reveal.

So who would this mystery maharishi be?

Sean began: "All right, I've been in cable news for ten years now and the thing that really bugs me the most is I can never get a yes or no answer to a simple question. Tonight, we're going to try and solve all that."

Of course, one wonders what exactly Sean was trying to solve. His guests' vexing tendency for conveying useful information?

You see, yes or no answers are simply not meant for political debate. They're for questions like, "Do you want soup?" Indeed, they're intended not to enlighten but to entrap.

But Sean didn't see it that way. He was going to get simple, straight answers out of the Democrats once and for all. So who had agreed to this epic confrontation? Hillary Clinton? Dianne Feinstein? The woman of the hour, Nancy Pelosi herself?

"Now let's reveal who's sitting tonight in the Hannity Hot Seat," intoned Sean.

A loud drumbeat. The lighting changes dramatically.

"There it is," announced Sean, proudly. "Sitting across from me is Jane Fleming, the executive director of the Young Democrats for America. All right, now . . ."

Fleming laughed. We sighed. Is this the best he could come up with? Certainly there had to be a higher-ranking Democrat available for this hit piece. Perhaps a random delegate from the 2004 Democratic National Convention, complete with big foam donkey hat, Mardi Gras beads, and an American flag painted on her face.

Sean laid out the ground rules:

Here's simple rules. Okay, very simple. Rule number one. We're gonna give you eight simple yes or no questions. Okay? Then, rule number two. We're gonna have each, we'll each have twenty seconds to elaborate on three shorter questions and then, you know what, we'll turn it into a discussion between the two of us.

Wow. Shades of the Lincoln-Douglas debates.

Sean began:

HANNITY: Are you ready? Very, very simple, because, you know what, Nancy Pelosi wants to be the next Speaker of the House of Representatives. It's a powerful position, so I want to find out if you agree with some of the positions she's taken and maybe we can get some insight as to where she wants to take America. For example, Nancy Pelosi voted against reauthorization of the PATRIOT Act. Did she do the right thing by voting against the reauthorization?

FLEMING: Yes.

HANNITY: Yes. She voted . . . So you agree with her, huh? All right. She also said that she voted against the creation of the Homeland Security Department. Was it right to vote against, after 9/11, the creation of the Homeland Security Department?

FLEMING: Yes, and I hope we get to talk about that one.

HANNITY: We will. She said that even if we caught Osama bin Laden now, this is our third question, it wouldn't make us any safer. Was she right to say that?

FLEMING: Yes.

HANNITY: Wow. You're right there with her. Is Nancy Pelosi right, here we are, fighting a war on terror, to oppose the terrorist surveillance program?

FLEMING: Yes, well, I would expand . . .

HANNITY: Naw, no . . . all right. Now, here we go. Nancy Pelosi, she voted for the largest tax increase in American history, and she also voted against all the Bush tax cuts. Was she right on those issues?

FLEMING: Yes.

HANNITY: Okay. Nancy Pelosi, was she right against voting to build a border . . . seven hundred miles, the fence on the border?

FLEMING: Yes, and I really hope we get to talk about that one.

HANNITY: Okay, does Nancy Pelosi—she referred to the president of the United States as mentally unstable. She said that Republicans are immoral, corrupt, and they run a criminal enterprise. Does she have the temperament to be Speaker?

FLEMING: She has the temperament, but I think . . .

HANNITY: Yes . . .

FLEMING: . . . we need to get away from name-calling.

Yeah, we can get away from the name-calling in a minute, but first, Sean Hannity is a hack and his viewers are simpletons. Okay, now no more name-calling.

Of course, what Fleming should have said after Hannity presented his rules is something like, "I came here to talk about serious issues facing our country and they cannot be addressed by yes or no questions and twenty-second sound bites. So I bid you a good day, sir. I said, *good day!*"

Now, it's no mystery why the only person Hannity could get for this segment was a representative from the Young Democrats. The segment should have been called the Hannity High Chair, because this is how you address a two-year-old who's just thrown her sippy cup on the floor.

Still, Fleming was doing a pretty good job under the circumstances. And it was time for the twenty-second response round, which would really give her a chance to shine!

HANNITY: Okay. Let me just start with something real simple. Now we go into rule two here because I want to expand on this. If you're against the PATRIOT Act, if you're against the Homeland Security Act, if you're against the NSA program, how do you make America safer after 9/11?

FLEMING: Well, the reason why Democrats, and it just wasn't Nancy Pelosi, but the majority of Democrats voted against the Homeland Security creation, the creation of the Homeland Security, was because we believe in smart government, not bigger government, and I would think that as a Republican you would agree with that as well, and so creating a whole other level of bureaucracy doesn't make any sense.

That was a good answer under the circumstances, but it had the unfortunate downside of being false. The truth is that the creation of the Department of Homeland Security was first proposed by Democratic Senator Joseph Lieberman and Republican Senator Arlen Specter in October 2001. President Bush opposed its creation for eight months before flip-flopping on the issue in June 2002, suddenly announcing that he supported the DHS creation.

The cynical politicking that ensued was summed up nicely by E. J. Dionne Jr. in a November 2002 column in the *Washington Post:*

> The natural move from here would have been authentic bipartisanship to get a bill passed. After all, the differences between Bush and the Democrats were so small that Senator Phil Gramm (R-Texas) noted that 95 percent of the homeland security bill finally approved this week had been written by Democrats.
>
> But getting a department created before the election was clearly less important to the president than having a campaign issue. He picked a fight over union and civil service protections and Republican senators filibustered various efforts to reach a compromise on the issue. In late September, Bush went so far as to charge that the Senate—meaning its Democratic majority— was "not interested in the security of the American people."

That, in essence, shows the danger of relying on yes or no questions and sound bites. They're useless, and they misinform. And that's precisely why Sean Hannity loves them.

Sean plowed ahead:

HANNITY: But wait a minute, I just asked you a simple question. You voted against the PATRIOT Act, the Homeland Security Act, against the NSA program.

FLEMING: Because those things were not going to make us safer.

HANNITY: All right here's my twenty seconds. But my point is, you know, Republicans, we're saying you guys are weak on the war on terror. I asked you a question about what are you going to do to make America safer. If you're against those things, give me three quick things in the next twenty seconds that you would support to make America safer . . .

FLEMING: Okay.

HANNITY: . . . after 9/11. Go. Twenty seconds.

FLEMING: With our borders we would have this new technology that would actually be almost a virtual fence, because a fence is not going to cut it. And I would make sure that we actually enforce the laws that are already on the books. Under Bush, in 2004, we only find . . .

HANNITY: So a virtual fence.

FLEMING: . . . three employers, we only find—and enforce the laws that are already on the books. We only find three employers for undocumented workers. I know there were more than three employers that had undocumented workers.

HANNITY: Here's the bottom line, if we can't for example, if terrorists are calling into America and you're against that, if you're against the PATRIOT Act which we now know has stopped terrorist attacks, if you're against building a fence, it proves my point that Democrats have no plan. And what you say is we'll build a virtual fence. That's the best you can do? After 9/11, the best you can do is a virtual fence. Your next twenty seconds.

FLEMING: I was talking specifically about the fence, but there's lots of other things we can do, too. Let's talk about Iraq. How about let's start to begin a redeployment process? We went in there to take Saddam out of power, we went in there to put an Iraqi government, democratic government in place. We've done those things. Why are we still there? The violence is increasing. Our presence has actually increased violence rather than decreased it. And let's let the Iraqi government stand on its own two feet.

HANNITY: You know, 'cause it's amazing to me, now here's my point on Democrats, and we're in the discussion phase here so you can interrupt me at any time. I think Democrats, I think you prove it tonight, except for your one or two minor suggestions, when it comes to the single biggest issue of our time, I see weakness, I don't see any strength or any ideas, and I think ultimately the American people pay attention to that and they look at the Republicans, I think that's where they win in this election. You get the final twenty seconds.

Yes, the Democrats really are intellectually bankrupt, aren't they?

Sean Hannity gave the second-highest-ranking member of one of the party's satellite organizations a handful of yes or no questions and a few twenty-second answers to elaborate on the numerous intricate facets of the war on terror, and this is all they could come up with?

Hey, don't make Sean ask even fewer yes or no questions of the Democratic coroner of Sheboygan County, Wisconsin, 'cause he'll do it! Then won't they look foolish.

OPPRESSED WHITE MEN AND THE BLACK MAN WHO'S KEEPIN' 'EM DOWN

AT FIRST GLANCE, voter suppression doesn't seem like a Sean Hannity kinda story. Spoiled ballots, hinky voting machines, long lines in heavily Democratic districts, voter purges—it all sounds more like grist for the left-wing rumor mills.

So when the next segment began, forgive us if we thought for a moment that the demon that keeps Sean's soul trapped on the astral plane and his body in thrall to the underworld had at last relented and allowed his humanity to shine through.

He began:

Now, since the founding of our country individuals and groups have tried to influence the vote by using strong-arm tactics. For example, in the 1860s New York's Tammany Hall used intimidation against Irish immigrants. After the gold rush in California, Mexican and Chinese Americans had their voting rights threatened, and tactics included poll taxes and literacy tests and even physical violence. And despite being free from slavery as a result of the Civil War, African-Americans continue to struggle for the right to vote.

Of course, Bizarro Sean would not stay long. Regular Sean continued:

Now, in a shocking twist, the government is charging African-Americans with voting fraud in Mississippi, a state that helped to give the birth of voting rights and the Voting Rights Act. We sent our own Rudi Bakhtiar to Macon, Mississippi.

BAKHTIAR: (voice-over) Beautiful Macon, Mississippi. Population three thousand one hundred, give or take a few. A no-stoplight town with a big problem.

AFRICAN-AMERICAN WOMAN: We don't care what color they is. The people just want a fair election.

Wait, wait, wait. We appear to have glossed over a lot of stuff here. Sean was talking about slavery and Jim Crow, and now, after everything that's happened since those dark periods in our nation's history, he's gonna jump in with a story on this? It's like ignoring Uganda for thirty years and then finally filing a report when someone keys Idi Amin's car.

Sure, it's man-bites-dog, but it's a pretty small man and a pretty big dog.

BAKHTIAR: Do people around here talk about him at all?

WHITE WOMAN IN CLOTHING STORE: Yeah. They talk about him.

BAKHTIAR: They do? What do they say?

WOMAN: White people don't like him.

Is it unfair to point out that he's a black man in rural Mississippi? It is? Okay, then let's move on.

BAKHTIAR: (following an African-American man who's talking on a cell phone) . . . Just a couple of questions.

(Man waves her off and shakes head.)

BAKHTIAR: (voice-over) Ike Brown is the Democratic executive committee chairman of Noxubee County, a region where blacks outnumber whites about three to one. In violation of the hard-won Voting Rights Act of 1965 [at this point, black-and-white video is shown of African-Americans marching with a "We Shall Overcome" banner], Brown is the first black man charged by the U.S. government with suppressing votes—white votes.

Yeah, you know why he's the first black man to be charged? Because it's not a national epidemic, you boobs. But this plays perfectly into the white-man-as-victim narrative that so many Fox viewers love.

Now, we're not saying this isn't a story, but there are bigger fish to fry than a few voters getting harassed in a few local races in a tiny Mississippi town.

For instance, why doesn't Hannity interview Greg Palast, who has done some intriguing reporting on widespread Republican suppression of largely African-American, Democratic votes, including through the use of "caging lists" meant to target black communities for voter challenges?

Oh, that's right. He did. Here was that exchange, from October 29, 2004:

HANNITY: Greg, do you consider yourself a reporter or just a Democratic operative?

PALAST: Well, I'm definitely not a Democratic operative. In fact . . .

HANNITY: You're not a Democrat? You're not voting for John Kerry?

PALAST: Actually, the—no, I'm not. But the . . .

HANNITY: You're not voting for John Kerry?

PALAST: I'm staying out of this business.

HANNITY: Because I could tell you're voting for John Kerry, so don't—let's not act like you're some big objective reporter. Because you sound like every walking, talking cliché that I've heard every liberal say. And you're not giving facts. You're drawing conclusions based on your interpretations of events. Isn't that true?

After a segment where Bakhtiar questions a white man who says Brown didn't want to let him run for sheriff, she continues:

BAKHTIAR: (voice-over) Brown is a felon who served nearly two years for tax fraud. In Macon for some twenty-six years, he is a powerful political presence.

SCOTT BOYD, LOCAL NEWSPAPER PUBLISHER: When Ike Brown moved to Macon there were only one or two black elected officials countywide. Today there are only one or two white elected officials.

Didn't they point out earlier that the district was predominantly black? So doesn't the fact that there were only one or two black elected officials in the county seem a bit odd?

But now it's an outrage because there are only one or two white elected officials?

Now, again, if Brown is doing something illegal, he should be prosecuted. But let's get some perspective on this story at least. We can begin by accusing Hannity and Bakhtiar of being Republican operatives and walking, talking conservative clichés.

Bakhtiar later tracks Brown down on the street and confronts him in person:

BAKHTIAR: Have you intimidated white voters? Did you move people from one district to another?

BROWN: (talking on cell) I'm trying to talk on the phone, lady. Don't be hollering in my ear.

Classic.

Bakhtiar should have continued with, "Please, sir. Please hang up the phone. We're trying to influence a national election here by calling attention to a trivial scandal that affects literally tens of people in rural Mississippi."

Now, let's say that this report is right. Then Brown will have to answer to the authorities as well as his own conscience.

But what the hell does this have to do with the big picture when it comes to the midterm elections? Is this sort of thing systemic? Is Jim-Crow-in-reverse now a permanent part of our electoral process?

Are straight white men across the Deep South being forced to submit videos of themselves dancing at weddings to prove they're not dorks before being allowed to vote in presidential elections?

Not likely. But if they were, you can be pretty sure Sean would be all over it.

HANNITY AND A BUNCH OF STREET WALKERS

FINALLY, AFTER A *Hannity & Colmes*–style shouting match and another pointless Jaywalking rip-off, Hannity went to his promised segment on the public perception of His Honor.

Boy, was it an eye-opener:

I think he's wonderful.

I think he is one of the most dangerous people on the air right now.

Sean is sexy.

Sometimes the things that he says kind of get me a little angry sometimes.

I think he's handsome.

I'm really not a big fan of Sean Hannity.

I think Sean Hannity thinks the way I do. I know he does.

I think he's kind of harsh and aggressive and arrogant.

Sean is sharp. He keeps me interested in the news.

I like his straightforward style and I like the way that he just lays it down, you know.

He's just number one, that's all I can say.

Sean Hannity, not my favorite. Big thumbs down.

He's a patriot and he loves this country.

I think he's a windbag of a gorilla.

Sean Hannity ought to be president of the United States as far as I'm concerned.

Sean Hannity, he's the best of the best of the best. He's intelligent, he's handsome. I know he can't dance, but he's still the best.

It's weird that no one mentioned "freakishly insecure."

THE B-SQUAD

▼

13

THE TURNCOATS ARE COMING!
THE TURNCOATS ARE COMING!

MAKE NO MISTAKE about it. When Fox says it's fair and balanced, what it really means is it likes a rigged game.

While any idiot can see the network tilts to the right on everything from electoral politics to celebrity news, its anchors and reporters will occasionally give lip service to the other side. Unfortunately, this is typically done with an unmistakable nod and wink to their conservative Republican base.

Indeed, they're kind of like the girlfriend who promises to rent both a romance and an action flick on her way home from work and then shows up with *Steel Magnolias* and *The Bodyguard*. Technically, she didn't lie, but she's not exactly building trust either.

In much the same way, Fox loves to invite guests with Democratic pedigrees whose last liberal impulse was supporting Jimmy Carter's efforts in the SALT II talks or arguing that kinky sex fetishes should be a private matter between leading political campaign strategists and their prostitutes.

In short, they love a turncoat. Unfortunately, the quality of their recruiting efforts leaves a bit to be desired. It's not quite like snatching Wernher von Braun away from the Nazis at the end of the war. More like Werner Klemperer.

PART I: DICK MORRIS

WHEN POLITICAL PUNDIT Dick Morris appears on Fox, he's usually introduced as a "former Clinton adviser." A more fitting title would be "former Clinton adviser who was forced to resign because he forgot to tell his wife that he liked sucking hookers' toes."

Yes, it was back in August of 1996 when Morris left the Clinton campaign amid very disturbing and incredibly funny revelations that he was banging prostitute Sherry Rowlands. It also came out that Morris had let Rowlands listen in on conversations between him and the president.

We know what you're thinking: perfect credentials for a Fox News contributor. But come on, Fox News wouldn't hire a Democrat who had worked for the Clintons, would they? Well, not unless he was a backstabbing lout. Enter Dick Morris.

Morris is frequently brought on as the counterweight to a conservative guest.

You'll get combinations like Morris, Ann Coulter, and former *Wall Street Journal* editorialist David Asman. You know, so there's balance.

During his numerous Fox appearances, you'll hear him spout such far-left rhetoric as: "Oh, God. I love Karl Rove. He deserves better. He's magnificent. He elected Bush. The country owes him a debt" (*The O'Reilly Factor*, October 20, 2005).

We're not sure what's more embarrassing: The toe-sucking thing or that statement.

Diddly-Squat and Other Things You Can Learn from Dick Morris and Bill O'Reilly

Morris frequently visits *The O'Reilly Factor* to discuss any and all things Clinton. He especially has it in for Hillary. He even wrote a book, *Rewriting History*, that was a direct response to Hillary's bestselling *Living History*.

Now, if we ran a network and wanted to see a fair discussion of one of the most powerful women in the country—one who could very well end up being the first woman to head a major party's presidential ticket—we'd make damn sure no more than 50 percent of the participants in that discussion had either perved out with a whore in a hotel room or jerked off to an employee's voice over the phone while simultaneously threatening to defile her hoohoo with fried chickpeas.

But on April 14, 2005, these two little men were sniping at the junior senator from New York like a couple of impotent Cliff Clavins who just got turned down for dates to the annual postman's ball:

MORRIS: There is a very interesting fight shaping up in oh-six in New York State. Because Hillary, you know, has to run for reelection to the Senate before she runs for president.

O'REILLY: Right.

MORRIS: I personally would advise her to skip it and just run for president. What does she need a reelection fight for? But I've heard that there's some possibility that a pro-choice, pro-assault-rifle-ban, pro-affirmative-action woman might run against her—Jeanine Pirro, the attorney general—district attorney of Westchester, who's on Fox News a lot.

O'REILLY: Yes.

MORRIS: That would be something.

O'REILLY: That's in the air. That's in the air. And you know, but Hillary has so much money. But that would be a competitive race. And if that happens . . .

MORRIS: Because Hillary needs to run against someone like a Gingrich.

O'REILLY: Yes.

MORRIS: Hillary needs to run against somebody like a Gingrich, who's anti-choice, and you know, pro anti-gun-control. But again, someone who in essence is so much like her on the policy issues, Hillary would find herself fighting herself.

O'REILLY: It would be interesting. But I think Hillary might take your advice—if Ms. Pirro does declare—she might say, "I'm going to run for president."

Now, anyone can miss on a prediction. For instance, after our last book was published, we were certain O'Reilly would kill us—most likely staging it to look like a freak elk-hunting accident or a black-market Hello Kitty buy gone bad. But that just made sense. And it certainly wasn't based on our own vindictive desires.

But Morris's and O'Reilly's fever dream? Well, let's just leave the land of delusion and travel forward in time eight months, where the sky is still blue, O'Reilly's still an idiot, and Hillary is still a force with which to be reckoned.

On December 21, 2005, the Associated Press reported: "After weeks of pressure from her own party to drop out, Republican Jeanine Pirro abandoned her struggling campaign to unseat Sen. Hillary Rodham Clinton and announced Wednesday that she will run for New York attorney general instead."[1]

A Quinnipiac University poll released around that time showed that Clinton was ahead of Pirro by a margin of 62 percent to 30 percent. Now, Morris and O'Reilly might consider that a "competitive race," but where we come from that's called "a landslide."

So what we saw from Morris and O'Reilly was not analysis or even honest speculation but merely wishful thinking. By that we mean the kind of wishful thinking that pimply faced high schoolers have about Angelina Jolie. So once again, Morris and O'Reilly were faced with the realization that their fantasies were just that—fantasies. And now they were left embarrassed and, let's face it, a little sticky.

You Say Tomato, I Say Ketchup Ball

When Morris isn't sublimating his sexual dysfunctions through error-filled, misogynist political analysis, he can be found expounding some of the most blatant, bizarre spin on Fox (and that's saying something).

On March 16, 2006, as sectarian violence continued to grow in Iraq, the media tried to put a name to the ongoing turmoil. Terms like "insurgency," "sectarian violence," and even "civil war" were bandied about. Of course, Morris had a more creative term for it:

ALAN COLMES: You call the bombings of mosques, you call the targeting of civilians by some of the Shiites, you call the corpses being dragged through the street, you call that a negotiation?

MORRIS: Yep. I sure do, Alan. I didn't invent the Iraqi style. You know, they say divorce, Italian style? This is negotiation, Iraqi style. What's going on right now is the Shiites and the Sunnis are trying to get the upper hand militarily in the street so as to get the upper hand in the coalition government.

Why did Dick stop at calling it a negotiation? Why not an elegant cotillion . . . with hand grenades?

Of course, Morris's characterization is not just absurd—it's insulting and racist. The implication is that the Iraqis are not civilized like us, with our well-manicured lawns, two cars in every garage, and sexy-toed whore in every shed.

Then again, maybe Morris is just trying to influence the vernacular, like when the Bush administration tried to change "suicide bomber" to "homicide bomber" and O'Reilly tried to change "liberals" to "S-Ps," "conservatives" to "T-Warriors," and "loofah" to "falafel."

You can almost see it—a redneck is sitting in a dive bar in Montana when he walks up to a guy who appears to be checkin' out his old lady, and says, "Let's you and me have ourselves a little negotiation . . . *Iraqi style.*"

Just Half the Facts, Ma'am

The mission of the turncoats is to forward conservative talking points while maintaining at least the appearance of fair-mindedness.

Dick Morris's "former Clinton adviser" designation works beautifully to this effect: "Hey look, even this Clintonista thinks the Democrats have gone off the deep end! Boy, they must really be out of touch!"

Yes, and it might work even better if Morris weren't a slimy political operative who lies all the time.

From the August 29, 2006, edition of *Hannity & Colmes:*

MORRIS: And [the American public] see Iraq as unsolvable; they think that on balance we probably should have gone in, maybe, but what are you going to do about it? But the PATRIOT Act, the NSA wiretaps, the seizure of bank deposits, data mining, they all support that and the Democrats oppose it.

There is, of course, a glitch in Morris's argument here. We like to refer to it as "a hole so big, Alan Colmes was able to point it out."

COLMES: That's an interesting theory, Dick. I want to talk to you about Kerry in a second, but first what you just said about Democrats opposing wiretapping and data mining, they don't. They oppose doing it without a court warrant.

MORRIS: Yeah, okay, okay.

COLMES: They oppose doing it without oversight over the presidency, that's all.

MORRIS: Take it on your—take it on your own terms, and I don't want to get into a debate.

COLMES: But that's the issue.

MORRIS: We did that two weeks ago on the show.

Ah, we didn't realize mid-August was fact-based analysis week on Fox. Apparently, they're back to their regularly scheduled deliberate misinformation and half-truths.

Of course, what Colmes said is irrefutable. Morris knows it

and can't deny it. He was caught spouting dishonest talking points in the service of God-knows-what personal grudge and has nothing left to say.

The "I don't want to get into a debate" line is especially rich. You're on f-ing *Hannity & Colmes,* you twit. It's a debate show. That's all it is. It's not a particularly good debate show, but the point is it's basically a forum for debating politics and little else.

If you want to go on a program whose purpose is to spread lies based on nothing but false premises and faulty analysis, try *The O'Reilly Factor.*

PART II: PAT CADDELL

ON THE AUGUST 22, 2005, edition of *The Big Story,* John Gibson introduced his guest Pat Caddell, placing a curious emphasis on Caddell's political background:

> **GIBSON:** As we have been discussing, the war in Iraq has taken a huge toll on the president's poll numbers. You can be sure the Democrats will try to figure out how to take advantage of that in 2006 and, of course, in 2008.
>
> But there is a serious rift within the Democratic Party over the issue. Here to talk about it, former Democratic pollster Pat Caddell—former in the sense that you're not working, doing anybody's polls now.

But just to stress his point, Gibson added, "But he's still a Democrat and he's still a pollster."

For the record, Caddell was a pollster for Jimmy Carter. So he isn't necessarily a Democrat any more than the guys who felt up Jenna Bush back in high school are Republicans.

Indeed, Caddell sees nearly every appearance on Fox as a chance to criticize the Democrats and commend the Republicans. On this night, he took the Dems to task over their Iraq War criticism, claiming they never "laid out and said, this is our plan. This is what we would do. I mean, that is one of the reasons John Kerry was not elected president, because of this belief."

He continued:

> Listen, so much of the Democratic Party is waiting for the deus ex machina to deliver them to power. And what you—when you don't have—when you start abandoning principles and simply look for the tactical gain, you have got a problem. And that's part of a problem in the party. We are having a debate over tactics here. We are not having a debate on principles.

Now, whether the Democrats have abandoned their principles in favor of parochial, short-term political interests is a matter of interpretation. It could be that one of their principles is "Next time, let's not just invade a country for no reason and see what happens."

But as a Democrat himself, Caddell should have known that the Republican caricature of the Democrats as a party with "no plan" on Iraq was at best an oversimplification.

For instance, here's John Kerry in a speech the *Washington Post* published on its Web site in September 2004 under the mystifyingly vague headline "Kerry Lays Out Iraq Plan":

> All across this country, people ask me and others, what we should do now every stop of the way. From the first time I spoke about this in the Senate, I have set out a specific set of recommendations from day one, from the first debate until this moment. I have set out specific steps of how we should not and how we should proceed.

This was followed by several specific recommendations as to what the president should do in Iraq. Sounds like a plan to us.

Republicans might not have liked it, as it departed from their own plan, which was basically, "let's keep doing the same stuff and hope Jesus comes flying down one of these days with an Uzi full of ass-kickin' love," but it *was* a plan, even if it didn't resonate with the electorate. After all, what was Kerry supposed to say he'd recommend when it came to that escalating mess? "Hey, guys. You're kicking ass over there. But could you kick ass a little faster?"

So when Caddell says the Democrats are not having a debate on principles, one wonders what he means. That they shouldn't call a spade a spade when it comes to Iraq? To our minds, saying President Bush is a hopeless dipshit fuckup who does almost everything wrong is a pretty fair organizing principle.

The following night, Gibson read a letter from a viewer: "On yesterday's discussion on the conflicted Democrats, Gary Mottola in Brooklyn, New York: 'Pat Caddell is so reasonable and honest that I'm surprised that the party of Howard Dean, Hillary Clinton and Ted Kennedy still allow him to be a member.'"

Finally! A reasonable Democrat. One who clearly states that the party lacks a plan and has abandoned its principles. Oh, Pat. If only there were more like you.

And on the Left, We Have Jerry Falwell

On the January 27, 2006, installment of *Hannity & Colmes,* we were treated to this lead-in: "We continue now with Ann Coulter, and joining us is Democratic pollster and old friend, Pat Caddell." Dear Lord, why not just bring on Medusa and Judas?

HANNITY: Can I ask, do you really think it's good for the Democratic Party to go through hearings like they did, get the negative reaction of the American people. Just prior to that, you had Dean saying we can't win the war, Kerry saying we're terrorizing women and children in Iraq. Do you really think the face of the party now has got to be Kerry, Kennedy, and Hillary?

CADDELL: I'll tell you, I sometimes feel like my party, the way it was once described of the liberal Republicans, the people who shoot their own wounded.

So you've got Ann Coulter on as a guest and to counter her you bring on a guy who claims the Democrats are people who "shoot their own wounded."

Can anyone else see how farcical this is? Why not just bring on the CEO of R.J. Reynolds to rebut the radical prosmoking agenda of Philip Morris?

This is typical of Fox thinking, of course, but that doesn't make it right. When a guest is introduced as a Democrat and proceeds to spout right-wing propaganda, it's just dishonest—like when O'Reilly goes on *The Tonight Show* to plug a book and acts moderately sane for nearly eight consecutive minutes.

Still, Caddell *is* more liberal than Ann Coulter.

Poached Democrats à L'Orange

On August 7, 2006, Alan Colmes and Pat Caddell discussed the rise of challenger Ned Lamont in the Connecticut Democratic senatorial primary.

While it turned out that Democratic primary voters actually preferred Lamont to incumbent Democrat Joe Lieberman before voters statewide reelected Lieberman as an independent, Caddell was nevertheless sure they were poised to make a huge mistake:

COLMES: Pat Caddell, look, you know people say, "Oh, the death of the Democratic Party, if Lamont wins it will be the antiwar party." Lieberman's saying Democrats are strong on defense, you don't have to be on the far left. You're strong on defense if you're a Democrat even if you don't agree with the war. You can be antiwar, feel this is the wrong war, the wrong place, the wrong time, and be strong on defense.

CADDELL: Well, that's possible, Al, but that's not what this is about. Look, Joe Lieberman, who's not necessarily my favorite person but, my God, he has a certain amount of integrity. Six years ago he was by acclamation nominated to be the vice-presidential candidate of the Democratic Party and tomorrow a whole part of the party wants to purge him. And that's just the beginning and we're ninety days away from a very critical election and the Democratic Party is going to start eating its own? I mean, this is ludicrous!

It's nice to know that when the Democrats shoot their own wounded, they're willing to eat them, too. What's more, they use every part of the Democrat, including the bones for a delicious, zesty soup stock.

Of course, it's also possible that Lieberman was out of touch with his own party, and that his support of the Bush administration on Iraq policy was not just out of synch with Democratic principles but a little loony as well.

Obviously, the war in Iraq was a deal-breaker for the majority of Democrats in Connecticut. Lieberman didn't see it. And Caddell apparently didn't want to.

Amor Republicanos de Homos

When Caddell isn't challenging Colmes, he can often be found seeking common ground with Hannity. It's particularly entertaining when he steps up as the Cassandra for his party, predicting utter doom if Democrats don't start thinking more like Republicans.

Of course, Hannity is more than willing to serve as his Greek chorus. Indeed, it might be great theater if it weren't scripted like a Log Cabin Republican soap opera . . .

Cut to low-angle shot framed by swaying palm fronds and a bright necklace of stars festooned against a deep indigo sky (Sean Hannity and Pat Caddell walk hand in hand as the sun sets on a Malibu beach).

HANNITY: I see the Democrats imploding with this extremism.

CADDELL: (eyes downcast, then turning to meet Hannity's gaze) So do I. My concern is we are not standing for something.

HANNITY: (clasps Caddell's hands into his own) Bingo.

CADDELL: We're haunted by—what we do is wallow in our

hatred. And it is self-destructive. The fact of the matter is, there's many things to criticize here, and it could go on for hours, but you've got to have some kind of reasonable, legitimate debate in this country. And we're not having it.

Camera pulls to a tight shot (They kiss.)

Curtain. (Adapted from a March 31, 2006, transcript of *Hannity & Colmes*.)

PART III: ZELL MILLER

WHEN DIXIECRAT SENATOR Zell Miller announced he would support President Bush in his 2004 reelection bid, there was a collective creaming of the pantaloons over at the Fox News Channel.

On September 2, 2004, Bill O'Reilly invited Dick Morris on his show to discuss Miller's speech at the Republican National Convention.

Let's just put it this way: It's really friggin' scary when Dick Morris comes off as the voice of reason.

MORRIS: Last night I thought was just over the top. I think it was too negative. These people liked it . . .

O'REILLY: Loved it.

MORRIS: . . . but the voters kinda feel maybe Miller has a grudge or something. I don't think . . .

O'REILLY: But it was so entertaining.

MORRIS: Well, it was if you're a party faithful.

O'REILLY: I think anybody would be. I'm not rooting for anybody. I've been out watching this guy going boom, boom, boom.

MORRIS: And I know Zell. [He] was a client. He's a great guy.

O'REILLY: I believe what Gingrich said is true. He was genuinely angry and wanted to show it.

O'Reilly wasn't rooting for anybody? That's like saying the fans in the end zone at the Oakland Coliseum might secretly be pulling for the Broncos.

Of course, given his Zen-like detachment, it's something of a puzzle what O'Reilly found so entertaining about Miller's speech. It must have been when he said the Democratic Party was "motivated more by partisan politics than by national security." That was entertaining for sure.

Or it could have been when Miller said of John Kerry, "As a senator, he voted to weaken our military. And nothing shows that more sadly and more clearly than his vote this year to deny protective armor for our troops in harm's way, far away."[2] That was a hoot.

Of course, we thought O'Reilly hated those bomb-throwers. You know, those dishonest weasels who toss around defamatory remarks based on quotes and facts taken out of context.

He can't stand Michael Moore or Howard Dean. So why does he find Miller so entertaining?

Guess.

Even Dick Morris—whose Machiavellian outlook would have made Lee Atwater scratch his own face off—thought the speech was "over the top," "too negative," and only appealed to the "party faithful." Oh, but not Bill. He found this pack of distortions "entertaining."

Oh, and in case you're wondering what an opportunistic two-faced liar Zell Miller is, here's what he said about John Kerry in March of 2001:

> My job tonight is an easy one: to present to you one of this nation's authentic heroes, one of this party's best-known and greatest leaders—and a good friend.
>
> He was once a lieutenant governor, but he didn't stay in that office sixteen years, like someone else I know. It just took two years before the people of Massachusetts moved him into the United States Senate in 1984.
>
> In his sixteen years in the Senate, John Kerry has fought

against government waste and worked hard to bring some accountability to Washington.

Early in his Senate career in 1986, John signed on to the Gramm-Rudman-Hollings Deficit Reduction Bill, and he fought for balanced budgets before it was considered politically correct for Democrats to do so.

John has worked to *strengthen our military,* reform public education, boost the economy and protect the environment. *Business Week* magazine named him one of the top pro-technology legislators and made him a member of its "Digital Dozen" [emphasis added].

Gee, sounds like Zell Miller might be one of them no-good flip-floppers.

In December of 2004, Miller announced that he'd be joining Fox News as a contributor. It was as shocking and disillusioning as the next O'Reilly sexual harassment suit.

Eat Your Vegetables and Grow up to Be a Big Fat Liar

When *Fox News Live* anchor E. D. Hill wrote her book *Going Places: How America's Best and Brightest Got Started Down the Road of Life,* she included life lessons from luminaries such as Dolly Parton, Randy Owen (of the popular country band Alabama), Ronnie Milsap, and, of course, Zell Miller.

She learned a lot from Zell, as have we all.

Here's what she told Fox's John Gibson on the November 3, 2005, edition of *The Big Story:*

as he is growing up, his mom tells him, "Zell, if you want your dessert, you have got to eat your spinach." Didn't matter what she was talking about, "If you want dessert, you've got to eat your spinach."

And what that means is, you know, we all want the good stuff in life. We want the big job, we want the great relationship, but are we willing to do the things we need to do to get there? Or do we just expect it to be given to us, without tackling the smaller jobs, without, you know, working hard?

If you want to go to a great college, you have got to study hard. If you want a great, love-of-your-life relationship, you have got to work at it. And so that was the whole moral of that story, was if you want your dessert, you have got to eat the spinach.

We don't know what's worse, the triteness of the saying itself, or the fact that E. D. felt the need to explain it.

Then again, this could be a rare opportunity for the spinach industry. They ought to approach the former senator about an endorsement deal. If there's anything that might get consumers to forget about *E. coli*, it's Zell Miller.

NOTES

1. Pirro's campaign for attorney general would eventually be dogged by several seamy allegations, including that she had eavesdropped on her husband and was seen giggling at a New York City cop's funeral. She lost.

2. This criticism of Kerry's vote on body armor, which the administration exploited to great effect in the 2004 election, is a blatant and deliberate distortion. According to a September 3, 2004, *Washington Post* article:

> President Bush, Cheney and (Zell) Miller faulted Kerry for voting against body armor for troops in Iraq. But much of the funding for body armor was added to the bill by House Democrats, not the administration, and Kerry's vote against the entire bill was rooted in a dispute with the administration over how to pay for $20 billion earmarked for reconstruction of Iraq.

> In short, Kerry wanted to pay for the appropriation by rolling back tax cuts to the wealthy, whereas Bush did not. Kerry's "no" vote, then, was part of a political negotiation, not—as Miller surely knew—a callous ploy to leave our soldiers exposed. Indeed, President Bush himself had threatened to veto the entire $87 billion supplemental appropriation if his version of the bill didn't pass.

> One can also fairly wonder why President Bush would send our troops into harm's way without the appropriate equipment to begin with.

> Either Miller knew this and still agreed to spread lies about his own party's candidate, or he's too stupid to understand it, which means he's also too stupid to be allowed to give influential speeches on national television.

14

THE ISLAND OF MISFIT EXPERTS

IN THE PREVIOUS chapter, we looked at the "Democrats" Fox relies on to create the illusion of balance in its programming.

Of course, when you're as fair as Fox News, you can't just let crazy left-wingers like Zell Miller and Dick Morris monopolize the discourse. You need some ecological balance—someone willing to step up and club the baby seals when they breed out of control.

Much as Fox unearths the most reactionary, right-wing Democrats you'd ever find outside of a Reconstruction-era Klan meeting, it regularly invites conservative guests whose clear but unstated role is to make the network seem restrained by comparison.

They're kind of like the bad vaudevillian comedian who uses a ventriloquist doll to mouth his crudest, most controversial jokes. The dummy says things the comic could never say, because he knows he'd be hooted off the stage. But somehow when the dummy says it, it comes off as cute and funny.

That, in a nutshell, is why Ann Coulter, Michelle Malkin, and Bo Dietl appear on Fox as often as they do.

BO DON'T KNOW DIDDLY

RICHARD "BO" DIETL is a highly decorated former New York City policeman who currently runs a private investigation firm.

While he may be a great source on a story about a missing college student, we're not sure what the hell he's supposed to know about foreign policy.

It's difficult to describe Bo in print. He's basically Andy Sipowicz without the polish. Indeed, we're guessing at least 50 percent of his gray matter originated as either sweet custard or raspberry filling.

Here's how Neil Cavuto described him on the April 25, 2005, edition of *Your World:*

> You know, I've had a theory about my friend Bo Dietl for years. He comes across as this rough, tough guy, some critics say a not-so-bright guy—that he mixes words and syllables. I do that. Anyway, he does. But my theory on Bo is this. He does so deliberately, so that you underestimate him, maybe even dismiss him.

Now, we don't underestimate Bo Dietl just because he makes Yogi Berra sound like Christopher Hitchens. No, we underestimate him because Fox has taken a workaday former New York detective who is well-versed in the inner life of the NYPD and consulted him like he was Madeleine Friggin' Albright.

On July 7, 2006, Dietl drew on his keen understanding of international law and weighed in on the detention of enemy combatants:

> I think that this liberal bunch of people out there worrying about these people over here in Gizmo prison down there, worrying about a guy being blindfolded, are they worried about those poor people that were going to work this morning to

make money for their family that were blown apart, probably children also? Did they worry about them?

We shouldn't worry so much about these murderers that are over there in Guantanamo Bay. We should worry about crushing them out, because under their philosophy, under bin Laden's philosophy of Al Qaeda and this philosophy, you cannot coexist with them. They want us wiped out. So, we should wipe them out first, no matter what we got to do. Intelligence.

We're not quite sure why Bo threw the word "intelligence" in there, other than for irony's sake. (At best, it conveys the misplaced pride of a four-year-old child who has successfully inscribed the word "poop" on his mother's dining room wall.)

But while Guantanamo Bay has often been referred to in short-hand as *Gitmo*, it is rarely called *Gizmo*. So why is Fox soliciting expert analysis from someone who would need to clap erasers after school for extra credit to pass a ninth-grade civics class?

Well, his view that everyone at Gizmo is guilty and we need to simply "wipe them out" fits the prevailing Fox wisdom like a glove. In other words, "you appear to be an idiot—here's the washroom key."

On the October 8, 2005, edition of *Geraldo at Large*, Geraldo asked Bo to elaborate on his call for the racial profiling of Muslims:

RIVERA: You're talking about a kind of profiling, not that I have anything against it, but would you be random-searching grandmas here with their baby strollers?

DIETL: You have to realize one thing. We have rights. At this point right now people are trying to kill us and kill our democracy the way we know it. Our rights have to be a little supsendi-tated, you know what I'm saying, Geraldo?

Um, does anybody?

Of course, one wonders what the Founding Fathers would have

thought if they knew that the civil liberties they fought and died for might simply be supsenditated one day. Dietl continued:

> We have to realize that I don't mind them searching me. I'll feel more comfortable if I am going to go on a subway train if I have a bag and they search it good, at least I know they are searching bags.
>
> I [inaudible] about their rights now, because they're coming here. They were here before. This is their target and they're going to come back and they are they are going to do something [inaudible] Geraldo, that they would come and they would put two plancs into the World Trade Center like that. Let's stop being complacent. They're coming back here. Let's band together and let's do what we've got to do so it doesn't happen again.

Now, Bo's suggestion that we suspend civil liberties until there are no acts of terrorism in the world is an interesting one. The "let's do what we've got to do" plan may seem rather open-ended and all-encompassing, but we have to hand it to Fox for bringing on a no-nonsense former cop to lay it out for us.

Still, Dietl is at his best when he goes even further afield—say, into the realm of comparative religion. Here he was on the August 14, 2006, edition of *Your World,* doing his best St. Augustine of Hippo impression:

> And Neil, the bottom line is, [Islam] is a Johnny-come-lately religion. Christians and Jews have been around for sixteen hundred years, fifteen hundred years before. When they're having a religion talking about killing people, I think we should reevaluate people who pray to someone who wants to kill you.

Hey, everyone, Bo looked up a fact! And got it wrong! Christianity actually preceded Islam by 600 years while Judaism preceded Islam by around 1,800 years.

Now, you can certainly make the argument that Scientology is a Johnny-come-lately religion, but Islam? He's kidding, right?

Then again, Fox has always been a fairly safe haven for Islam-bashing. Certainly, nearly every Fox pundit and contributor has made (as has Dietl himself) a crack about the "seventy-two virgins" that some would-be Muslim martyrs believe await them in heaven.

Yes, what a silly group of people those Muslims are. It's far more likely that a semiskilled Jewish woodworker and itinerant preacher who was executed by a preindustrial Mediterranean empire for sedition two thousand years ago is somehow responsible for the ready conveyance of an oblong leather ball across a series of parallel chalk lines in defiance of eleven men in differently colored jerseys.

But before you start cracking on the Koran for its violence, you might want to read the Old Testament, which, to be honest, makes *The Texas Chainsaw Massacre* look like an episode of *Eight Is Enough*.[1]

And if you're going to argue that the oldest religion is the most valid, then we all lose to Hinduism anyway.

IF EVER OH EVER A WITCH THERE WAS . . .

FOX NEWS LOVES Ann Coulter. We don't mean they love booking her on their programs. We mean they love her. Like a CEO loves his mistress.

They have no intention of marrying Ann and giving her her own show, but they like keeping her around as their whore.

And why not? She does everything the wife won't do—the things that, in their cocktail party–fueled reveries, they can usually only fantasize about.

She fulfills every sick, twisted need and then some. Indeed, when she released her latest antiliberal polemic, *Godless*, it was the golden shower that Murdoch, Cavuto, O'Reilly, Hannity, Gibson, and all the rest had been aching for.

So despite finding herself in the center of a media maelstrom over her claim that four 9/11 widows who had fought for the creation of the 9/11 Commission were "witches" and "harpies" who were "enjoying their husbands' deaths," Coulter reached deep within and found the energy to re-spew her bile on the June 8, 2006, *Hannity & Colmes.*

After Democratic strategist Laura Schwartz said, "the everyday reality is that these women did not seek their celebrity status; they're not trying to hang onto fifteen minutes of fame," Coulter responded like a caged baboon about two minutes before you pull the Thorazine dart out of its neck:

COULTER: They absolutely did.

COLMES: They didn't seek to be celebrities.

SCHWARTZ: Absolutely not.

COLMES: Do you think for one second, Ann . . .

SCHWARTZ: What? They willed their husbands to be attacked?

COULTER: Did they just trip into that *Vanity Fair* photo?

COLMES: Let me ask you this. Ann, do you think they—for one second—these women wouldn't give up whatever notoriety . . .

COULTER: They just woke up one day and suddenly they're on the *Today* show.

COLMES: Please answer my—please answer my question.

COULTER: They didn't ask for that.

COLMES: Hold on one second. Decaf, next time. Do you think these women, for one second . . .

COULTER: You're saying crazy things.

COLMES: Decaf, please. Calm down. Do you think for one second these women would not give up every piece of celebrity and notoriety they have to have their husbands back?

COULTER: Oh, I don't know. At this point, to give up two million dollars . . .

COLMES: To have their husbands back.

COULTER: . . . and to go back to cooking meals and not be . . .

SCHWARTZ: Oh, my God, what are you saying, Ann?

COLMES: They wouldn't do that to have their husbands back?

SCHWARTZ: These are women that had husbands . . .

COULTER: . . . appearing in *Vanity Fair*. They're clearly enjoying their celebrity status.

COLMES: They would not give up—I want to be clear on this. They would not give this up to get their husbands back?

COULTER: I don't know. I can't read into their hearts. But it isn't as obvious to me as it apparently is to you.

COLMES: Really?

COULTER: They're taking limos around . . .

SCHWARTZ: Oh, Ann, you were never in these marriages . . .

COLMES: You've got to be kidding me.

Now, what's more likely here? That four women who suffered through one of the most tragic and heartbreaking things a human being can endure are delighted the tragedy occurred, or that a woman known for selling her soul and integrity for cash is projecting her own sick outlook on an innocent group of widows?

Seriously, what is Ann accusing these women of? Manipulating the media and engaging in ghoulish exploitation of a tragedy without their union cards?

But as head of the vile media whore guild, Coulter was simply not going to wilt in the face of criticism. Nor was Fox willing to let a good thing go.

These accusations were exactly what Fox wanted. They needed someone to come on the air and say that any and all dissenters—even those whose heartache and indignation were unassailable—were somehow beneath reproach.

And to prove it, they would invite Coulter on the air numerous times after the release of her book. Indeed, over the next twelve weeks, Ann would appear on *Your World with Neil Cavuto* no less than nine times.

For instance, on July 20, 2006, Cavuto conducted separate interviews on the Israeli-Hezbollah conflict. So, who would his producers invite on to lend insight to the discussion? If we had to guess, hmmm, let's just say former Secretary of State Warren Christopher and, for a wild card, maybe Avi Bell, a professor at Bar Ilan University in Israel and an advocate of Israel's right of self-defense. Yeah, we don't know who he is either. It took us ten seconds to find his name on Google, but the point is he's an expert of sorts on the issue—not a lunkhead former cop known for his clumsy malapropisms or a screeching Teutonic banshee whose face would be more at home on the bow of a Viking longship than in your living room.

But no. The two people Cavuto invited to shed light on the ongoing turmoil in the Middle East were, of course, well-known international relations experts Ann Coulter and Bo Dietl. (Dietl, incidentally, suggested in his segment that Muslim Turks are conspiring to "overpopulize" Germany).

In probing the depths of Coulter's expertise, Neil managed to assemble the six most unnerving syllables to ever pass human lips: President Ann Coulter.

CAVUTO: President Ann Coulter has a situation now where the head of Hezbollah says, "We'll release your prisoners if you release ours. We can start talking."

COULTER: I think the point from both Hezbollah and Hamas has to be: Are you going to give up on your single-minded quest to drive Israel off the face of the map? Because otherwise this is

just going to keep going, keep going, keep going. I mean, that's
the point. Israel keeps giving up territory in return for—can we
please just have some land here? And as long as the Islamic terrorists who are of a piece, of what we're fighting against, refuse
to acknowledge that, I mean, that isn't an agreement worth
happening. It's just a matter of time of waiting until—until the
next soldiers get captured or the next bomb gets launched. And
that's what I'd say right after my first act in office, which would
be to deport all liberals.

CAVUTO: Go for it. That would be a very interesting . . .

COULTER: Number one. Then my deal with Israel.

You see, like any good whore, Ann gave her sugar daddy everything he wanted, and a happy ending to boot.

Then again, sometimes they like to bring her in just for an
afternoon quickie. Indeed, sometimes they simply need a voice
that will jibe perfectly with their own talking points.

On August 24, 2006, *Your World with Neil Cavuto* guest host
Brenda Buttner announced that Ann, once again, was in the hiz-
zouse: "The NSA wiretapping program, Gitmo, the PATRIOT
Act, the war in Iraq—most Democrats are against all those. So
Ann Coulter wants to know exactly which parts of the War on
Terror are Democrats for? She's author of the best-seller *Godless*.
Hi, Ann. Thanks for being here."

After a brief greeting, Buttner continued: "Well, you do a great
job in your editorial of—kind of listing it all out, and when you
do, it's very interesting to see—they're really good at saying what
they're against, aren't they?"

What followed was the usual list of distortions: Democrats are
against the NSA spying program, Democrats reject the PATRIOT
Act, Democrats have no plan to fight terrorism, women with
Adam's apples are not necessarily trannies, and so on.

For example, Coulter said, "They're against the NSA spying
program, listening, or following phone calls made from Al Qaeda

phone numbers," without noting that Democrats simply oppose the use of *warrantless* wiretaps.

But as Coulter chirped away, Buttner cooed and giggled and declined even a perfunctory challenge to her sham analysis.

Hey, if nothing else, it's nice to see that Fox's resident whore is willing to do girl-on-girl as well.

MALKINAVELLIAN

MICHELLE MALKIN IS often introduced as a Fox News contributor. A better title might be "associate media whore."

Of course, her favorite john these days is Big Daddy Bill O'Reilly.

If ever O'Reilly needs validation, Malkin is eager to come on his show and regurgitate his favorite themes and talking points. She's the Lennie to his George, the Ron Palillo to his Travolta, the Madame to his Wayland Flowers, the tahini to his falafel.

Indeed, Malkin uses well-worn O'Reilly terms such as "smear merchant," refers to liberals as "unhinged," and generally spouts far-right misinformation on issues ranging from immigration to media bias to not-whore-being.

On July 13, 2005, she blinked twice and appeared on *The Factor*, poised to put a pleasin' on her master:

> Well, when it comes to coverage of terrorism, the BBC has as much credibility as *The Daily Show* here in the United States. And they've really made themselves the laughingstock.
>
> And their behavior in the past week, especially immediately after the 7/7 attacks has really, really exposed them for the unfair, unbalanced, and unreliable journalistic enterprise that a lot of people in Britain have come to realize they are.

Now, a little background. O'Reilly has frequently dismissed *The Daily Show* (which has not been shy about mocking him), claiming the program is primarily watched by "stoned slackers" and "dopey college kids," even though *Daily Show* viewers have been shown to be better educated than *O'Reilly Factor* viewers and better informed on election issues than cable news viewers generally.[2] Not to mention that the median age of *Factor* viewers is roughly twice that of *Daily Show* viewers.

So while O'Reilly's viewers may be less informed and less educated than Jon Stewart's viewers, at least they're near the end of their sad road.

Malkin's *Daily Show* crack, then, was the equivalent of dirty pillow talk. It was just what Bill needed to ease his buffeted ego after being intellectually bested by a network that airs *Mannequin 2: On the Move* twice a day.

Still, O'Reilly's decrepit audience needs something to hate other than the British media and funny Jews, so on May 30, 2006, Malkin appeared on *The Factor* to discuss San Francisco, the big liberal thorn in Bill's paw:

> They are really on another planet. And I think if you look at the unique history of San Francisco, it became an epicenter for hippies and socialists and all sorts of anti-American riffraff starting from the fifties and through the sixties, the Beat Generation made it its home. Haight-Ashbury, the Castro district and those hippies took over the city. I mean, you really do have the nutballs running the asylum in San Francisco. They took over all the power centers and the public institutions.
>
> And they kicked out normal Americans in the middle class. They've made it completely unaffordable for people with regular values, values like you and I share and most of your audience share. And what's left are these folks who hate the military, hate Bush, have nothing but contempt for our traditions and our history, and then blame the messenger when somebody turns the mirror on them.

Now, the second half of that quote is so bizarre it almost defies elaboration. Apparently, in Michelle's head, the San Francisco housing market operates in a bubble where the laws of supply and demand no longer exist and where Realtors now accept only specially minted gay doubloons.

Yes, in Malkin's world, a U.S. city of more than three-quarters of a million people all got together one day and said, "Hey, we should start hiking up the prices of our houses to keep out conservative middle America! We don't want folks selling their trailers in Alabama and buying up our Victorian townhouses. So what do you say we price a 1,300-square-foot two-bedroom in Pacific Heights at a million-two and go from there? That should keep out Ma and Pa Kettle."

But could Malkin actually believe the absurdities that come out of her mouth? Or maybe—and this is much more likely the case—she assumes that *Factor* viewers are so obtuse that she can rewrite both economic laws and the laws of human nature, and no one will notice. (And we're not even going to get into the fact that she considers herself and O'Reilly to be "people with regular values.")

Still, she loves to please her daddy, as any whore would. So she spouts back his talking points and, with her "hate the military" reference, soothes his harried conscience in the wake of his controversial terrorists-should-fly-into-the-Coit-Tower plan.

Charming.

And what a fine example of Malkin's and O'Reilly's "regular values."

NOTES

1. If you don't believe us, check out 2 Kings 2:23–24 just for starters.
2. According to a September 2004 CNN.com story, "*Daily Show* viewers are 78 percent more likely than the average adult to have four or more years of college education, while O'Reilly's audience is only 24 percent more likely to have that much schooling."

    Also, according to a 2004 Annenberg Public Policy Center survey, *Daily Show* viewers were better informed on election issues than national news viewers and newspaper readers.

THE CASE STUDIES

▼

15

A FOXHUNT FOR GAYWAD COWBOYS

MUCH **AS FOX** News hearkens back to the good old days when men were men, women were women, and queers either stayed in the closet or played rhinestone-encrusted pianos in sequined hotpants while publicly affirming their deep, abiding fondness for vaginal intercourse, we also, to some degree, bemoan the modern balkanization of America's progay and anti-gay factions.

Don't get us wrong. As authors, we're squarely in the progay camp. Indeed, we're both dedicated political progressives, Joseph is openly gay, and, though heterosexual, Tom ain't exactly burying the needle on the ole' masculinity meter.

But these days, there are just too many anti-gay folks masquerading as something else. Indeed, there seem to be at least twelve distinct and descending categories of people in this country when it comes to gayfriendliness:

1. Homosexuals who are free and open about their homosexuality and who feel no regret or shame about their sexual orientation.

2. Heterosexual men who are secure in their own sexuality and see homosexuality as a legitimate lifestyle choice on a par with heterosexuality. They favor gay adoption, gay marriage, and free and open access to the mythical enchanted underground lesbian fortress of solitude in northwest Greenland.

3. Heterosexual women who love gay men, and who consider there to be a certain cachet in counting them among their friends. (Indeed, the popular culture features numerous examples of the classic straight woman/gay friend dyad, including Grace Adler and Will Truman from *Will & Grace*, Carrie and Stanford from *Sex and the City*, Julia Roberts and Rupert Everett from *My Best Friend's Wedding*, and Liza Minnelli and pretty much anyone she dates.)

4. Clueless older women who wonder why that charming, funny man who planned their daughter's wedding can't find a nice girl to settle down with.

5. Men and women who consistently betray a squeamishness about homosexuality, but nevertheless concede that gays should be afforded a modicum of respect and granted certain minimum legal protections in exchange for shutting their big gay traps about their sexual orientation.

6. Men and women who say gays should be left alone, as long as they don't try to gay-ify their kids or plead for special rights, such as the right to rent homes and apartments, work in harassment-free environments, or walk down the street without being hit in the head by a Slurpee.

7. Closeted gays and bisexuals who are so deeply ashamed of their sexual preferences that they feel the need to marginalize every gay icon that comes down the pike, from George Michael to Ellen DeGeneres to Tinky-Winky. They think homosexuality is sick, wrong, and a threat to all normal, red-blooded American males, such as that handsome young gentleman from *Who's the Boss?*

8. Religiously motivated, predominantly fundamentalist men and women who profess to hate the sin but love the

sinner and who decry the perfidious homosexual agenda
that's being forced down their and their neighbors'
throats.

(Of course, when confronted with other biblical proscrip-
tions, such as the eating of shellfish, they will point out that
(a) unlike homosexuality, these other activities are not
heavily promoted by well-funded, well-organized interest
groups endeavoring to foist their lifestyle on the culture,
and (b) they can't argue with you right now because they're
late for their weekly prayer fellowship at Red Lobster.)

9. Unreconstructed rednecks who are completely out in the
open about their bigotry and who tell virulent anti-gay
jokes, implicitly or explicitly condone gay-bashing, become
visibly agitated in the presence of homosexuals, and make
no apologies for their hatefulness.
10. People who wave "God Hates Fags" signs at the funerals of
AIDS victims.
11. The KKK circa 1870.
12. John Gibson.

Of course, Fox is well aware of the increasingly nuanced attitudes toward homosexuality in this country and so they're loath to
simply break out the playground banter on the air. What you get
instead is a thick, rich nougat of homophobia served up with a
thin candy coating of tolerance.

Indeed, if you monitor Fox for any length of time, it becomes
abundantly clear where its allegiances lie. Top NSA code breakers
employing sophisticated decryption technology would have a
tougher time completing a *Highlights for Children* word search than
most viewers have in deciphering Fox's anti-gay agenda.

So when the critically acclaimed *Brokeback Mountain* became an
unlikely cultural phenomenon in the winter of 2005/2006, gar-
nering eight Oscar nominations, posting robust box-office numbers, and generating positive word of mouth from sea to fabulous
sea, Fox started spinning like Paul Lynde's head at a Greek naval
barracks.

Of course, considering that it broadcasts to numerous countries and all fifty states and not just Trent Lott's dad's house, Fox naturally had to dial its homophobia down to the level of an Alabama skinhead with Tourette's.

Oh, but it was still a wonder to behold.

SOMETHING WICKED THIS WAY CUMS

BEFORE YOU START reading the next excerpt, grab a piece of paper and a pencil. First, draw two circles. In the first circle write "bombings and assassinations," in the second circle, "homosexuality." Draw the circles so that they overlap, but only to the degree to which you think these two subjects share commonalities. (Yes, alert readers will recognize this as a Venn diagram.)

Now shade the overlapped section and draw a straight line from the shaded area to the margin. In the margin, compute the area of intersection relative to the area of the whole using standard Euclidian plane geometry and assuming a value of 3.14159 for pi.

Finally, if you actually did any of that, send us the link to your Geocities Peter Jackson tribute page because we've got a bunch of old Dungeons & Dragons shit to get rid of.

And now, here's Fox:

Films dealing with homosexuality, homicide bombings, political assassinations, the list goes on and on. Hollywood, going with a lot darker themes this year, and they're courting some controversy.
—*Fox News anchor Gregg Jarrett,*
reporting on the Oscar Best
Picture nominees, March 5, 2006

Of course, to be fair, many people do equate homosexuality with brutal murder. But most of them live in Central Asian caves, not Manhattan apartments. (Remember, this wasn't just a bit of ill-timed off-color office talk; some budding James Joyce apparently wrote this down and put it on a TelePrompTer.)

Now, we have no idea what Dan Rather's religious leanings are, but he's considered by a great many Americans to be the news media's reigning symbol of liberal bias and has more than once been a lightning rod for conservative criticism.

So imagine if Rather, in his last weeks on the air in 2005, had reported on an upcoming Oscars ceremony that featured films such as *The Aviator, Hotel Rwanda,* and *The Passion of the Christ,* by saying "mental illness, genocide, and Christianity. Hollywood, going with a lot darker themes this year, and they're courting some controversy."

Outraged Christians would have opened their pocketbooks so wide that Pat Robertson would have been on the phone buying that gold-plated bidet he's been trying to acquire from the Sultan of Brunei before Rather finished his sentence.

But this comment by a nondescript Fox News Channel news anchor was barely noticed. Granted, *Passion of the Christ* was controversial, mostly because of perceived anti-Semitism and a generous helping of gruesome violence. Likewise, *Brokeback Mountain* exposed a wide cultural rift. But no one in his right mind would have referred to Christianity as a dark theme, and in particular, no respectable journalist would have put it on equal footing with death and destruction.

So how does Fox get away with marginalizing an entire segment of the population? Well, that's easy. They're simply held to a lower standard.

Now, this wasn't just a boneheaded slipup on the part of Fox. Indeed, Jarrett prefaced his analysis with, "They're the best movies of the year, allegedly. Most of us, though, haven't seen them."

Clearly, Fox was signaling to its most loyal viewers that theirs was a friendly little clubhouse—a place where elites are scorned, traditional values are affirmed, and Adam and Steve pass the time talking about baseball and pussy.

Yes, Fox was declaring 2005 the year of the Hollywood elite. And in the forefront of it all was a little film about two cowboys playing pitcher and catcher.

HOW MUCH GAY PORN IS TOO MUCH?

LEADING THE CHARGE of Fox's Light-Loafered Brigade was John Gibson.

Fox's Web site describes Gibson's show, *The Big Story,* as "a one-hour program that provides in-depth coverage and analysis of the day's top stories." Well, apparently the big story on the evening of January 2, 2006, was Gibson's distaste for hot male-on-male action: "But I think most people do not want to go into a darkened room with a tub of popcorn and munch away watching two guys get it on. I just don't."

That's great, John. And this is a fine argument against the mainstreaming of hard-core gay porn. But suggesting that *Brokeback Mountain* is a film about two guys getting it on kind of misses the point. You might as well say *Romeo and Juliet* is a story about parkin' the ole' Pink Cadillac.

Basically, *Brokeback Mountain* was about an unconventional relationship set against the backdrop of a repressive place and time. It was more a tragic love story than a tawdry sex romp. In fact, the film's sex scene, which more closely resembles a wrestling match, was far more implicit than explicit. So millions of people—a great many of whom are heterosexual—were able to relate to the film, because just about everyone has been challenged—and hurt—by love.

Then again, Gibson is probably right that the majority of Americans don't want to watch Jake Gyllenhaal and Heath Ledger have sex, implied or not. But we're guessing even fewer would want to watch the exceedingly pigment-challenged Gibson breathlessly awaiting yet another vigorous conjugal rendezvous while sprawled out on the basement rec room pool table as his wife appends Moby, his favorite strap-on. Indeed, watching Gibson even under the best of circumstances is a chore. The guy's yapping head alone is enough to strain your average retina. If he exposed any more skin, you'd basically have to start watching him through one of those boxes people use to view eclipses.

So if a multiscreen theater were offering the two options side by side, we're guessing that Gyl and the Ledge Man would outdraw

Gibson and his old lady by a wide margin. (Remember, John: freaky albino newsmen who live in glass houses shouldn't throw stones.)

Then again, there are a lot of things in art and cinema that make people uncomfortable. In 1989, Jodie Foster won an Oscar for playing a victim of gang rape in the powerful film *The Accused*. Now, a moronic commentator might have said, "I think most people do not want to go into a darkened room with a tub of pop-corn and munch away watching a woman get violently gang-raped." That may be true, but it's totally meaningless. Indeed, such a comment cynically seeks to dismiss the larger merits of a film by simply dwelling on its most discomfiting moments.

The point of a sex scene is not necessarily to titillate viewers. Often such scenes are used to show intimacy, detachment, impul-sivity, aggression, or a range of other emotions. The sex scene in *Brokeback* merely establishes the nature of the relationship that exists between the two characters near the beginning of the film. It's not about intimacy and love but about self-denial, repression, even anger. Gibson doesn't know this, primarily because he didn't see the film but also because he's a simpleton.

Of course, the above remark was hardly an isolated comment. Earlier, on December 9, Gibson had been discussing the film with a Fox correspondent who had actually seen it, when he uncorked this beauty: "Which is harder to watch, the pulling out the finger-nails of *Syriana* or Heath and Jake inamorata in this?"

Oh, that John Gibson is a joker. Then again, we're quite certain it would be easier to have our own fingernails pulled out than to watch ole' John in the act of heterosexual Christian lovemaking.

I DON'T WANT HIM, YOU CAN HAVE HIM . . .
OR WE CAN SHOOT HIM

WHERE JOHN GIBSON led, Bill O'Reilly followed. For some reason, sex 'n' violence were foremost on Bill's mind as well:

According to friends of mine who have seen *Brokeback*, the key scene takes place in a pup tent. Apparently, two shepherds "bond" in said tent. If I do see the movie, I know what will run through my mind during that scene: What would Clint [Eastwood] and Lee [Van Cleef] and Eli [Wallach] have done had they stumbled upon the tent? I believe gunfire might have been involved.

Okay, we get it, Bill. You're heterosexual. So heterosexual, in fact, that the mere thought of gay sex puts you in the mind of three rugged movie stars simultaneously discharging their long guns upon discovering two guys humping in a tent. You've proven your point. *You are straight.*

Still, it takes a rare breed of homophobia to hear about a gay love scene and only be able to imagine the two characters getting brutally murdered. It's almost as curious as believing that the key scene in a two-hour, fifteen-minute film about love denied is a brief, awkward encounter in a tent. That's a little like judging a journalist's entire career by the time he allegedly masturbated to his producer's voice over the phone.[1] Again, it misses the point.

But the absolute weirdest thing about O'Reilly's statement here is that it wasn't made extemporaneously. Bill sat down at his desk and conjured this little inferno of genius for his weekly column. It wasn't part of a memo maliciously leaked by a disgruntled employee who was trying to embarrass him, as you might have suspected. No, he wanted everyone in America to know that this is how he thinks.

Indeed, this is yet another window into O'Reilly's twisted psyche. We can't help wondering if he had the same thoughts as he watched *The Birdcage* . . . you know, Nathan Lane and Robin Williams prancing around only to be shot in the face—their blood and brains spattering against the walls—their lifeless faggot bodies slowly slumping to the floor.

Good times, good times.

TILDA SWINTON ALONE DOES NOT AN OSCAR FILM MAKE

WHEN THE DAZZLING intellects over at Fox weren't getting totally grossed out by the thought of two boys kissing, they were doing their best to dismiss *Brokeback* as an "agenda" film. You know, the effete, hopelessly out-of-touch coasts were heaping praise, publicity, and prestige on a dreary little art film that was destined to make diddly in the red and purple states.

Conservative commentator and Fox News contributor Charles Krauthammer did his best to sum up the prevailing attitude at the network in a January 2, 2006, appearance on *Special Report with Brit Hume*: "*Brokeback Mountain* will have been seen in the theaters by eighteen people, but the right eighteen, and will win the Academy Award."

Of course, by the time Krauthammer had looked into his crystal ball, *Brokeback* had already made $15 million stateside, exceeding its $14 million budget in less than a month of limited release.

The fact that the movie opened to packed audiences in cities such as Green Bay, Wisconsin, showed that it was not going to be rejected in the heartland. But the film would ultimately prove a hit by any measure. For instance, by the end of its theatrical release, it had grossed $178 million worldwide. And during its seventh week of release, when the film was in wide distribution (1,196 theaters), the per-theater revenue was $6,213. Compared to the seventh-week grosses of *The Chronicles of Narnia* ($2,262 per theater) and *Star Wars: Episode III* ($2,860), two of the three films Bill O'Reilly would contrast with *Brokeback* to tar it with the dreaded "agenda film" brush, it was doing pretty well for itself after all.

Indeed, in his *Brokeback* column, O'Reilly wondered why the Academy would snub all those big earners:

These days, Hollywood considers itself not only a place of entertainment, but also a cultural trendsetter. There is no question that many showbiz types would like to banish any societal stigma associated with homosexuality. Thus, a mainstream movie that portrays gay conduct as nuanced and complicated, as *Brokeback* reportedly does, contributes to a more broad-minded approach to homosexuality—a more accepting view.

So that's what's in play this year at the Academy Awards—a social and political statement. And that's why *Star Wars* and *Harry Potter* and *Narnia,* the three largest-grossing movies of the year, are not in the Best Picture running. Spectacular movies often make tons of money, but they do not advance any cause. Gone are the days when *Gone with the Wind*–type entertainment ruled the Hollywood day.

First of all, what would Bill prefer to a nuanced portrayal of homosexuality? A cartoon? When Bugs Bunny marries Elmer Fudd in *Rabbit of Seville,* does O'Reilly consider that pushing the envelope?

Secondly, *Star Wars: Episode III, Harry Potter and the Goblet of Fire,* and *The Chronicles of Narnia* were at best mediocre films. They were not skipped over by the Academy because of some veiled social agenda; they were skipped over because the first was a flat, disappointing conclusion to a beloved franchise, the second was a cookie-cutter installment in a blurry sequence of nearly indistinguishable films, and the third was a tepid adaptation of a classic children's fable.

But this is a familiar O'Reilly tune. Just as Bill thinks his own show's ratings are presumptive proof of his talent, intellect, and moral superiority, he believes that any stale popcorn flick that pulls in beaucoup box office is necessarily a worthy offering.

Well, at the risk of sounding elitist, we submit a simple, two-word refutation of this notion: *Patch Adams.* [2]

But honestly, even to compare *Harry Potter* with a film such as *Capote* is absurd. Most people understand this. But O'Reilly and his Fox News cronies are like hyper eight-year-olds hopped up on Wild Cherry Pepsi and Sour Patch Kids, nervously fidgeting in their seats and shouting, "Why is that guy talking funny?"

But maybe Bill is on to something. Perhaps *Capote* would have benefited from a rousing game of Quidditch or a few lightsaber battles dripping in CGI. Perhaps we should hope for a more O'Reilly-friendly sequel replete with action sequences, big-budget effects, and some gunplay. We can see it now: *Capote II: Butt Pirates of the Caribbean.*

THE REAL CULTURE CLUB

O'REILLY'S MOSAIC WISDOM continued to roll down from the mountaintop:

> But I also think the entertainment industry should be up front in explaining what films it values and why it finds them especially worthy. Most Americans are not gonna see *Brokeback Mountain* because they don't relate to the subject, and if Hollywood is now in the "culture-shaping business," it should admit it.

In 1997, *The English Patient* cleaned up at the Oscars. Back then, O'Reilly no doubt wondered why *Independence Day, Twister,* and *Mission: Impossible* were not in the running for Best Picture. Gee, there must have been some sort of agenda in play. Why did Hollywood value films that the general public didn't?

Well, because big-budget films about wild and woolly tornado researchers with hearts of gold battling evil tornado researchers who skulk around in black vans are more palatable to audiences than art films about mapmaking English burn victims.

For much the same reason, Wendy's sells more salads than the Waldorf-Astoria. Seriously, since when did we start to value the work of artists based on their mass appeal?

If it were up to the general public, major metropolitan galleries would hang limited-edition Thomas Kinkade prints next to Picassos and Il Divo would be launching the new season at the Lyric Opera of Chicago.

And if it were up to O'Reilly, he'd win the Pulitzer Prize and the National Book Award every year. Luckily, awards voters don't pay much attention to Nielsen numbers. Why? *Because that's not their job.*

GUESS WHO'S COMING TO THE OSCARS

NOW, IT'S INTERESTING that Fox's commentators would so cavalierly dismiss *Brokeback Mountain* as an agenda film. Of course, in a way they're right. The movie is definitely not neutral on the question of whether fags should have their heads bashed in, so in that respect it's hardly fair and balanced. But, once again, that's hardly the point.

Imagine if Fox had been around in 1967 when *Guess Who's Coming to Dinner* was released. That's a film that certainly played better on the coasts than in the South and Midwest. And it also touted an agenda that appealed to a minority of the population, as there were very few interracial marriages at the time and several states actually still had antimiscegenation laws on the books, which were ruled unconstitutional by the Supreme Court that same year.

So was *Guess Who's Coming to Dinner* an agenda film? Yes, and proudly so. But would Fox have it dismissed based on that criterion alone? Well, we don't know, of course. But they certainly could have done so without risking all that much, and a significant portion of the population would have enthusiastically cheered them on.

In fact, we can just about imagine it:

I think most people do not want to go into a darkened room with a tub of popcorn and munch away watching a black man and a white woman tell her parents they want to get married. . . .

According to friends of mine who have seen *Guess Who's*, the key scene takes place when a black man visits the home of his white girlfriend to announce their engagement. If I do see the movie, I know what will run through my mind during that scene. . . . I believe gunfire might be involved.

Yeah, sounds pretty appalling, doesn't it?

NOTES

1. This should actually be seen as a cheap plug for our first book, *Sweet Jesus, I Hate Bill O'Reilly*, rather than a cheap shot at Bill. After all, if we really wanted to cheap-shot Bill, we'd bring up his madcap adventures in Thailand.
2. We realize some of you might like this movie. Tastes are subjective and widely varied, which is what makes America great. So if for some reason you happen to be a *Patch Adams* fan, please substitute another high-grossing Robin Williams movie that totally sucks ass, such as *Robots*.

THE WAR ON THE WAR ON CHRISTMAS

The War on Christmas is real and, taken to the extreme, turning Christmas into a second-class holiday would kill much of the retail specialty stores. The next target would be Easter.

—*Tobin Smith, panelist on Fox News's weekend business show* Bulls & Bears, *December 3, 2005*

In today's consumer society, this time (of the year) is unfortunately subjected to a sort of commercial pollution that is in danger of altering its true spirit, which is characterized by meditation, sobriety and by a joy that is not exterior but intimate.

—*Pope Benedict XVI, Vicar of Christ on earth, December 11, 2005*

YOU'D THINK BILL O'Reilly would have learned his lesson by now. After being roundly ridiculed in 2005 for his war on Christmas fantasy—including during an infamous dustup with beloved snarkmaster David Letterman, who dismissed much of O'Reilly's manufactured outrage as "little red and green stories"—O'Reilly was at it again less than a year later in his absurdly Manichaean manifesto, *Culture Warrior.*

In the book, O'Reilly took on those in the press who challenged him the previous year for claiming that Christmas was under siege not only by far-left elements and secularists but by commercial interests such as Wal-Mart that had substituted secular greetings for the overtly religious "Merry Christmas."

As proof that the war was real, O'Reilly cited some lawsuits that had challenged government entities' sponsorship of Christmas, and the reluctance of several big-box retailers to use "Merry Christmas" in their advertising.

We know what you're thinking. How long before the storm troopers crash through your skylight to confiscate your contraband reindeer sweater, illegal gingerbread paraphernalia, and decorative mince pies?

Of course, it's curious that O'Reilly could have looked at the "more than thirty separate newspapers" that attacked him by name for defending Christmas traditions without really understanding what any of them were saying.

No one denies that the ACLU regularly challenges religious displays and expressions (including those involving Christmas) that are sponsored by local governments nor that some retailers prefer the more generic and inclusive "Happy Holidays" to the expressly Christian "Merry Christmas." The quarrel is over the meaning of all this.

O'Reilly and his Fox cohorts see it all as a big assault on Christmas. We disagree.

Who's right? Well, if you're willing to ignore history, theology, logic, common sense, common courtesy, the evidence of your own senses, the light-up singing Santa on your neighbor's lawn, and the simple truth, O'Reilly's arguments might have a certain superficial appeal.

If not, you're an unwitting foot soldier in this country's ongoing battle against winter fun and frolic.

Now, it goes without saying that if there is an actual, calculated war against Christmas, the secularists really suck at it. Honestly, they're worse than Rumsfeld. Indeed, we saw our first Christmas-related television news story on October 7 of last year (apparently, Christmas was "just around the corner") and the first Christmas retail ad at least a week before that. So, whatever their intentions, the Christmas resistance clearly isn't gaining much ground.

But there simply isn't a war on Christmas. And while it's impossible to prove a negative, we're gonna give it our best try. Following are eight reasons why we believe there's no such war—and why Fox's commentators actually owe Jesus Christ an immediate and abject apology.

1. Retail Sales and Secular Holiday Greetings Are Not Proxies for a Holiday's Spiritual Vitality

It's a cliché, but it goes without saying that if Jesus returned to earth and saw how commercialized Christmas had become, he'd spit Starbucks Holiday Blend from his No Spin Savior sixteen-ounce ceramic coffee mug.

But the brain trust at Fox still insists on viewing fourth-quarter sales and secular greetings at department stores as the proverbial canary in the coal mine of Christmas.

In an ironic twist on biblical tradition, on December 3, 2005, the money changers were busy driving out Jesus.

On Fox's *Bulls & Bears,* host Brenda Buttner complained, "The war on Christmas: Could the left win its crusade against Christmas and does that threaten our stock market and entire economy?"

Regular panelist Tobin Smith offered, "The war on Christmas is real and, taken to the extreme, turning Christmas into a second-class holiday would kill much of the retail specialty stores. The next target would be Easter. This definitely does hurt the economy. Retailers have fallen under the pixie dust spell of consultants, and this idea of being politically correct becomes this insidious little disease."

There are at least four things wrong with this theory. First, the left is not waging a crusade against Christmas (more on that later).

Second, saying "Happy Holidays" at retail stores is not going to make people throw up their hands in disgust and walk out without their items, vowing a life of asceticism and a more solemn approach to Christian feast days (any more than not being Irish keeps a guy from drinking enough Guinness on St. Patrick's Day to anesthetize an alpaca).

Come on, haven't these folks ever seen a Tickle Me Elmo stampede? Are we to believe these roving packs of mothers—who on a bad day could fend off a Panzer Division with a cache of Koosh balls and a plastic lightsaber—would stop dead in their tracks upon spying a nonsectarian holiday greeting despoiling the housewares section?

Third, you couldn't turn Christmas into a second-class holiday at this point if you passed a constitutional amendment banning it. At worst it would turn into a pagan/secular solstice festival without the economy-killing harping of know-it-all ministers who think it's become too commercialized. Know why? Because Hasbro has to move Weebles shit, that's why.

And what do they mean by a second-class holiday, anyway? One that doesn't last for three months and isn't defined almost exclusively by retail sales? Something like, say, Veterans Day? You know, the holiday that honors all those men and women who fought to protect Tobin Smith's and Brenda Buttner's right to have fatuous conversations about holiday retail sales?

Fourth, what the hell do retail sales have to do with the health of Christmas anyway? Retailers better hope to hell there's *not* a Christmas revival—that is, a renewed focus on the meaning of the day itself—because it would kill their bottom line.

On November 28, 2005, Bill O'Reilly summed up the growing impiety of America's big-box retailers with his latest encyclical:

> Ten years ago, almost everybody said "Merry Christmas" in America, but now that's changed. It is happy holiday time. Christmas is a forbidden word to some. . . .
>
> Every company in America should be on its knees thanking Jesus for being born. Without Christmas, most American businesses would be far less profitable. More than enough reason for business to be screaming "Merry Christmas."

You know, he's right. We're being ungrateful. Let's put Christ back in the retail sector, shall we?

Thank you, Jesus, for being born. It's really been great for retail business in late-twentieth- and early-twenty-first-century America. We now have superstores that manufacture goods in impoverished countries that pay substandard wages for hot, grueling, often debilitating work, and pass the savings onto your humble servants.

Oh blessed son of God, your faithful flock awaits your return to judge the living and the dead so we can show you the top-of-the-line Weber Summit Platinum D6 outdoor gas grills with six stainless-steel burners, and the enclosed, heated swimming pools with swim-up bars we bought ourselves for your birthday. And our awesome backyard barbecues will have no end.

Oh sweet baby Jesus, we commemorate your birth and the gifts of gold, frankincense, and myrrh you received by buying our own dirty gold and conflict diamonds; designer fragrances with huge, unnecessary markups; and novelty sex oils that never fail to get a big laugh when unwrapped at our hilarious, booze-soaked office Christmas parties—which the secularists, in their anti-Christian zealotry, want to turn into "holiday" and "winter" parties. Oh, Lord Jesus, please give them all painful, chronic, incurable diseases that in no way impede their ability to get to the mall.

It's all in your name, oh eternal son of the living God. Thanks a bunch. Even if we don't know anything about your teachings or your church, we do shop. So thanks again for the awesome fourth-quarter sales. You rock. Keep it coming.

We ask this in Jesus's name.

Amen.

P.S. Bill thanks you, too, Jesus. Your Spin Stops Here Tin filled with Soft Mint Puffs[1] is on the way.

2. The Secular Holiday Symbols Fox Defends Under-mine Rather than Support the True Spirit of Christmas

Fox might be a little more credible as a protector of the one true faith and smiter of the sinister secularists if its defense of sacred Christian holidays weren't continually embroidered with images of Santa Claus and the Easter Bunny.

On November 30, 2005, O'Reilly launched into yet another impassioned defense of Christmas: "We've been reporting, as you know, on the many attempts to diminish Christmas throughout America. Now it's time to look at the other side. Millions of Americans are fed up, angry that Christmas is under siege by secular forces, and some are fighting back."

Sounds like a clarion call to all those Christians out there who are sick and tired of their holiday being diluted by secular influence. Unfortunately, while Bill was bugling, he showed two rather incongruous graphics. The first was a decorated tree with the words "Christmas Controversy" underneath. The second included the words "Fighting Back" with a picture of a pissed-off Santa.

Now, we're not theologians, but we could open a drive-through seminary that would pump out people with a firmer grasp of Christianity than Bill. O'Reilly fails to understand that Christmas trees and Santa are the two primary symbols of the *secularization* of Christmas.

Indeed, there is at least some scriptural evidence that putting up a Christmas tree is expressly forbidden by God (see Jeremiah 10:2–8).

But Bill is not defending the Bible here. He's defending *A Christmas Story*. O'Reilly is well aware that more of his viewers know Ralphie's mother's warning about shooting his eye out than Jesus's warning about a camel fitting through the eye of a needle. People are scared of losing the Christmas of their childhood, not their right freely to observe a religion they don't know anything about under the protection of a Constitution they don't understand.

Still, O'Reilly is not alone here. Fox in general seems rather confused about the true symbols of Christianity. No, they are not Christmas trees, Frosty the Snowman, the Coca-Cola bears, or Rudolph the friggin' Red-Nosed Reindeer. Protecting these symbols does nothing for Christianity. In fact, some would say these are all assaults *against* Christianity.

For example, the Christmas tree has distinctly pagan origins, and Frosty's death and resurrection at the hands of Professor Hinkle and Santa Claus, respectively, skates dangerously close to blasphemy, when you think about it.

3. "Happy Holidays" Has Been Around Forever and Never Offended Anyone

One of the pillars of Fox's argument that secularists are out to destroy Christmas is that some retailers have suddenly taken to saying "Happy Holidays" instead of "Merry Christmas" under pressure from the usual suspects (liberals, atheists, Jews, homos, etc.).

On November 30, 2005, as a guest on *Your World with Neil Cavuto*, O'Reilly was making his case for the phrase "Merry Christmas" as the sole proper consummation of the country's numerous November-through-December retail transactions:

> Then the business community says we don't want to offend anybody so we're not going to say "Merry Christmas." We're going to say "Happy Holidays," all right? That offends millions of Christians, see? Eighty-five percent of the country calls itself Christian. Fifteen percent of the country—you figure these people could do the math if they're CEOs. Eighty-five percent Christian; they are into Christmas, okay? That's their big day. Fifteen percent aren't. Now of those fifteen percent, maybe one percent are totally insane. They're nuts. They're the ones who are offended. So what it comes down to is that these CEOs and big companies—big companies like Wal-Mart, Sears, Kmart—will not say "Merry Christmas" in their stores or advertising to cater to one percent of Americans who are insane.

The message being, apparently, that if you make a big deal out of what the underpaid clerks and greeters at Wal-Mart say to their customers after Thanksgiving, you're "totally insane."

Of course, while O'Reilly and his viewers may act like children, they've actually been around a long time—long enough, anyway, to know that "Happy Holidays" has thrived alongside "Merry Christmas" for at least as long as Adam and Noah lived with triceratopses and T-Rexes. Indeed, it's a phrase that goes back as long as just about anyone in this country can remember.

We could go ahead and research its first usage but, frankly, that would be kind of dumb and a waste of time.

However, in *Culture Warrior,* while responding to a critic of his annual war-on-Christmas coverage, Bill managed to pull a little more dirt onto the pit of stupid he'd dug himself into.

Shortly after scolding the American stores that "prohibit" the words "Merry Christmas," O'Reilly took on *Washington Post* columnist Harold Meyerson, who'd "rallied the S-Ps" (Bill's abbreviation for "secular progressives") in one of his articles.

Here's O'Reilly quoting Meyerson:

> Now the Fox News demagogues want to impose a more sectarian Christmas on us, supplanting the distinctly American holiday we have celebrated lo [lo?] these three score years with a holiday that divides us along religious lines. Bill O'Reilly can blaspheme all he wants but, like millions of my countrymen, I take attacks on Irving Berlin's America personally.

Bill's response: "Attacks on Irving Berlin's America? Easy on the eggnog, Bud—I am an Irving fan. He wrote the song 'White Christmas' when he could have called it 'White Holiday.'"

Ha ha ha ha ha ha ha ha ha. Whoo. That's rich, Bill. Oh, those silly PC liberals. When will they ever learn?

Of course, as you know, "White Christmas" was introduced in the 1942 film *Holiday Inn,* which also featured the beloved Christmas classic "Happy Holiday," which includes the familiar lyric "May the calendar keep bringing/happy holidays to you." Nineteen forty-two, Bill. That's more than sixty years ago, or slightly longer than you've been this dumb.

Of course, as alert bloggers pointed out at the time, in the midst of Fox's ongoing campaign against generic uses such as "Happy Holidays" and "holiday tree," the Fox News Web site offered its own "holiday" ornaments, including one with—you guessed it—an *O'Reilly Factor* logo.

4. The ACLU Fights for Individual Religious Expression, Not Against It

One of the central set pieces in Fox's fake war against the

anti-Christmas fascists is a series of lawsuits, mostly filed by the ACLU, that seek to curb the official government sanction of religion—in this case, as expressed through a religious holiday.

This is what John Gibson's book *The War on Christmas: How the Liberal Plot to Ban the Sacred Holiday Is Worse Than You Thought* is largely about.

Now, whatever the legal issues involved, it's easy to see how some people (Christian, nonreligious, or other) who have kids in public schools or who do business in government buildings would rather not have to confront expressly sectarian symbols, traditions, or doctrines in these particular contexts.

After all, who wants to see any arm of their government, which is supposed to be neutral, promoting particular religious beliefs?

Of course, Gibson might understand the difference between government protection of and government promotion of religion if he lived in, say, a Shinto-dominated country. However, in the introduction to *The War on Christmas*, after commiserating with small-town folk who haven't the wherewithal to stand up to slick ACLU lawyers, Gibson manages to torpedo his book's credibility in a single paragraph:

> These liberal groups give lip service to religion, but only as a completely personal activity that should be practiced and celebrated behind the closed doors of privately held property (evidently it would be preferred they were in windowless and soundproof rooms, lest some expression of religion escape into the air breathed by others).

That's an amusing theory, but the fact is, between an ACLU lawyer and Jesus Christ, only one is a strong advocate of public religious expression, and it ain't the one tap-dancin' on the Sea of Galilee.

As we pointed out in *Sweet Jesus, I Hate Bill O'Reilly*—and as both Gibson and O'Reilly consistently and conveniently fail to acknowledge—the ACLU has filed suit numerous times to protect individuals' rights to public religious expression. This includes a

February 2003 action that defended students who were punished for distributing candy canes with religious messages. What Gibson won't or can't understand is that the ACLU stands against the coercive profaith actions of governments *as well as* their misguided attempts to prevent individual religious expression.

So much for Gibson's thesis.

Jesus Christ, on the other hand, said in Matthew 6:5–6:

> And when thou prayest, thou shalt not be as the hypocrites are: for they love to pray standing in the synagogues and in the corners of the streets, that they may be seen of men. Verily I say unto you, they have their reward. But thou, when thou prayest, enter into thy closet, and when thou hast shut thy door, pray to thy Father which is in secret; and thy Father which seeth in secret shall reward thee openly.

So Jesus is telling those who pray to "shut thy door," just like Gibson's imaginary liberals. So by his own definition, Gibson's Christ hates Christmas, Christianity, and himself, whereas the ACLU appears to have no problem with them unless the government forces them on you.

Oh, dear Christ. Why do you hate Christians so?

5. Bill O'Reilly Makes Shit Up All Day Long

On the December 9, 2005, broadcast of *The Radio Factor,* Bill O'Reilly claimed that an entire U.S. town was plotting against the colors red and green: "In Saginaw, Michigan, the township opposes red and green clothing on anyone. In Saginaw Township, they basically said, anybody, we don't want you to wear red or green. I would dress up head to toe in red to green if I were in Saginaw, Michigan."

Needless to say, the town of Saginaw, Michigan, does not oppose red and green clothing. That is, unless Mr. Blackwell has staged a secret post-Thanksgiving village coup, in which case the town will also no doubt be banning wide lapels and the wearing of white after Labor Day.

According to WNEM TV 5, Mid-Michigan's News Leader, a television station that's presumably based in mid-Michigan where Saginaw is (a little journalism tip, Bill: that's the sort of fact it's okay to print without independent verification): "O'Reilly's comments are flat out not true. [Saginaw Township supervisor Tim] Braun goes on to say the township hall has red and green Christmas lights adorning the building at night."

Of course, we hardly need to point out that not only is O'Reilly full of it, but he's also been caught once again with his theological britches in a bind.

That is, there's nothing in the Bible about wearing red and green at Christmas. So Bill's hardly defending the Christian holiday here. Indeed, the colors red and green have about as much to do with the birth of Christ as Hermey the Elf and the Island of Misfit Toys.

6. John Gibson Makes Shit Up All Day Long

In the introduction to *The War on Christmas,* John Gibson writes, "A free expression of Christmas in this age is fast becoming impossible."

Our response: *Danny Thomas spit take* "Whaaaaaaaa!?" *Eyes stretch out of our heads, accompanied by cartoonish boingy sounds, at which point we're overcome with the vapors and faint dead away.*

Of course, what Gibson writes is hardly true, in part because of the ACLU's defense of our constitutional freedoms, and in part because our Founding Fathers established a secular republic instead of a biblical theocracy—a theocracy that could have easily interpreted the Bible as saying everyone should be forced at gunpoint to pray in their closets and that Christmas trees are forbidden pagan symbols.

7. If You're a Christmas Warrior, Eventually You'll End Up Sounding Like a Complete Ass

On the December 2, 2005, broadcast of his radio show, O'Reilly outlined his plan to terrorize, crush, and humiliate all those who stood against the holiday of generosity, peace, and love:

I am not going to let oppressive, totalitarian, anti-Christian forces in this country diminish and denigrate the holiday and the celebration. I am not going to let it happen. I'm gonna use all the power that I have on radio and television to bring horror into the world of people who are trying to do that. And we have succeeded. You know we've succeeded.

They are on the run in corporations, in the media, everywhere. They are on the run, because I will put their face and their name on television, and I will talk about them on the radio if they do it. There is no reason on this earth that all of us cannot celebrate a public holiday devoted to generosity, peace, and love together. There is no reason on the earth we can't do that. So we are going to do it. And anyone who tries to stop us from doing it is gonna face me.

Okay, you couldn't get more farcical than this if you were writing dialogue for a satirical novel about an insane serial-killer anchorman—because your editor would send back notes with a line through this paragraph saying, "No!—Over the top!"

For God's sake, he sounds like a cross between St. Thomas Aquinas and Travis Bickle.

Actually, though, Bill presents a perfect opportunity here for young, ambitious Fox producers. A Bill O'Reilly Christmas Special dedicated to generosity, peace, love, and crazy random threats could very well make the network a bundle.

8. Even Cal Thomas Thinks These People Are Full of Shit

Whatever else you want to say about him, *Fox News Watch* panelist Cal Thomas is a genuine Christian. By that we mean he appears to have actually read the Bible sometime in the last twenty years and, unlike some we could mention, doesn't think Christmas is all about kickin' ass and takin' names.

On December 13, 2005, Thomas appeared on *Your World with Neil Cavuto*. The conversation conspicuously departed from the usual Fox talking points:

CAVUTO: You're saying that, you know, the John Gibsons, the Sean Hannitys, the others are going too far in this thing. What do you mean?

THOMAS: I don't mention any names.

CAVUTO: Come on. Come on.

THOMAS: Hey, look, we shouldn't expect store clerks who are about the bottom line to wish whoever or whatever a "Merry Christmas," a "Happy Ramadan," a "Happy Hanukkah." They're there to make money, and the fact that they've cashed in on Christmas, which is about not the bottom line but the savior of the world. Not about lights on the tree, but the light of the world. And not about Xboxes, but about our sin boxes, if you will. Let them do what they do. But the people who actually revere the person who is supposed to be the reason for the season have a special way of worshipping and adoring him that have nothing to do with the crass commercialism . . .

CAVUTO: Yeah. But, Cal, this is not about the person behind the cash register, the person who's stocking toys. This has to do with the organizations themselves, the Wal-Marts and the big stores that seem to have an inherent policy not to say the words, "Merry Christmas."

THOMAS: I don't care, Neil! I don't care what they say. Their holidays are on April 1, April Fools' Day, okay? I won't mess with them if they don't mess with me. Let them do whatever they want. They're stores! They're selling stuff! They're increasing the bottom line.

CAVUTO: Cal, you're a deeply religious man. I know you personally, and you're one of the most decent guys I know. Now, do you, when you go searching for Christmas cards and have a tough time finding Christmas cards, or go to stores and have a tough time even hearing the word "Christmas," does that bug you as a religious guy?

THOMAS: Not at all, Neil. I'm not expecting it there. I hear it in church. That's fine. That's no problem for me.

First of all, we'd like to know where Neil is shopping. The Socialist Workers Party outlet mall? If he can't find Christmas cards in stores in December, he's got bigger problems than getting punked by Cal Thomas. Hey Neil, try looking somewhere other than the lingerie department for once.

The point, which Thomas makes rather well, is that *churches* provide spiritual guidance, not the government or Wal-Mart. And whether Wal-Mart says "Merry Christmas" or substitutes the tried-and-true "Happy Holidays" is really irrelevant. They'd no more scrub their stores of Christmas stuff than they'd stop selling beef in Texas. Jesus is big business, and they know it.

But it just makes sense that you'd want to avoid saying "Merry Christmas" to someone who doesn't actually celebrate it. That would be like saying "Happy Bar Mitzvah" to Pat Buchanan. No, it's not really offensive—just kind of stupid. That doesn't make you hostile to Christians or Christianity.

WAR IS OVER, IF YOU WANT IT?

IN THE FALL of 2006, with both sides firmly entrenched, the war on Christmas seemed at a bleak impasse. And with liberals poised to take control of Congress, traditionalists across the country were, if anything, on the run. How could Fox ever win its holiday war now? Surely all would be lost, and the nation would be forced to endure another Chrismahanukwanzakah. Yes, it was only a matter of time before the Burgermeister Meisterburger sacked Christmas Town and reinstated his drear anti-Christmas regime.

Then again, the nice thing about a nonexistent war is that it's really easy to declare major victories.

On November 9, Sean Hannity announced, "Finally a signal that the war on Christmas may be over, straight ahead."

On the same day, John Gibson proclaimed, "What a difference a year makes."

O'Reilly summed it up on his November 13, 2006, broadcast: "as you know, last year there was a culture war battle between people who wanted to say 'Happy Holidays' and not say 'Merry Christmas' and those of us who want to maintain the Christmas tradition without interference."

So what was the tipping point that heralded a cease-fire on this particular front of the culture war? Was there now a nativity scene on every courthouse lawn in the country? Were children singing "Away in a Manger" in every Massachusetts public school? Oh no. D-Day came for the anti-Yule fanatics when Wal-Mart announced it would now say "Merry Christmas" to shoppers as they purchased oversized canisters of popcorn divided into sections of caramel, cheese, and plain.

Oh, there would certainly be more battles to come. Secular insurgents might try to push their hedonistic agenda on an unsuspecting public by banning green leg warmers or changing the lyrics to "Frosty the Snowman." But the tide had turned—because Fox had deemed it so.

Still, it seemed that Fox's outrage against those who bastardize this most holy of holidays was particularly selective.

On the December 6, 2006, *O'Reilly Factor,* Bill brought glad tidings of great joy to all his people:

You know, it seems now every day we report on some left-wing display on a college campus in America. Well, now here's a right-wing display. The Young Conservative group at the University of Texas has put up this holiday display. No, it's not a manger scene. It's a solstice barn. Instead of Joseph and Mary tending to Jesus, they've got Gary and Joseph. The wise men are Lenin, Marx, and Stalin. And the display is dedicated to the ACLU. And I almost forgot, the angel on high appears to be Nancy Pelosi.

Ridiculous? Ho ho ho. I love the solstice barn.

Yes, lovely. Perhaps for Easter some guys at Hillbilly U will nail an effigy of Howard Dean to a cross. Oh, and look—a hyssop stick holding a sponge soaked in Shiraz. How droll. Yeah, we're sure Bill and the kids at Fox News would find that hilarious as well.

Of course, if you think Fox is ready simply to declare victory over the secularists and drop the Christmas war for good, well, we've got a gingerbread condo at the North Pole to sell you.

The war-on-Christmas spirit will live on as long as morons the world over still believe and Fox News pundits in Manhattan need a bullshit issue to exploit.

Indeed, just two weeks after saying the anti-Christmas forces were in retreat, on November 28, 2006, O'Reilly once again rallied the troops: "Now for the top story tonight, the city of Chicago versus the nativity scene. You got to believe me on this. I had hoped these Christmas controversy stories would be very limited this year. I really wanted to get away from them. But no, more insanity in the air."

Oh, Bill. We couldn't have said it better ourselves.

NOTES

1. This is an actual product.

17

CRAZY + POLITICS = FOX

IN **FEBRUARY 2001,** Fox television aired the notorious documentary *Conspiracy Theory: Did We Land on the Moon?*

The hour-long program was essentially a forum for the world's small community of moon-hoax believers to spin their pet theories. Of course, its claims were quickly debunked by members of the not-completely-insane community.

But while the documentary aired on the Fox television network and not Fox News, its provocative, stentorian intro did have a familiar ring to it:

The following program deals with a controversial subject. The theories expressed are not the only possible interpretation. Viewers are invited to make a judgment based on all available information.

Tonight, we investigate the most extraordinary event of the twentieth century. Man landing on the moon. But believe it or not, some people say it never happened. Decide for yourself, as we explore the evidence, analyze official government photos, examine the films, and hear the testimony of one former astronaut who's not afraid to speak his mind. Could the government have orchestrated the deception of the century? You be the judge.

In other words, "We Report, You Decide."

Yes, could the small army of people who worked on the Apollo Program have been paid off to keep quiet about the hoax, continuing to keep a lid on it for more than thirty years, even though revealing details of the conspiracy would have brought any one of a possible thousands of whistle-blowers rock-star attention, an indelible place in American history, and a series of lucrative book deals?

Hey, it's an open question. We're just bringin' ya the info, Chachi.

Of course, the government being the government, NASA actually agreed to pay journalist James Oberg $15,000 to write a rebuttal of the most widely circulated conspiracy theories. Oberg's commission was canceled when members of the not-insane community heard about the book and complained that it would simply dignify the hoax theorists' claims.

So what does this all have to do with Fox News? Well, we mention it only because we feel it illustrates three important points:

1. It's possible to convince some people of just about anything, no matter how crazy, if you have no shame about peddling nutty theories and propaganda as plausible scenarios. Indeed, due no doubt in part to the Fox special, Oberg estimated, in a 2003 article for *Skeptical Inquirer*, that perhaps 10 percent of Americans now disbelieved the Apollo landing.
2. Rupert Murdoch will put just about anything on TV if there's a buck in it. If he could get a higher share and a better demo by replacing Sean Hannity with a monkey who spent an hour each weeknight throwing poo at Alan Colmes, you better believe that's what he'd air.[1]

3. Blatantly obvious things require no rebuttal unless you're surrounded by idiots. If 90 percent of Americans rejected the historicity of the moon landing instead of 10 percent, Oberg probably would have continued to receive funding. But, ultimately, convincing the submental 10 percent was deemed not worth the effort.

So what, then, to do with Fox News's frequent and blatantly false claim that it's "fair and balanced"? That depends. If you're at a family gathering and your brother-in-law suddenly gets in your face, screaming that Fox is the only news source that's unbiased, you should probably just set your drink on his brow and quietly walk away.

If, however, you find yourself in a social setting where you're surrounded by idiots, you may feel compelled to trot out specific evidence of Fox's absurd right-wing bias.

So at the risk of becoming the James Obergs of media criticism, we dedicate this chapter to anyone who at least occasionally finds himself in one of those awkward social situations where he's about the only functioning chip on the motherboard.

Hope it helps.

MY KINGDOM FOR A SIXTEEN-YEAR-OLD WITH TEXT MESSAGING

WHILE SOME MIGHT see Fox News as a sort of conservative Trojan horse, it's actually more like a transvestite prostitute—a right-wing echo chamber whose true nature is glaringly obvious to all but the most deeply and willfully delusional.[2]

Sure, they have a few nearsighted "clients" who don't know the difference and some who'd rather not ask too many questions. But with the exception of Bill O'Reilly—who, like Buffalo Bill in *Silence of the Lambs,* is crazy enough to think he might actually be what he pretends to be—we're guessing no one at the network really takes the "unbiased" claim all that seriously.

But that doesn't mean they can't keep repeating it. And it

doesn't mean they can't, under the shadow of objectivity, mobilize their conservative base to trumpet the day's talking points right along with them.

Indeed, the first rule at Fox is that there's nothing that can't be successfully spun—no Republican bad news that can't be made to look like Democratic liability, and no Democratic victory that can't be turned to mush.

Take the Mark Foley scandal of October 2006. When the Florida congressman was caught up in an e-mail and instant messaging sex scandal—quickly dubbed "Pagefuckergate" by the liberal media—the GOP was sent reeling.

But Fox had a nutty plan. If they could just reposition Democrats as the bad guys . . .

No, no that would be just too crazy. How could they possibly take a scandal where a Republican congressman asked a teenage page "did you spank it this weekend" and "where did you unload it" and twist it around so the Dems looked like the villains?

Oh, where there's a will . . .

The Democrats

On October 6, 2006, *Fox & Friends* ran a segment titled "The Mark Foley Scandal: Who Knew What & When?" The guest that morning was Republican Senator Saxby Chambliss.

Now, *Fox & Friends* has always had a knack for spinning stories via suggestive screen titles. On this day, Fox viewers were treated to the oddly bland "Mark Foley exchanged e-mails with a teenage boy" and the oddly accusatory, though somewhat vague, "Are political parties exploiting the Foley fallout?"

Two things right off the bat. One, "exchanged e-mails" is about as soft as you could possibly lob that ball. Come on, kids. Don't be coy. You didn't say Bill Clinton "gave of himself" to an intern. You presented pretty much every detail of that episode short of the genome sequencing on the dress stain. Be fair.

But even better is how this story suddenly became an albatross for the Democrats. Never mind that there was growing evidence of a high-level GOP cover-up. The real story was that a political party might have tried to use a lurid, high-profile sex scandal for political gain!

Oh, but there were even graver portents.

F&F co-host Steve Doocy asked the question that was on the tip of every Republican-talking-points-kissed tongue: "Is this an October surprise? You think somebody on the way-left did this?"

He added, "There are so many stories out there, Senator, that you know this might have the fingerprints of some outfit on it."

Can you get less specific with your rumors there, Steve? Something that's at least falsifiable? Could you give a name? An organization. One fact?

Maybe Steve Doocy has a single, infertile testicle the size of a crushed persimmon. See, that's what we call a testable assertion and thus a basis for responsible media speculation.

Come On, Already. It's Been Thirty-Six Hours Since Then

Within days of the story breaking, there was talk of a backlash against Democrats if they dared point out the rich irony that one of the Republicans' most visible child advocates was trolling for boys.

Fox News Channel's Bill Sammon spelled it out on October 7, 2006, as co-host of *The Beltway Boys*: "And if there is a backlash—if voters do perceive that Democrats are exploiting a genuine tragedy for—for political gain, I think that's going to hurt Democrats."

Now, just to refresh your memory, our last Democratic president was impeached by a partisan House after getting painted into a corner by a partisan independent counsel who turned a partisan investigation of a land deal into a partisan witch hunt over a sex scandal involving two consenting adults, out of which Fox News et al. have made partisan hay for going on nine years now.

So, yes, how dare the Democrats turn this into a partisan issue?

Of course, just a few days earlier, Sammon had been peddling the same GOP palliative on *Hannity & Colmes*: "But there's also the danger that the Democrats will overreach, that there will be a backlash against this unseemly, sort of gleeful celebration of this scandal."

Get that? It's the Democrats who are being unseemly. Not the guy spankin' it to Hardy Boys mysteries.

And we're not quite sure where the gleeful celebration took place. Did we miss the coverage of Democrats filing out of their offices, gathering on the Capitol steps, and singing "Ding Dong, the Witch is Dead"?

Wasn't Nixon a Democrat?

Certainly anyone who works in the hectic world of daily newspapers or broadcast journalism knows that mistakes are sometimes made.

Typos and misstatements are an occupational hazard. Usually, typos are quickly cleaned up and factual errors corrected.

Then there are the times when the error seems just a little too perfect to be accidental.

On October 3, 2006, on three separate occasions, during two different segments, Bill O'Reilly showed video of his fellow culture warrior, boy-crazy congressman Foley, accompanied by the tagline "Former Congressman Mark Foley (D-FL)."

That's right, kids. Foley, that darling of the right and champion of child protection, was labeled a Democrat as soon as it came out that he's got a hankerin' for adolescent boys. This is what we in the business call "a lucky accident."

Now, remembering Fox viewers' penchant for getting things spectacularly wrong—demonstrated, for example, by the University of Maryland Program on International Policy Attitudes study we discuss in Chapter 1—one fairly wonders what effect this might have had on the largish segment of the O'Reilly audience that sees Democrats as perverts to begin with.

Consider also that the median age of O'Reilly viewers is seventy-one. That's the *median*. So for every *Factor* fan who was young enough to avoid fighting in the Battle of Inchon, there's a much older guy screaming about "secular progressives" over his fifth brandy and ginger ale. Any chance he's gonna hop over to the Huffington Post or Air America to get a different take on the story?

So we're guessing that the average O'Reilly fan was sleeping well that night with the knowledge that the creep in Florida trying to bed boy pages was a Democrat after all.

How Dare the Democrats Expose a Child Predator?

During *Special Report with Brit Hume's* October 11 Grapevine segment, Hume revealed a shocking piece of information about the Democrats and Mark Foley:

> The *Washington Post* acknowledged today that one of its sources for sexually charged computer messages from former Florida Congressman Mark Foley was a former page who supports the Democratic Party. The *Post* writes that its source, and the former page who talked to ABC News, might not have come forward had Democratic operatives not divulged less sordid e-mails upon which the original stories were based.

So, in a nutshell, what he was actually saying was, "And he would have gotten away with it too if it wasn't for those meddling kids."

Seriously, was Hume really trying to deflect attention from this 100 percent Republican scandal by accusing the Democrats of tattling?

Fine. Let's bring in Mike Brady and get this tongue-lashing over with.

Of course, the fact that top Republicans had some of the pieces of the Foley puzzle in their hands for months before the scandal broke was somehow fading in importance.

Apparently, that a congressman would want to buy presents for and trade pictures with teenage boys was only a little disconcerting.

Then again, maybe there's a way to find some sort of moral equivalence between a breaking story about a congressman consorting with minors and a nine-year-old scandal involving consensual relations between two adults. That might get those jackals off the GOP's back, huh?

Say, Sean Hannity, what do you say we rub that magic lamp one last time?

"You know something? And I don't want to bring Clinton into it."

Aw, Sean. Ya just did, now, didn't you?

FOX TAKES ON THE WAR PROFITEERS

WE'RE ALWAYS WILLING to give Fox the benefit of the doubt. No, seriously. In fact, on August 21, 2006, O'Reilly kicked off his program on a very promising note.

Over the tagline "War Profiteering," his camera followed a man walking down the street being dogged by a reporter: "How much money have you made marketing death like this?" the reporter demanded.

Then Bill teased the segment: "Is this man exploiting dead American soldiers?"

Wow, was Bill finally going to do a story on greedy corporations that exploit the war for profit? Had we been wrong about him all along? Maybe Bill really is fair and balanced. Heck, maybe he was going to nail Custer Battles, a company that allegedly defrauded the U.S. government out of millions in Iraq!

Well, no, maybe later.

At Fox, they're more interested in striking the root: Guys who sell $18 antiwar T-shirts with the names of dead soldiers on them.

We had to wait awhile, but eventually, somewhere in between a JonBenet Ramsey segment and another plug for *Culture Warrior,* Bill got to his promised story about people who benefit financially from the tragic deaths of young innocents:

O'REILLY: Personal Story segment tonight, an antiwar activist named Dan Frazier has been selling T-shirts with the names of seventeen hundred military killed-in-actions on them. Also on the shirts, the words, "Bush lied, they died." That action has outraged Judy Vincent, whose son, Marine Corporal Scott Vincent, was killed in Iraq. She believes Frazier is doing a terrible thing. . . .

O'REILLY: All right. Joining us now from Tulsa, Oklahoma, is Judy Vincent. Did you ask this guy to take the name of your son off the shirt?

VINCENT: I did talk to him twice, and I never could get through to him. His line was either busy or there was no answer.

O'REILLY: Were you able to—were you able to leave a message?

VINCENT: No. I didn't.

O'REILLY: This didn't go through. You saw him. I mean, he wouldn't [answer] any of our questions, and you know, he's a fanatic. We know that. When did you first—when were you first made aware of this, and then how did it hit you when you found out your son's name was on the shirt?

VINCENT: Well, we all became aware of it in June of 2005 when he got his site up and running to sell his wares on the Internet. And when I [saw] it, I was outraged and just sickening. And . . .

O'REILLY: How much did he charge you for the shirts?

VINCENT: He sold the last batch, marked them down to ten dollars.

O'REILLY: They were eighteen dollars—eighteen dollars originally. Nobody's buying them. I don't think a lot of people are buying these things.

VINCENT: Well, he's printing new ones now.

O'REILLY: Yes.

VINCENT: He's added more names to the shirt, a total of more than twenty-five hundred. And he's back selling them for eighteen dollars.

O'REILLY: You took your anger to the Oklahoma legislature. What happened?

VINCENT: I took my anger to my state representative, and we got together and I directed a deal. And Oklahoma governor signed the bill, the bill into law of May of this year.

O'REILLY: What does the law say?

VINCENT: And—it's illegal to use the fallen without our permission.

O'REILLY: Illegal to use anyone killed in combat without a family member's permission for profit—profitable gain? Is that it?

VINCENT: Yes, sir, that's right.

O'REILLY: Okay. I think Louisiana also has a law like that. It may be unconstitutional, because [of] free speech. We don't know yet. But he operates out of Arizona, this guy. And, as you said, he's selling off the Web site. So you'd have to get him on a federal beef. Unless he came through Oklahoma or Louisiana. Then you could arrest him. Because the law did pass. Is it in play?

VINCENT: Yes.

O'REILLY: Are the Feds going to do anything about him?

VINCENT: Governor—not Governor Boren—Congressman Boren introduced a law into Washington July 11 of this year. And currently, they are on recess, though we're just waiting to see . . .

O'REILLY: How it goes.

VINCENT: . . . how it would go very . . .

O'REILLY: Okay. Now, I'm not going to speak for Frazier, because he could have spoken for himself. We sent our guy out there to get an interview with him, and you saw he wouldn't answer any questions. But I'm sure he would say, "Listen, I'm just doing this to save lives. I'm an antiwar guy. I want to save lives." And how would you answer that?

VINCENT: I don't think what he's doing is the voice of everybody else. It's his own personal opinion. He can use his opinion, but he doesn't need to use the fallen in any way, shape or form.

O'REILLY: Do you feel it's insulting to the memory of your son for him to do this?

VINCENT: I think it's a very dishonor [dishonest]. He states, too, that it's a memorial. Well, I don't think it's much of a memorial, putting my son's name on an eighteen-dollar T-shirt.

O'REILLY: All right. We're sorry for your loss. Thank you very much for appearing.

VINCENT: Thank you.

O'REILLY: And this Frazier guy, you saw him.

Ouch. Down goes Frazier!

O'Reilly, with his several minutes of cable network exposure that normally costs advertisers mere tens of thousands of dollars, has no doubt struck a fatal blow to this guy's multidollar home-based screen-printing business. Those antiwar pinheads are on the run now!

Now, we don't want to make fun of Vincent, whose grief and outrage are at least as legitimate as Cindy Sheehan's, but there's no way in hell this law is constitutional. Even O'Reilly can see that.

Indeed, if you had to arrest anyone who profited from the Iraq War, Fox News would pretty much have its own wing at Sing Sing.

Of course, to be fair, this is not the first time someone has been accused of war profiteering on O'Reilly's program.

On July 15, 2004, Bill ran a letter from a viewer in Ohio: "Mr. O, thanks for taking on the misrepresentations of [Michael] Moore. In my mind, he's nothing more than a war profiteer."

Bill had no response.

So we're guessing the folks at Halliburton are sleeping easy these days, knowing Bill remains cable's top-rated news personality.

As for Dan Frazier? Well, all we can say is: if he were a real American, he'd secure a lucrative contract to supply T-shirts for Operation Iraqi Freedom and then overcharge the government millions of dollars for them.

I LEFT MY FIRST FEMALE SPEAKER OF THE HOUSE IN SAN FRANCISCO

ON AUGUST 28, 2006, as part of Fox News's ongoing campaign to turn Nancy Pelosi into a cross between Vlad the Impaler and Wavy Gravy, Brit Hume spent part of his Grapevine segment fretting over the California congresswoman. In a piece titled "Don't Mess with Nancy," he quoted a *Time* magazine article, saying: "Nancy Pelosi likes to be seen as a kindly old grandmother, but the House Democratic leader is really an aggressive, hyperpartisan liberal whose hard-knuckle style rivals that of former Republican leader Tom DeLay."

Unfortunately, Hume left out a key phrase. The *Time* article had actually said, "The 66-year-old San Francisco lawmaker is an aggressive, hyperpartisan liberal pol who is the Democrats' version of Tom DeLay, *minus the ethical and legal problems of the former Republican House leader*" (emphasis added).

Yes, with the midterm elections looming, suddenly Nancy Pelosi was Fox's new *ogre du jour*—an assertive San Francisco chick with liberal values and more power than O'Reilly, Hannity, and Gibson put together. Alas, the He-Man Woman-Hater's Club was in a tizzy.

As we discuss in Chapter 7, O'Reilly warned his viewers of the San Francisco values Pelosi would bring to America, juxtaposing a discussion of congressional leadership with video of gay guys dressed as nuns dancing around a presumably gay Jesus.

And on October 11, Bill was beating the drum for his radio audience, insisting that a Nancy Pelosi speakership would ultimately prove to be the toothless Georgia mountain man to our nation's unsuspecting Ned Beatty:

> You know, I don't really care who wins the election in November. The only thing that bothers me is the Supreme Court, because I don't want secular-progressive judges on the court, and they're more likely to come about if Nancy Pelosi and her crew are in there. And I don't like San Francisco values.
>
> But again, that's up to you. You want San Francisco values, you vote in the Democrats because Pelosi becomes Speaker of the House. Frightening to me, but I—you know, you're smarter than I am as far as these things are concerned. You vote for who you wanna vote for. I'm not gonna tell you who to vote for.

I see the world in black and white. Nancy Pelosi never does. I think that's dangerous in a time of terror. I think there are villains who want to kill us. You know, and if you don't accept that, your odds of dying go higher.

O'Reilly doesn't care who you vote for, but if you decide to vote for the Dems, odds are you're gonna die, most likely gruesomely. But seriously, it's up to you.

We're not saying Bill is nuts, but rumor has it that Buddy Squirrel is filing an antitrust suit.

Of course, Bill's little "I'm-just-a-simple-caveman" shtick was hardly new. Less than a year earlier he was running the same dog-and-pony show on behalf of one Republican instead of all of them:

Now, next Tuesday voters in New Jersey will elect a governor. The choice is between Senator Jon Corzine, a Democrat, and Doug Forrester, a Republican. Now, *The Factor* doesn't endorse political candidates. We feel that you know your local people far better than we do. But in this case Forrester will push for Jessica's Law; Corzine will not.

So if you live in New Jersey and you care about the kids, in my opinion you gotta go with Forrester. Corzine is a classic liberal, a man who believes there's gray in pretty much every issue. We believe there is no gray in adults sexually assaulting children. You do it one time, you go to jail for twenty-five years. That's Jessica's Law. That's what's needed in New Jersey and every other state in the Union.

—*Talking Points Memo, November 3, 2005*

Okay, let's break this down:

1. *"The Factor doesn't endorse political candidates"*
   Really? Wow, we could have sworn that you . . . okay, we'll take your word for it.
2. *"you gotta go with Forrester"*
   That's an endorsement, Bill. And you're on *The Factor.*

3. *"So if you live in New Jersey and care about the kids"*
   Wow. Moral clarity really kicks ass, doesn't it?
4. *"Corzine is a classic liberal"*
   Actually, a "classic liberal" would be more along the lines
   of John Stuart Mill. Stick with "far-left Nazis" and "rabid
   dog," Bill. It's just so you.
5. *"That's what's needed in New Jersey and every other state in the
   Union."*
   So vote Republican, but only if you care about the kids. If
   you're pro-child-death, the Democrat is your guy. It's practically a referendum.

Oh, just so you know, O'Reilly's impotence was once again on
grand display. Forrester lost. Yeah, nice job there, Boss Tweed.

On October 15, Brit Hume was taking a slightly more resigned
tone. He had a unique take on possible Democratic gains in the
midterms:

> Let's talk about this possibility—it seems likely now, in almost
> all cards that the Democrats will get control of the House,
> which will bring us two years of Speaker Nancy Pelosi, who is
> not a popular figure or respected figure nationally.
>   Her behavior will be more visible than ever, more conspic-
> uous than ever. What effect does that have on the possibility of
> Hillary Clinton being nominated or even elected in 2008? I
> think it is a very good question. I suspect the effect would not
> be terrifically positive.

We're not quite sure what the message is here. If the Dems take
back the House, Pelosi will be the Speaker, but that would hurt the
'08 election? So if you want Democrats to win the '08 election you
shouldn't vote for Democrats in this election?

Do we really want to jeopardize Hillary's chances? Hume certainly doesn't want us to. Perhaps Fox News is secretly rooting for
ole' Hill. She does get an awful lot of coverage on Fox. In fact, *The
Big Story Weekend* host Julie Banderas aired this teaser on the

October 21, 2006, program: "Hillary Clinton in cahoots with Al Qaeda? Could this really be true? Well, her Republican opponent for the Senate seat is here and he's going to tell us why he believes she is actually helping America's most-wanted terrorist group."

Okay, so maybe they're not exactly rooting for her.

Now, even if you do believe there's an institutional liberal bias in the media, you have to admit that Fox is not an equal and opposite alternative. You'd never hear anything comparable on CBS, NBC, or PBS.

No, what Fox does is not just the death of journalism—it's silly, immature, and childish.

For instance, imagine if Blair from *The Facts of Life* was running for class president (episode 22) against Jo, and then Natalie, who wants Blair to win because she feels bad that Blair's cousin Geri has cerebral palsy and wants to be a stand-up comedian (episode 18), uses her position with the school paper (episode 118) to write an article saying that a vote for Jo is a victory for the boys' school, Bates Academy, because Jo is practically a dyke anyway and you might as well just have a man as class president. Well, that breaks every rule of journalism and eighties sitcom story arcs.

Come on, it's as obvious as the glassy expression on Tootie's face after she got into Blair's wine that one time.

THE FUTURE OF CRAZY

DESPITE FOX'S BEST efforts, the Democrats routed the GOP in the 2006 midterm elections, seizing control of both houses of Congress and throwing open the hellmouth portal that separated the rest of America from San Francisco values.

It was a major setback for Fox's intrepid liberal-hunters, and it was tattooed all over their faces—faces that might charitably have been described as glum.

Alessandra Stanley of the *New York Times* called the election-night atmosphere at Fox "funereal." She was being kind.

It was as if a Boeing 747 full of House and Senate Republicans had crashed in the Florida Everglades and Fox was watching them escape into the alligator-filled swamp via live chopper-cam, all the while being forced to report on each passenger as they were eaten.

But like a jilted lover who had just been dumped by an entire country, by day two Fox had quickly shifted from denial to anger.

For instance, you would think that Carl Cameron, Fox's chief political correspondent, would have had a lot to discuss, given that Congress had just swung to the Democrats for the first time since the network hung out its shingle in October 1996.

Instead, we were treated to gems like, "And just think about it. Every time San Francisco has a gay pride parade, Nancy Pelosi is not going to want to be in her hometown and still be Speaker of the House."

Remember, this is coming from a correspondent, not a commentator. But then that's what viewers are missing with the big three networks. Somehow, Katie Couric can do an entire segment on the historic significance of the first female to become Speaker of the House and not once mention gay street festivals or show video of drag queens. But, hey, that's the liberal media for ya. Fox doesn't make that mistake.

John Gibson took a different tack. He focused on the fact that most exit polls showed the Iraq War as foremost in voters' minds. In his My Word segment, he placed the blame for the massacre not on the fuzzy-headed populace but on the wily left-wing: "The Democrats and libs have been feasting on red meat for weeks, months, and it took its toll on the electorate. If you tell people they are losing a war long enough, they believe it, evidently. As an aside, it must be interesting news to our troops in Iraq that they're losing."

Now there's a nice double shot of delusion. First, Gibson seems to think there's some sort of mythological Iraq War that none of us see where things are going swimmingly. Second, look at the message we're sending the troops. Voters want a new direction? It's like they're saying the troops aren't trying hard enough.

So put yourself in the shoes of Gibson's offended troops. Imagine you're holed up in a foreign desert, facing rising sectarian violence and mounting casualties, and there doesn't seem to be any exit strategy. And even though your service commitment is over, you're not allowed to leave. Then some bastards start talking about a new direction. Screw that! We're staying the course, dude.

Apparently, Gibson thinks any change in strategy is a negative signal to the troops—a vote of no confidence from Uncle Sam. And why would Gibson want change? In his mind, we're winning. But what is winning? Gibson never defines it.

Perhaps it's when we finally get a Chili's in Ramadi. Or at the very least one Abercrombie & Fitch in the Anbar province. Then we can finally call it a day.

Still, it was our old pal Bill O'Reilly who screeched the loudest the day after Black Tuesday. O'Reilly invited Charles Schumer on *The Factor* to talk about the Democrats' big day. Schumer discussed Pelosi while at the same time trying to skirt O'Reilly's absurd characterizations:

SCHUMER: I think, you know, a lot of people, maybe yourself included, judge Nancy Pelosi wrong. She is from San Francisco, but she comes from a strong Italian-American political family from Baltimore, and she's a very pragmatic person. She's not going to do things . . .

O'REILLY: But I don't want dinner with the woman. I just want her not to support unfettered abortion, legalize narcotics and other things, and her district does. So I have to judge her by her district, not by—again, I'm not looking for a big Italian meal from Ms. Pelosi. Although if she invites me, I'll consider it.

SCHUMER: She may vote her district, but she is going to run the Democratic Party in a way that's pragmatic.

O'REILLY: I hope so, because if she doesn't, you know who's going to be right on her butt, don't you?

Of course, we have no doubt that Bill will be on Pelosi's butt for the next two years. We can't think of anything that would divert him from his silly culture-war drama, wherein the evil Pelosi tries to impose her San Francisco values on an unsuspecting nation but is nightly foiled by the fearless Falafel Man and Loofah Boy.

Yes, we see little getting in the way of O'Reilly demonizing Pelosi for the next two years, short of Hillary Clinton divorcing Bill, marrying George Soros, and then running for president. Yes, George Soros as First Lady. That would do it.

Still, it's interesting to see Bill's megalomania go so far unchecked that he's willing to put the most powerful female politician in the history of our country on notice the day after the election. Stephen Colbert could really just recite O'Reilly transcripts verbatim at this point.

But Pelosi was really secondary to O'Reilly's chief concern: the Democrats' ability to go after the Bush administration now that they control Congress:

O'REILLY: Is she going to try to investigate and Waxman, Henry Waxman, going to try to investigate all these things and create scandals? Are they going to . . .

"Create scandals." Interesting choice of words there. Why wouldn't O'Reilly want there to be an investigation of government contracts in Iraq and possible war profiteering? Sure, Halliburton's dealings may not be as bad as the many depredations of the novelty T-shirt industry, but shouldn't war contractors, and anyone who may have facilitated them, be held to account if they've unfairly exploited the Iraq conflict? Is it bad to discuss war profiteering when we're at war? Would it be better to table it until peacetime?

And what of possible political interference in regulatory decisions by the FDA and EPA? Or what about disaster response failures? Have we really seen any measures adopted in the aftermath of Hurricane Katrina that would give us confidence in our government's emergency preparedness?

The checks and balances inherent in a two-party system are essential to its effectiveness, but O'Reilly has already decided that there's no validity to anything the Democrats might bring forth and that any oversight role they might take on would simply be a spiteful attack on the administration.

For his part, Schumer replied specifically to concerns about the war:

SCHUMER: Well, look, again, let's be realistic here and let's do what's right. There should be some oversight. The war in Iraq isn't going well, by most people's judgment. To call in some generals and say why isn't Iraqization working?

O'REILLY: I'm not talking about that. I'm not talking about that. I mean, we—the country is giving the Democratic Party a chance to improve upon the Iraq performance and the performance of a lot of other things. And I respect that. As an independent voter, I hope you succeed. I do. I want the country to be the best it can be. But . . .

SCHUMER: As do we, Bill.

O'REILLY: I don't want sleazy little investigations by hyperpartisans ripping up the executive branch for partisan political reasons. Am I unreasonable there?

That O'Reilly can say "as an independent voter" with a straight face shows that he is clearly suffering from dissociative identity disorder. He has so abandoned his own reality that he might as well say "as a Puerto Rican Jew."

You also gotta love his use of "sleazy little investigations" to describe any instance of congressional oversight. No spin, Bill. Awesome job.

But the Fox Democrat-bashing was just warming up. Bill gave us a sneak peek into the future:

O'REILLY: Okay. But I just want to know. You're—so I can call you up and I can hold you accountable for what happens in Iraq the next two years? You're my guy?

SCHUMER: No, you can't do that, because I'm not the commander in chief, and that's the president. And he should still be held accountable.

So what will we see from Bill and the Fox News gang over the next two years? While on election night 2006 Fox was still reeling from the serpent-sharp sting of a thankless nation—which had watched Fox's Pelosi-thon but churlishly tossed the president's party out on its ass—we have no doubt our favorite cable news network will rise like a mentally unhinged, fire-breathing phoenix to terrorize the left again. Indeed, they're already well on their way.

This could even be a rare opportunity for Murdoch's troops. If Iraq progresses further into turmoil, what better scapegoat to point to than a newly minted liberal Congress? Indeed, the Democrats and Iraq's post-Pelosi troubles would go together like the peanut butter and jelly in Goober Grape. Sure, it would be a cheap, pointless marketing gimmick, but that doesn't mean plenty of people still wouldn't buy it.

But the more pressing question for our friends at Fox is this: can the Bush administration largely be absolved of any and all sins now that the Democrats share power with the president?

Let's take a look into O'Reilly's little Magic 8-Ball brain.

Ooooh . . . "Yes, definitely."

NOTES

1. Whether anyone would notice the format change is another question entirely.
2. Anyone who remains unconvinced of Fox's extraordinary right-wing tilt (to borrow a phrase from Fairness and Accuracy in Reporting) can look to at least two surveys that examine the network's sources.

   The first, from FAIR, monitored nineteen weeks of *Special Report with Brit Hume*, which Fox had called its signature political news show. While the survey is from 2001, it's still relevant, because even then the network missed no opportunity to repeat its slogans "we report, you decide" and "fair and balanced," and Hume himself has continued to hew to conservative ideals.

   Indeed, here's just one Humeism, from August of 2003, that proves once and for all that it *is* physically possible to fit a mature adult human male inside Karl Rove's rectum. See if you can find the logical fallacy:

   Two hundred seventy-seven U.S. soldiers have now died in Iraq, which means that statistically speaking, U.S. soldiers have less of a chance of dying from all causes in Iraq than citizens have of being murdered in California, which is roughly the same geographical size. The most recent statistics indicate California has more than 2,300 homicides each year, which means about 6.6 murders each day. Meanwhile, U.S. troops have been in Iraq for 160 days, which means they're incurring about 1.7 deaths, including illness and accidents each day.

Now show it to your five-year-old son. If he figures it out, give him a cookie.

Anyway, FAIR found that, during the survey period, *Special Report* featured sixty-five guests who were avowed conservatives out of a total of ninety-two guests—"that is, conservatives outnumbered representatives of all other points of view, including non-political guests, by a factor of more than 2 to 1," wrote the study's authors.

The program's partisan tilt was even more extreme: "Of the 56 partisan guests on *Special Report* between January and May, 50 were Republicans and 6 were Democrats—a greater than 8 to 1 imbalance. In other words, 89 percent of guests with a party affiliation were Republicans."

In addition, a May 2006 study by Media Matters monitored the number of Republican/conservative and Democratic/progressive guests on *The O'Reilly Factor* from January through April of 2006. The results, available at http://mediamatters.org/items/200605220001, betray a striking imbalance, with conservative guests outnumbering liberals by a more than two-to-one ratio in nearly every month studied.

Of course, O'Reilly has often touted the fairness of both *The Factor* and Fox, once claiming, "if you do an analysis every day of the voices and the time given to stories and people, you'll see that liberal people get just as much time as conservative people on the Fox News Channel, and the commentators are pretty much split down the middle on their ideological bent."

Now, as O'Reilly would be the first to tell you, Media Matters and FAIR are both liberal media watchdog groups, but it would be hard to bias these surveys. They simply counted the number of Republican and conservative guests on Fox's shows and compared them to the number of Democratic and liberal guests—something Fox itself seems somehow incapable of doing.

A FINAL THOUGHT

▼

18

SWEET JESUS, WE LOVE *FOX NEWS WATCH*

TO SAY THAT Fox News is a wholly dysfunctional organization utterly devoid of any merit would be wrong. Even Pol Pot was rumored to be really great with the grandkids. And much like the brutal leader of the Khmer Rouge, who exterminated three million Cambodians, Fox News, too, has a small bright spot.

Each week, Fox airs *Fox News Watch*, by far the best show on the network and one of our favorites on cable news.

While the format is not new, the show is a big departure for Fox. Hosted by Eric Burns and featuring liberals Neal Gabler and Jane Hall and conservatives Jim Pinkerton and Cal Thomas, it's a refreshingly civil and informed review of the week's media coverage.

It's also the only Fox program that's truly fair and balanced. The panelists run the gamut from the far-left Gabler to the far-right Thomas. But even with this clash of ideologies, you'll see more nuanced coverage of stories here than anywhere else on the network.

LIVING UP TO THE MANTRA

ON OCTOBER 7, 2006, while discussing Bob Woodward's *State of Denial*, the *Fox News Watch* panel gave us a surprisingly impartial take on the controversies surrounding the book:

PINKERTON: Jacob Weisberg in the *Financial Times* had a piece where he went through the descriptions of Rumsfeld in the 2002 book, the 2004 book, the 2006 book, and concluded that Woodward is just a weather vane. And as the media wind had turned against Bush and the administration, so has Woodward.

BURNS: All right. We're all talking about Woodward's book. Everybody, Jane, is familiar with at least some of the charges. There have been denials of some of these charges from the Bush administration. Have they been given enough attention in the media?

HALL: I think so. I read that, I mean, Condoleezza Rice's response—Andrew Card pretty much acknowledged that what he had said to Woodward was true. Woodward has documentation. I think the bigger question is the one you're raising. If the purpose is to serve the American public, then why hold on to this for a big book, and why not get it out there sooner, in your newspaper? That's what we're supposed to do. Information wants to be free. That's according to Jim Pinkerton.

PINKERTON: Well put, Jane. Woodward can be accused of being an opportunist and a snake. But he gets his facts right. I mean, as he said on *Larry King*, he said, I have seven hours of taped interviews with Andy Card. And they—let him try to deny it. Andy Card hasn't really denied anything. I mean, that's the point: Woodward does get them on the record.

Now this is the kind of reasoned exchange that brings depth and understanding to a story. Notice there's no "some people say that this book is anti-American" or "isn't Bob Woodward really just hurting the troops, and might he be guilty of giving aid and comfort to Al Qaeda?"

But more important, you have people breaking across partisan lines, with Jane Hall wanting to explore why Woodward withheld important information for a book and Pinkerton giving Woodward credit for his thoroughness.

Certainly, this isn't too much to ask of a news network. And, to the program's credit, it's the norm at *Fox News Watch*.

GET THEE BACK, LIBERAL

NEAL GABLER IS the only unapologetic far-left liberal on Fox News. The only one.

But that doesn't mean he always toes the party line. For example, on September 23, 2006, he harshly criticized former New Jersey governor Jim McGreevey, a Democrat, who had cheated on his wife and given a well-paid position to an alleged lover before revealing he was gay:

GABLER: Yes. And he—and he chose women's shows primarily to do this so that he—he would—he could talk about his integrity and everything. Look, what he did was shameless. It was disgusting. And hold onto your seats. Sean Hannity gave him the best interview by nailing him and asking about how he treated his wife.

BURNS: All right. Could we get a shot of me please? I am literally holding onto my seat.

GABLER: Last time I'm ever going to say anything nice about Sean Hannity.

Of course, Gabler's relationship with other Fox News figures is not quite so amicable. Indeed, it's instructive how Fox's biggest gun views Gabler's position with Fox. As the only significant liberal counterweight to Fox's right-wing propaganda (and as part of the most balanced, nuanced programming on the network) he's received special notice from Bill O'Reilly—which points up exactly how much of an exception-that-proves-the-rule *Fox News Watch* really is.

On February 20, 2006, O'Reilly had Burns on *The Factor.* Needless to say, it was time to smear the only unapologetic far-left liberal on Fox News.

> **O'REILLY:**   Impact Segment tonight. Both *Time* and *Newsweek* have covered stories about the Dick Cheney hunting accident. Nothing much new. *Time* magazine poll says fifty-two percent of Americans feel Cheney handled the situation appropriately. Forty-two percent say he did not. But overall, Dick Cheney's approval rating is just twenty-six percent. Not good. Now there are all kinds of irresponsible statements being made about the vice president, one of which occurred this weekend on the Fox News program *News Watch.*

O'Reilly played a clip of Gabler saying, "This could be a conspiracy. And in this very sense. Look at what this did. This got Abu Ghraib off the front pages, it got Chertoff off the front pages. While we're here talking about the idiocy of him shooting his friend, we're not talking about the major, major problems that this administration is having. That's clever PR. That's not bad PR."

Now, the way O'Reilly presents this, it almost sounds as if Gabler was saying Cheney shot a man in the face deliberately to distract people from Abu Ghraib. That's clearly not what he was saying. He was saying the White House may have manipulated coverage of the story (and the coverage of how it was handled) to drown out other, potentially more damaging news—which is the kind of thing that's done in politics all the time.

Gabler also cited a blogger, Jay Rosen, who said Cheney didn't "make a mistake" by delaying the announcement of the incident. Rosen claimed that Cheney is known for his contempt of the press and this was just part of his m.o.—a way, in Rosen's words, to "*roll back* the press as a player within the executive branch, to make it less important in running the White House and governing the country." After Cal Thomas facetiously mentioned possible conspiracies surrounding the administration's handling of the incident, Gabler made his comment—which O'Reilly edited to remove references to Rosen (who, in his blog post, never used the word "conspiracy") and to Cheney's decision to delay talking about the incident.

Gabler's use of the word "conspiracy" was probably ill-advised, but he was making a larger point about the administration's relationship with the media.

Then again, even if Gabler could be accused of suffering a genuine on-air meltdown, O'Reilly of all people should have been expected to cut him a little slack. But you know our Bill. After claiming Gabler was "out of control," O'Reilly criticized Burns for failing to challenge him:

> But look, you should have come back and said to Gabler, look, you have—this is a watchdog program. I like your program, Eric. I think you do a nice job. All right? But you got a guy like Gabler, and this is the second time this guy did this. The first time he smeared me about the Christmas controversy.

Ah, there you have it. Inside every out-of-control pundit is a devil who's criticized O'Reilly.

Of course, what O'Reilly referred to was not a smear at all. It occurred during a December 3, 2005, *Fox News Watch* discussion about the alleged war on Christmas. Gabler was merely stating the obvious: "Eric, we are at war. There's Darfur. There's an AIDS crisis. And you're worried about whether people are saying Merry Christmas or not?"

Always one to call a spade a spade, Gabler went after what he saw as the core of the issue: "I want to talk about the media angle, because we've avoided it; it's the elephant in the room—it's Fox News. Come on. It's O'Reilly; it's Hannity; it's Gibson. They're demagogues who realize that at Christmastime, you can—you can rebel."

He added: "They'll do it every Christmas. They did it last Christmas; they'll do it next Christmas."

Neal Gabler, you bastard! Smearer! Smearer!

Of course, O'Reilly hates anyone who calls him out on his silliness, especially on his own network. But it's interesting that he'd give Cal Thomas a pass when Thomas was echoing similar themes during the same discussion from a Christian conservative perspective:

> But I will say, today's my birthday; I'm not looking for anybody to celebrate my birthday. People say "good morning"; I'm not saying, "Wait a minute! Why aren't you wishing me a happy birthday?" Let's give the secularists their holiday on April 1, and leave the rest of it to me. I don't care what the culture does; they don't mean it anyway. They're trying to exploit Christmas to make money.

And that's why we love *Fox News Watch*. You have the panel's most conservative member essentially agreeing with its most liberal member while refusing to buy into the network's absurd talking points.

Still, O'Reilly saved his best venom for the liberal: "This guy, Gabler, who you shouldn't have on your program, by the way. If I—and I don't run Fox News, but I'd fire him in a heartbeat and I'd bring in a responsible person. He traffics in personal attacks, this guy. He brings in insane stuff."

It occurs to us that that may be O'Reilly's real problem with Gabler. He's intruding on his territory.

HEY, CRAZY IS NONPARTISAN

WE STARTED OFF this book by saying that we weren't interested so much in bashing conservatives as in casting a critical eye on conservatism as it's filtered through the most tawdry, soulless, and crazy-ass news network that's ever propagandized a nation.

So we think it's only appropriate to give a Christian conservative the last word.

On the June 17, 2006, edition of *Fox News Watch*, during a discussion of Fox competitor MSNBC's struggle to find an identity, panelist Cal Thomas summed it all up rather nicely: "You touched on the important thing: the loss of identity. All of them are trying to copy Fox now, to be honest. They wanted—many of them are doing more tabloid, more big-lipped blondes and all this kind of stuff. There's only so much of that trailer-trash pie to go around."

You said it all, Cal. You said it all.

Acknowledgments

▼

MEDIAMATTERS.ORG AND NEWSHOUNDS.US are two of the biggest thorns in the side of Fox News and two of the finest media watchdog groups on the Web. They made researching this book both easier and more fun.

Al Franken and Keith Olbermann have continued to serve as sources of inspiration, and, perhaps most importantly, have helped stoke the fires of Bill O'Reilly's insanity, from which we've drawn considerable warmth.

Matthew Carnicelli, our brilliant agent, and Carl Bromley, our witty and urbane editor, were instrumental in guiding this project to completion. We can't thank them enough.

We'd also like to thank our families and friends for their support and encouragement over the last year. They know who they are.

Index

▼